MW01611015

Odyssey of High Hopes

A Memoir of Adversity and Triumph

Cyrus A. Ansary

Washington, D.C.

Published in the United States of America
by Lambert Publications, LLC.

ISBN 978-1-7326879-7-4 (Hardcover)
ISBN 978-1-7326879-3-6 (Paperback)
ISBN 978-1-7326879-5-0 (Kindle eBook)
ISBN 978-1-7326879-4-3 (ePUB eBook)

Interior design by Booknook.biz

ALSO BY CYRUS A. ANSARY
George Washington: Dealmaker-In-Chief

*The Story of How the Father of Our Country
Unleashed the Entrepreneurial Spirit in America*

Author's name?
Ansary
To rhyme with AnswerMe.

DEDICATION

To Ashley, Brad, Chris, Doug, Eric, Evan, Jan, Jeff, Justin, Karen, Kelsey, Kevin, Linnea, Maxi, Nancy, ParyAnn, and Will.

Table of Contents[1]

---

[1] *Odyssey of High Hopes* **is a memoir in three distinct slices of the author's life—Books I, II, and III.**

.

Book I

An Enduring Quest

Life is either a daring adventure, or nothing.

—Helen Keller

Prologue

It was a long, rough morning and a scene worthy of an Alfred Hitchcock spy thriller. Earlier, a cold front had rolled down from the fields of Soviet Central Asia, coating the streets of Tehran with a foot of snow, but this day turned out sunny and beautiful with a mild breeze blowing in from the Alborz Mountains north of the city. The sidewalks were by now almost clear. As I kept skulking about in my neighborhood of small houses and many shops, thoughts uncommon to most teenagers raced through my mind. My preoccupation was with the stranger for whom I was keeping an eye out. He often made his appearance at midday. I had picked him out of the throng of pedestrians near my home in Tehran.

Balding, middle-aged, slightly pudgy, and dressed in a nondescript suit, the man could blend into any crowd. He was, however, not your average everyday mystery man. He walked with a purposeful stride and wore a perpetually preoccupied look. I guessed he was a foreigner. The city was home to many nationalities at the time, so he could be from anywhere, but I fervently hoped he was an American. I had urgent need of a U.S. embassy connection.

The side street on which I lived and where the mysterious stranger walked was a narrow pedestrian lane. Tehran had more than its share of such picturesque and winding streets. This one was bisected by a shallow irrigation ditch into which the city would periodically run water. The adjoining homeowners would then direct the flow to water their gardens or to fill the tiny backyard pools common in that section of town. Too narrow for automobile traffic, the lane was used by pedestrians as a cross street between two broad avenues.

I had no idea where the man was coming from each time I saw him, nor where he was going. I'd have to follow him to find out if he was someone who could help me. I was fourteen, and to be thinking of tailing a stranger, I had to be desperate. And that I was.

Chapter One

Scent of Roses and Poetry Games

There is an old saying, sometimes attributed to Aristotle, that the unexamined life is not worth living. I never believed it. Life comes in endless shades and shapes, each as precious as a soft summer breeze. I was particularly eager to examine my father's life, but it remained an enigma to me.

Other children I knew showed little interest in their parents' early history. Some fathers liked to talk about the hardships they endured while growing up, and how fortunate their children were. These—and other stories that always started with "when I was your age"—bored the kids to no end, but I was not jaded in that way. Intuitively, I felt that my life was defined as much by Father's experiences as by my own. I wanted to know about his family and friends, the world he had been born into, and the incandescent culture of his day.

Father, however, showed no inclination to lift the veil on his upbringing, smiled cryptically at my questions, and changed the subject. So I turned to Mother for the snippets of his life she knew about. Patiently listening to her stories, I was able in time to pull together a rough sketch of Father's boyhood. Still, these brush strokes never attained for me the crispness of a Rubens portrait. Rather, they were more like a painting dominated by dark colors and obscuring shadows.

Orphaned at six, Father found his upbringing placed in the hands of an abusive older brother. His new guardian took sadistic pleasure in beating him. He never knew when the next blow would fall. Battered, hopeless, and unwilling to be trapped in this nightmare any longer, he ran away from home at the age of nine.

I wondered how Father survived without family or friends in one of the most inhospitable areas of the world, the Persian Gulf region of Iran in the early twentieth century. During the years when most children's lives revolved around family, friends, school, and play, he must have been desperately scrounging for food and shelter. Who comforted him when sick or injured? And how did he avoid cruel adults? What was it like to hide under bridges and ducts, always on the run, and never to have a decent set of clothes or shoes? I had loads of questions but few answers. Obviously, the memories were too painful for Father to resurrect. His abhorrence of the turmoil of his early days played out now in a determined search for order and stability even in small things.

Father was slight of build, trim, and wiry. He stood proud and erect and was rarely without a white shirt, suit, and tie. He had a round face, a strong chin, a clear forehead, and thinning hair. In time, he became bald. Unafraid of physical confrontation, he was almost combative. He looked like a man who had been tested by life's challenges and had emerged unscathed. It probably accounted for his favorite saying, which was something along Nietzsche's old line that "suffering ennobles." Father would know, I always thought.

You'd think his early struggles for survival would have left Father with no chance for intellectual pursuits. And yet he taught himself to read and write Persian, his native tongue. Along the way, he also developed fluency in English, Hindi, Urdu, and Arabic. And enough French and German to order dessert. Amazingly, through the long arc of his life he never lost his sense of humor—undoubtedly what saved his sanity.

Father's reluctance to reminisce about his childhood did not keep him from waxing eloquent about the cities he had visited. As a child, I loved hearing him talk about the travels of his youth. Being the last-born of four children, I had precious few opportunities for quality time with my parents. How Father had ended up in India I never knew, but he did talk about the country. Calcutta and Bombay, where he had spent parts of his youth, he described as hot and crowded. He must have walked hundreds of miles as a young man visiting several countries.

By 1921 he had worked his way to Basra, a major city in Iraq near its border with Iran. There he found a job as a telegraph operator. He was twenty-one at the time. The only photo of him at that age showed a fresh-faced and skinny young man with a small mustache, wearing a bow tie on a detachable white collar and a funny hat that was the fashion in the country where he worked. Archaic finery, but probably the style in the early 1900s.

Later, Father worked at the Anglo-Iranian Oil Company in Ahvaz, a city on the Iranian side of the border with Iraq. It too was hot and tropical, but he felt lucky to have a job. Once settled there, his thoughts turned to romance, and he began searching for a wife. The city was filled with the families of sunbaked oil workers and peasants, but he had no interest in looking among them for a mate. He asked for a month's leave and then expanded the radius of his search by about 250 miles.

Eventually, he zeroed in on Shiraz, a medium-sized city in southern Iran. There he heard about the eldest daughter of one of the local grandees. Without ever seeing her or even a photo of her likeness, he mounted a full-fledged campaign to win her father's

consent to marry her—not easy to do for a stranger in Shiraz. Acutely aware of the passage of time before his leave ran out, he importuned several influential people in town to intercede for him.

Improbably, he eventually succeeded in securing my grandfather's permission to marry my mother. He was twenty-seven, she

9

eighteen. The night of their wedding was the first time my mother and father laid eyes on each other.

By then Father's leave from his job was over, but when he tried to return with his new bride to Ahvaz, she balked. An early experience had left her fearful of losing her loved ones, so she was resistant to any move away from her family. In 1918, when she was nine, the influenza pandemic infected hundreds of millions worldwide. With no vaccines, an estimated 50-100 million people lost their lives. It was one of the deadliest natural disasters ever to befall the planet. Mother suffered irretrievable losses of her own. In a single two-day period, she bore the indescribable pain of watching her mother, grandmother, and older sister die agonizing deaths from the virus. The overwhelming grief left her with a deep-rooted attachment to the remaining members of her family.

Now she was married to someone who lived in a different city, but she would not give up her beloved Shiraz without a fight. Not exactly the submissive Persian bride Father may have expected, she argued that Shiraz was infinitely more pleasant than the smelly Ahvaz oil fields. Where would he like to rear the family they were planning, she asked? She was persuasive, so he promised to relocate as soon as he could line up a job in Shiraz. It was not a difficult promise to make. The oil company was hardly an ideal place to work, as the British class-and-caste culture treated the local staff no better than servants. A couple of the English overseers, set apart by their square jaws and muttonchop whiskers, were often quick to resort to flogging, even for minor infractions.

Father took Mother to Ahvaz, where their first child was born in 1927. He was named Hushang, but Father affectionately called him Hushy (to rhyme with sushi) when he was small. (Later I'd want to call him Hugh, but he refused to let me shorten his name.)

True to his promise, Father gave up his job soon after and moved his family to Shiraz.

The new town may have been only a few hundred miles from Ahvaz, but it might as well have been on a different planet. While Ahvaz was hot, dry, and dusty, Shiraz had a temperate climate and lush gardens. Father found a job at the government-owned Bank Melli ("melli" being the Persian word for "national"), the only financial institution in the country. With no formal education, he had to start at the bottom. There he learned about money and interest rates, collaterals and secured loans, and other arcana of finance.

In the ensuing years, Mother bore three more children, another son, Bahram (whom I came to call Barry) born in 1928; Pary, my sister, born in 1931; and me, born in 1933.

Once settled with work and family, Father maintained a rigid schedule at home: Breakfast at 7 a.m., lunch at 1 p.m., lights out at 10 p.m. Amazingly, his turbulent childhood led to an uncanny level of self-control in adulthood. He loved beer, for example, but he rationed himself to a single bottle before dinner on the last Friday of every month. He looked forward to it, counted the days, but then the one beer was *it* until the next month.

With his children, Father maintained strict discipline, but he was also often thoughtful and tender. His method of rearing us was to ensure that we had an intellectual bent, that debate and dispute were our daily fare, and that we were imbued with deep professional ambition. An orphan, he had learned to operate in a world he'd never dominate, and wanted to pass on to us a few nuggets he had picked up the hard way. But when he tried to impose his own daily regimen on his rowdy and inquisitive chil-dren, he totally struck out. We loved him, but we laughed at his quirks, openly made fun of them. It was ironic, but he didn't seem to mind.

And so we were living in Shiraz, a town of about thirty thousand residents, known for its literature, flowers, and beautiful sunsets. It also had pleasant weather; extremes of temperature were rare. In the spring, its crystal pure air was permeated with the sweet scent of red roses, and at night the sky shimmered with the glint of a million dazzling stars against the dark backdrop of space. Even as a child I was amazed at how brilliant the moon looked. There may be nicer places on the planet, I used to think, but not many.

In the center of town there was a large round pool with a fountain spewing water in the air, the sunlight reflecting off it like diamonds. The people congregated there every evening, with loads of children playing and families socializing.

The population of Shiraz included a tribe of mountain people. They were goat and sheep herders. At the approach of summer, they'd break camp and move their flocks higher in the mountains. Growing up I often saw several groups of tribal men and women walking around in colorful attire when they came to town to buy provisions. They spoke their own dialect of Persian and tried to stick together. I was always curious about them and eager to learn about their lifestyle in the mountains, but they would not mingle with the other Shirazis. There were similar tribes in other parts of the country.

———•••———

Shiraz was also a city of poets and poetry lovers. The country's best-known poet, Saadi, who had poured his heart out in rhyme centuries before, was buried there. His works were translated into German by Goethe, and into English by Sir Richard Francis Burton. Another poet, Hafez, was also buried in Shiraz. Both their tombs attracted visitors from near and far. Still another, Ferdowsi, wrote a mythical history of Persia in a mind-numbing 50,000 couplets. It too was translated into English verse.

Another Persian poet was Omar Khayyam whose quatrains were translated into English by Edward FitzGerald. Having studied Persian while at Cambridge, he made Khayyam's Rubaiyat famous in the English-speaking world, of which the following is a sample:

> *A Loaf of Bread beneath the Bough,*
> *A Jug of Wine, a Book of Verse—and Thou*
> *Beside me singing in the Wilderness—*
> *And Wilderness is Paradise enow.*

Most of the adults in Shiraz were poetry buffs. There was an emotional attachment to verse, and the calling of poets was universally revered. In an era of deprivation, wars, and disease, the language and imagery of poetry were designed to change life's calculus. There were even games that tested a player's knowledge of verse. One player would recite a single line of poetry, the next player had to come up with a verse starting with the letter of the alphabet in which the previous line had ended, and so on with each succeeding player. Often ten or more people would participate, and unbelievably these games could last for hours. Poetry up the wazoo. Without radio, television, movies, sporting events, or even political theater, we were making do. As for me, having been consistently excluded from the ball games of the older boys on weekends on account of my age, I began boning up on Persian poetry so I could participate in the adults' poetry-recital contests. By the time I was ten I knew hundreds of lines of Persian poetry by heart, and soon started winning my share of the games.

Despite their archaic formality, the games were satisfying and fun; they also served as a fulcrum for the development of literary skills among the young, including me. In time, however, I'd learn that the rest of the country did not share the Shirazis' enthusiasm for poetry games.

Chapter Two

"Live the Life You Dream"[2]

With an area of 636,000 square miles, Iran occupies a territory larger than Britain, France, and Italy combined. Its population of 25 million in the early twentieth century included an ethnic mixture of Turks, Kurds, Arabs, Armenians, Assyrians, Baluchis, and various tribal groups. It was equally diverse in religion. Though a Muslim country, it notably included sizable Christian, Jewish, Baha'i, and Zoroastrian minorities.

Roughly 2,500 years earlier, Persia (as Iran was then called) was a vast and powerful nation. Founded by Cyrus the Great, the First Persian Empire connected almost 40 percent of the global population in 480 B.C. From its seat of power in Persepolis near Shiraz, Persia extended its rule across Asia and Africa: from Egypt to parts of India, and included modern-day Turkey, Iraq, Kuwait, Syria, Jordan, Israel, Lebanon, Afghanistan, and Bahrain.

In the seventh century, a man from the Arabian Peninsula by the name of Mohammad created a religion called Islam and declared himself its prophet. His Arab followers, driven by a messianic zeal to spread the new faith, conquered huge swaths of three continents, a feat even greater than that of Genghis Khan or Alexander of Macedonia. The Arabs then sent their armies to Persia, again and again, until they wiped out all resistance to their new faith. The penalty for refusal to convert was death. The reign of terror thus unleashed led to thousands of beheadings before the desperate

---

[2] Henry David Thoreau.

local population caved in, gave up their own faith, and accepted the new religion.

Even so, the Iranians still found clever ways to thwart the Arab raiders. They held on to their unique Persian culture and language, and then, in an act of ultimate defiance, created their own version of the religion. Thus was born the Shiite sect of Islam.

Before the Arabs came, the Persians belonged to a gentle and peaceful faith. Named after their spiritual leader Zoroaster, they were called Zoroastrians. Fleeing from the religious persecution emanating from the Arabian Peninsula, large groups of Zoroastrians began abandoning their homes in Iran and migrating to India in the seventh century. There they were welcomed by the Indian government, subject to three conditions: They had to speak Hindi, even at home and among themselves; they had to adopt the Indian form of dress for men, women, and children; and they had to make earnest and immediate efforts to assimilate into the local population. They agreed and soon became known in India as the Parsees (meaning Persians).

In time, the wisdom of the Indian government's requirements was borne out. Over the generations, the Parsees became fully integrated into the Indian population. When Britain's East India Company set up trading posts there in the seventeenth century, the enterprising Parsees learned the English business methods and discovered their own flair for commerce. Some of India's largest modern companies—such as Tata, Godrej, Mistry, Poonawalla, and Wadia—were started in the eighteenth and nineteenth centuries by the Parsee families. Today, they are some of the most philanthropic of all Indians. There are also large Parsee communities in England and the U.S.

A few pockets of Zoroastrians, however, remained in Iran and somehow escaped beheading by the Arabs. A small group of them happened to own a magnificent fruit orchard and cattle ranch in

Shiraz, and needed a revenue source. My grandfather, a prominent man in his day but reduced by financial misfortune, was a longtime friend to the Zoroastrian community in the city; he persuaded them to carve out a portion of their land and build a house on it for rental income. Father and Grandfather rented it on a shared basis. It was located on Zand Avenue, the broad thoroughfare in the center of the city. There was, of course, no running water, electricity, telephone service, or radio, and the roads were unpaved, but we didn't miss what we had never known.

The house itself was comfortable. Its central feature was a porch running the entire length of the lot with rooms coming off it. There was also a room with a well in it and a nearby cistern. Periodically, one of the older boys would pull up the pail from the well and pour the water into the cistern. A faucet at the bottom of the cistern provided drinking water for the family.

Grandfather's quarters were on the other side of the porch. He had been married before, to my maternal grandmother, one of the millions who had died in the influenza epidemic of 1917-18. She left behind three children—my mother and her younger brother and sister, both of whom now lived with us. Grandfather's second wife produced two children, a girl and a boy, but he divorced that wife before I was born. The boy, Mother's half-brother, also lived with us, as did my Great-Aunt Baji. And, of course, Grandfather and his current wife and their five children lived in the shared house.

That was still not the whole menagerie. From time to time, Father's nephews, two nice and polite teenage boys, lived with us. We also had a black and white terrier named Husky and a playful kitten no one had gotten around to naming. Somehow that jumble of people made for a tight-knit family, and I never felt crowded.

We slept in bedrolls on Persian carpets and rolled them up and put them away in the morning. In the summertime, all of us slept on cots on the roof beneath a palette of stars. We took baths at the public bathhouse in separate facilities for men and women.

The house had a large backyard with a most attractive feature, a private portal into the beautiful Zoroastrian garden and fruit orchard. For us children, that small inconspicuous door was our escape into the lush world beyond. The Zoroastrian owners were kind and tolerant and they gave us children the run of their property. We came to know every bush and tree and every rock and pathway in that private oasis. We climbed the ancient oak trees with limbs that reached toward the pristine skies of Shiraz, and reveled in the bronze and gold colors of the leaves in the flashes of sunlight. Flocks of sparrows were visible on the trees, and an occasional rabbit quietly nibbled on grass or peered through the vines. We gorged ourselves on the ripe apples, pears, grapes, walnuts, and goji berries on the fruit trees and bushes. Solid and serene, the house and the adjacent orchard bespoke comfort and contentment. I thought it was a blissful life.

Most food was expensive and sparse, particularly in the early days. So we learned to fill our tummies with bread, which cost little. Mother was always ready to go without, so some of us would have a little more. If there was one thing we learned from her, it was that there was sheer joy in doing for others, never with any expectation of a reward or benefit.

Preparing meals for the family in the basement over a brazier was an all-day affair. Aunt Baji helped Mother with the chores. Baji was really my great-aunt, but we called her Aunt Baji, it was simpler. A small person, she had never married. She was the hardest-working woman I had ever known and was totally dedicated to the family.

The national holiday was called Noruz, Persian for "new day." It had no religious significance, so everyone could participate. Noruz was held on the first day of spring, most often on March 21st. It was a celebration of the end of winter and a time for the gathering of family and friends, of festival and laughter.

Mother and Aunt Baji would labor for weeks making sweets for the guests. They would set a Noruz spread with traditional rice dishes. All of us children waited eagerly for Noruz, as there would be no school for a week. We could also have pistachios and other nuts, pomegranates, and homemade treats made with dates. There would also be a goldfish in a bowl of water for good luck, and a mirror as a symbol of light. Father gave each of us money. I got the equivalent of ten cents, while the others, being older, got more.

Mother and Aunt Baji also made new clothes for us at Noruz— the only jacket and trousers we boys got for a year. By the time a few months had passed, our new clothes would be in tatters, but we'd still have to wait for the next Noruz. We would also get a new pair of shoes then, again meant to last a full year. Glue being unavailable, the shoemaker used nails to keep the leather together, which hurt when they stuck out from the soles until we could hammer them down. Of course, as we were growing, with the passage of months the shoes became tight and uncomfortable, even painful. But we'd have to bear it. I looked forward to the day when, with a sigh of relief, I could remove the tight shoes of the year just past.

In those years, I was in the habit of retreating to the Zoroastrian garden and climbing my favorite oak tree, the tallest one around. High above the ground, forty feet or so, two branches created a perfect cradle where I found indescribable joy in spiritual solitude. As a gentle wind stirred the leaves, I basked in the feeling of freedom there; it was my moment of enchantment. Inspired by Father's stories, I'd dream of traveling to other lands for my education and carving out a fulfilling professional niche there for myself. I had an unquenchable desire to experience life in other cultures, and this became my dominant motivation early on.

Chapter Three

A Question of Seniority

My older brother Hushang was an exceptional boy. Among the Ansary children, he was the one who had won the genetic lottery. A classic overachiever, he had a faultless memory and an IQ that was off the chart. He also had the gift of the gab. Even as a kid, he could outtalk most people. You'd think he had kissed the Blarney Stone! Way back, when he was small, my grandfather predicted that Hushang would lead a life of rip-roaring achievement. As events would prove, Grandfather was prescient.

Mother adored her first-born, put him on a pedestal, and showered him with love and attention. Hushang was her golden boy. She was effusive in her admiration when he showed initiative or learned something new. She made sure he had the right playmates and friends, and her maternal instincts kicked in in full force to protect him from inadvertently getting into trouble.

I was not so fortunate.

Over time, Mother herself told me in bits and pieces the story of my desolate infancy. With a slight flush to her face, she spoke hesitantly and with reluctance, but I needed to hear what I had already suspected about my beginnings from my siblings' innuendos and taunts. This was not a ghost I could lay to rest.

Mother had had a difficult pregnancy with her first-born, and lingering health issues afterwards, including abdominal separation which failed to improve. When she had her second and third births, she fervently prayed for no more children, but it was not to be, as birth control was unknown in Shiraz. Besides, she was already at her limit running a large household. She cursed her luck when she became pregnant yet again. There was no rejoicing at my arrival, and she was in no mood to love and cuddle her new baby. Unable to airbrush out my existence, Mother turned me over to a succession of maids hoping they'd serve as wet nurses, each lasting for only a short time.

Impatient and exasperated, Mother then hired as my caregiver a stocky male servant named Sadeq who was known to be an angry and violent person. She felt she simply had no choice. Infant formula being unavailable in Shiraz at the time, how this man was supposed to feed the baby entrusted to his care weighed heavily on her mind. When she eventually checked up on me, I was "emaciated to the edge of starvation" and "showed signs of physical abuse." Belatedly, she tried to fire Sadeq but he grabbed me roughly under his arm and refused to leave, threatening "you'll never see your baby again." So, Mother gave in and kept him on.

My emotions swirled as she spoke. She related all this as if her mind could see no connection between me and the nightmare she was describing.

Struggling not to flinch, I was still shocked and depressed by her revelations; they were reminders of the bleak and loveless feelings that had dogged my earliest days and of the terror I still felt at the merest reminder of Sadeq. It was cruel fate that had made me the last-born of Mother's children. If I could have reverse-engineered my own birth then, I would not have hesitated to trigger it.

Past the infancy stage, my earliest memory was seared on my brain before I was two years old. Father had a midday break and would come home for lunch. Mother was the efficient homemaker all morning, cooking, cleaning, shopping, and sewing, but shortly before his arrival, she became a transformed woman. She would put on a pretty dress, comb her hair, and carefully apply makeup. A small woman with wavy black hair and luminous brown Persian eyes and delicate features, Mother would be standing by the door looking daisy fresh as Father arrived. She'd smile, take his jacket and hat, and sit with him as he ate the meal she had set out. I had no idea what they talked about; I'd assume he told her about his day and she reciprocated in kind.

Being too young for school then, I was the only child at home at these times. With unbridled enthusiasm, I'd do everything I could to get my parents' attention. I'd run around them, roll on the floor, jump up and down, and keep up a steady stream of one-sided infantile conversation, wishing to be included in their intimate *tête-à-tête*, but nothing worked. They had eyes only for each other. To my amazement, they didn't even seem to see or hear me, as if I were Casper the Friendly Ghost.

Later when I turned six I came down with respiratory diphtheria. With no vaccine available, I was a very sick child and had to spend a month in the hospital. Aunt Baji visited me there twice, staying more than an hour each time. I'd stare into the hall for hours to see if Mother was coming but she never did. Neither did anyone else from my family. I felt isolated, unwanted, and utterly alone.

In time I'd learn there was a strict protocol in the Ansary household, as there was in the local society, and it was based on seniority in rank or age. As the newest addition to the clan, I was relegated to the lowest rung of the ladder. Too young to understand social structure, I was only aware that I stood at the bottom of the household hierarchy and had to bear the consequences: As a small boy curious about the world, I repeatedly got into trouble or was injured, at times seriously, because no one was looking after me. The message of my lowly status was, of course, not lost on my siblings, particularly on brother Barry (about whom more later). It was all a lasting shock to this small boy's self-image.

Still, I came to understand that there were reasons for Mother's neglect, and that she had her own history. Over time I also realized she had her share of good qualities. Starved for parental attention, however, I hitched my affection to Father. He was a busy man and away a lot and I had to work for it, but he could be attentive to me as he was to all his children.

———•••———

Father was transferred to Isfahan, a thriving metropolis, when I was almost three. He rented a small house for us on a cul-de-sac in a residential part of town. We shared an alley with four other houses.

Shortly after arriving in town, I wandered alone out of the house one morning into the alley. No one had told me not to, and Mother was busy elsewhere. Someone, perhaps a construction worker, had left a section of a tree trunk on the ground. It was not fully sawed off, so a thin and long portion, almost like a handle, stuck out from the log. After giving it a few pulls, I quickly learned it was too heavy for me to lift.

Just then I caught a mesmerizing sight. A Persian cat and her four kittens came by in single file, the mother first, followed by the kittens, from largest to smallest. They seemed to be enjoying their outing, and were beautiful to watch. They held their heads high, their eyes forward, and lifted their feet in the synchrony of a parade, or the enchanting tableau of a feline ballet. My attention was caught by the smallest cat, the last in line and the closest to where I was standing. He was obviously proud of being with his family, and kept up. I well remember my joy at seeing him. I loved that beautiful furry little Persian kitten and wished he were mine so I could play with him.

Out of nowhere, a big boy suddenly appeared, probably a neighborhood kid. He was big compared to me, maybe my brother Barry's age, about eight. Spotting the kittens, he picked up the log and with no warning rushed over to the cats, raised the log over his head like an executioner and brought it down in a powerful blow on the smallest of the cats. As the others frantically scattered, the tiny kitten fell, howling in pain and exposing its stomach. The boy, as though gripped by madness, raised and brought the log down in rapid-fire fashion on the kitten's soft belly three times. With the last blow, the kitten's breath came out in a sigh. Effervescent with life and joy only moments before, he collapsed, limp and lifeless.

It had all happened in seconds, like a blur. The boy casually dropped the log, mumbling to himself as he walked away. I couldn't make out what he said, but it sounded as though he had just proven something and was proud of himself for it.

I felt paralyzed by the act of mindless savagery I had just witnessed. That boy obviously had a hole in his head where his capacity for compassion should have been. A part of me died that day with the innocent little kitten. Shaken to my soul, I quietly cried myself to sleep that night, grieving for the tiny being whose image was etched in my young mind for all eternity.

Chapter Four

Playing Banker

Father had never made it to Europe or America, but he often
spoke with reverence about Western society. His longing to
visit those distant places came through in his wistful tone. He
also believed that speaking Persian put Iranians at a disadvantage
in dealing with the rest of the world. Persian script was alien to
Europeans as it was written right to left, the opposite of Latin-based
languages. He cited Turkey as a model for modernizing a nation.
Atatürk had pulled Turkey into the modern world by, among other
measures, switching the Turkish alphabet from Arabic to Roman,
imposing a dress code, lifting the ban on alcohol, and passing laws
granting rights to women.

So, Father tutored his number-one son in English from early
childhood, and Hushang was fluent by the time he was ten. Father
was then transferred to a hardship post in a Persian Gulf port and
was gone for three years, leaving Hushang, ten years old, as the
man of the house. Shortly afterwards, Mother took sick and had to
be hospitalized. Four years old, I was too young to understand her
problem or to know whether it was serious. Hushang decided we
should visit Mother to see how she was doing. We four children
trooped down to the hospital and went in search of Mother's room.

The building was eerily quiet, men and women walking silently
in the halls. With white walls and brown wooden furniture and
odd odors, the place was fairly uninviting. In some of the rooms,
people were lying in beds looking pale and forlorn. I was just
following my sparrow-skinny but energetic older brother, sure he
knew where to go.

We had turned down a hallway when a tall gray-haired woman dressed all in white blocked our way. I recognized the uniform— she was a nurse, just like my aunt. I knew nurses were kind and gentle, but there was no welcome in this lady's demeanor. The lift of her eyebrows showed her displeasure, and she was looking down on my brother as though he was from another planet. Unfortunately, I couldn't understand a word she said. There was a clear language barrier.

Hushang, however, was not fazed. As I watched with wide-eyed admiration, he answered back in the same alien tongue. He was unafraid, voluble, and forceful. He talked so long that the English nurse gave up and walked off in a huff. We then proceeded to Mother's room, only to discover that she was in no shape for a visit from her raucous brood. We left quickly. Perhaps that was the reason children were not allowed in that wing of the hospital.

My aunt, Mother's younger sister, was a nurse in the same facility. She told us later that the entire hospital had been abuzz about the little Persian boy who had gone toe-to-toe with the head nurse and had told her in fluent English that he and his brothers and sister were concerned about their mother and just had to see her.

That day, Hushang went from being just an older brother to becoming my role model. I had to crack the puzzle of that strange tongue in which he excelled. Nothing would do but for me to attain the same skill in the same foreign language.

Studying English became my passion, but Father was away and there was no one to teach me. I forsook running, playing, and climbing trees in the Zoroastrians' orchard for any opportunity to pick up an English word or phrase. There was a camp of Indian soldiers near our home, and I started hanging around them as they chatted in English. I paid attention to the cadence of the language. I'd focus on the delivery of a whole sentence without knowing the words. I was even able, parrot-like, to blurt out a phrase with no idea what I was saying. The Indian men were tolerant and friendly. Sometimes they'd interrupt what they were doing to give me a language lesson. Another passerby, an elderly Canadian, happened to hear me struggling with simple English words and started interrupting his daily walks to work with me. I was not learning much, merely absorbing the atmosphere. Language teachers would probably call it training one's ear.

Father was still away when I turned five. He had signed up my siblings for kindergarten by that age, so that they could interact with other children and learn new things, but in his absence Mother did not think of it for me. Without playmates, I hung around the house all day, mopey and alone. One day, Hushang came home from school and announced that he had a book for me. His school had a library but no books were permitted to be taken out. Hushang had taken it without permission and had to put it back the next morning before its loss was discovered. It was a children's book, an unheard-of prize for a youngster in Shiraz. It had black-and-white drawings and some writing. It was my introduction to the world of words. For me, it was like the discovery of the first gravitational wave. Now I had another obsession—an attachment to books and reading. One I never overcame.

———•••———

In time, I started attending a boys' school in Shiraz named Nemazee School. It went from first grade through the eleventh grade, but the headmaster was nice enough to allow me to skip first grade after a test. The school was named for a mysterious benefactor, but no one I knew had ever met him. It was said that Mr. Nemazee was a legendary magnate from the Far East, that he was originally from Shiraz, and that he had made a fortune in shipping in Shanghai, Hong Kong, and other areas of the Orient in the 1920s.

Nemazee School was known for its emphasis on academics, but it had no sports programs. There was a gym in town, but it was for adults only and consisted of a small, dark, and dank basement room with a pit in the middle of the floor. Into this pit only one man could descend at a time. He'd then pick up the handle of a cylindrical weight in each hand and begin twirling both around his shoulders. Those who practiced this exercise soon developed massive shoulder muscles. It was a sign of manliness.

The absence of organized sports at school led to an impressive variety of attempts by the students to prove their athletic prowess. When I was in fifth grade, an upperclassman named Hassan bet one hundred rials ($1.50) that he could leap a *qanat*. Like the aquifers of ancient Rome, the *qanats* were a vast network of wells connected by underground rivers that brought fresh water from distant mountains to local farms; they also supplemented a community's water supply. Relics of a technology abandoned thousands of years ago, the *qanats* numbered in the hundreds in the country; dozens still survived in and around Shiraz. (And no, in case any reader should be wondering, there were no remains of virgins sacrificed to the gods in those wells such as you'd find, according to my science teacher, in the ancient Olmec and Maya ruins in Latin America.)

The *qanats* were forty to fifty feet deep, and at the top their diameter was twenty-five or thirty feet. Hassan, an eleventh-grader, was tall, lithe, and fast on his feet. He had the reputation of never walking away from a challenge. Nevertheless, short of an Olympic athlete, no sane person would attempt jumping across one of those wells. We all thought Hassan was just having fun. People were always betting with each other, mostly about small things. It was a cultural trait; it added a tang to ordinary conversations. Then another student took Hassan's bet, put up the money, and dared him to try it.

A buzz of excitement ran through the schoolyard as word of the bet spread. During the lunch break, several dozen boys, including me, followed Hassan on the way to the *qanat* about a mile out of town. It was a nice outing on a mild and sunny day, but most doubted that anything would happen. *Hassan couldn't be that foolish, could he?* It was a given that if he tried and didn't make it, his chances of survival from the fall in the deep well were slim to none.

At the site, the moment of truth had arrived. Unbelievably, Hassan hadn't been kidding; he really meant to try this crazy stunt. Seeing he was serious, several tried to talk him out of it. The boy who was putting up the money told Hassan he'd pay him *not* to jump, but he was adamant.

A hush fell over the crowd as he started limbering up. Tension seized the group, many still expecting that Hassan would try to find a face-saving way to bow out. He himself seemed oblivious to the buzz of the spectators. He was focused on his stretches and squats, still warming up. This lasted about fifteen more minutes. He then walked back some thirty-five or forty feet, turned around to face the *qanat,* and took several deep breaths. Then, like a sprinter in a long jump, he abruptly took off in a flat-out dash toward the well, leaped off the edge and was airborne… and came down on the other side. But just barely. Then he rolled on the ground in obvious agony, with the edge of a bone protruding from his right leg. Several rushed over to him. One of the upperclassmen said Hassan had a compound fracture.

Without qualified medical care, Hassan's bone was not set properly. He had a long recovery, missed a lot of school, and was handicapped with a permanent limp. Of course, he had not done the stunt for the money. Teenage kids had no ready outlet for their youthful energies; it led them to take high-risk pathways to compete.

While growing up, I got an allowance that was the equivalent of one cent every two weeks. My siblings, being older, got more. I'd want to spend mine buying treats after school like my classmates. I'd try postponing the pleasure, but the aroma of vegetables and chicken legs being cooked over an open fire by the ubiquitous street vendors was difficult to resist with money in my pocket. I'd end up splurging before the day was out, most often by buying a roasted ear of corn on the cob, dunked in a saline solution for extra flavor. I would then have to go without for fourteen more days before I got the next allowance.

We went to school six days a week and were off on Fridays. On Thursdays, school let out two hours early. We would then rush home to do our homework and get it behind us. That way, we would have all of Friday free for play. Then the entire clan would descend on our already-busy household—all the cousins, aunts, and uncles. The grownups would pass the time talking or playing cards, chess, backgammon, or poetry-recital games while sipping tea. The children, often as many as nineteen, would play, climb trees in the Zoroastrians' orchard, have a foot race, or play soccer in the backyard with a homemade ball made of strips of cloth.

Being small, I was always relegated to watching and cheering. Or I'd hang around the grownups, hoping they'd want to play their poetry games and would let me participate. Otherwise, I'd just listen in on their conversations. Most had government jobs and often complained of deadly-dull paper-shuffling. They also felt there were few other life choices for them.

After I started school, I had my own special friends. We were a gang of five—two Armenian brothers, an Assyrian boy, a Jewish kid, and myself. For us, it was the best of times, before our young minds were adulterated by prejudice. I picked up a few Armenian phrases and some Yiddish words, but the Assyrian kid, also a Christian, did not want to share his language with me.

———···———

Father was assigned to yet another city when I was nine and took all of us with him. He was to run a bank branch in a town called Abadeh, halfway between Shiraz and Isfahan. It was a small community, so he was a prominent citizen there. I saw him as a respected local leader and wanted to pattern myself after him. I emulated his walk and tried to act like him. He tolerated me as I watched him manage the local branch. He was always telling my brothers that the most fulfilling work would be to go into business for themselves, as he wished he had done when he was young. He did not know it, but he was spreading the gospel of the entrepreneurial life to his children.

Well, if business was good enough for my father, it was good enough for me.

So I decided to set up my own bank. I got hold of some blank sheets of paper and cut them into small rectangular pieces like the checks Father used at his branch. I called my bank the Commercial Bank of Iran and printed the checks by hand. I then co-opted a small subterranean closet at home as my office. You had to crouch down to get into it.

I called myself the president and appointed sister Pary as the teller. I invited her into my "office" and gave her a blank check to use. Filled with my own importance as a banker, I left her in the closet, then went out to play, not realizing that the closet could only be opened from the outside. Pary was locked in the dark and cramped space. She cried out, but no one heard her. By the time I got back—more than an hour later—she was in hysterics.

Thus my first attempt at going into business at age nine ended in disaster. Undaunted, I was sure I'd set up a real bank someday.

———•••———

While still in Abadeh, I had a most unhappy experience. My favorite cousin, a funny and playful teenager who had been living with us, came home one day with a bag of purple grapes. We all gathered around him. We loved fresh fruit, but the Zoroastrians' orchard was miles away in Shiraz. Here, fruit was expensive, and there was never enough to go around. My cousin said the grapes were for all of us to share, and he'd be washing and distributing them right away.

Just then Father walked in unexpectedly. One look at him and I knew something was terribly wrong. He said the grapes had been stolen. My cousin would have to be punished, and the grapes returned to the grocer. He said all this in a low tone, but none of us could miss the angry edge in his voice. Father took him to a room and closed the door. The sound of the blows left me horrified, in tears, and fearful.

Honesty and honor were Father's foundational principles, so I could understand his deep disappointment. It was still one of the worst experiences of my childhood. The lesson of Father's discipline, of course, was being conveyed equally forcefully to all of us that day. That night and for several nights afterwards, I envisioned my cousin's puffed-up face after his punishment. I felt that in his eagerness to do a good turn for us, he had made an all-too-human mistake. For the first time in my young life I was deeply critical of Father's method of teaching integrity. There had to be other effective but less painful ways of instilling morals in a boy.

Chapter Five

A Daunting Move

Perhaps because of that early hospital experience visiting Mother, Hushang announced he wished to study medicine upon graduation from high school. There was, however, no medical school in Shiraz. In fact, at the time no high school in Shiraz even had a twelfth grade, and the only institution of higher learning in the country was Tehran University, established nine years earlier in the capital city.

If Hushang were to finish high school and enter medical school, he'd have to do so in Tehran. Father decided the rest of his children would soon have similar educational needs. So it was best for the whole family to move to the capital city—a huge change for us. Father quickly went ahead to apply for a transfer to the bank's headquarters in Tehran, a city of over a million. We then waited weeks to see whether Hushang would get his wish.

The day Father's transfer came through, I happened to be sitting with him as he opened the envelope. The color drained from his face as he read the order. The transfer, not having been initiated by the bank, was approved subject to Father bearing all of his own moving expenses. That made the move a financial calamity. Nevertheless, Father was still determined that his eldest son would have the best education possible. We had lived comfortably on his modest income in Shiraz, but how would that work in big, expensive Tehran?

Father had managed adversity before, and he'd do so again. By the time he announced his plans for the move he had regained his resolve. The family would relocate as soon as the school year was out. For me, that meant finishing fifth grade.

Father went on ahead to Tehran to find lodging for us. About a month later, we vacated our happy home in Shiraz. We were sad about it, but also curious and excited about what awaited us in the capital city. Mother bought bus tickets for the six of us—four children, Aunt Baji, and Mother herself. When the day of the move came, the bus was overcrowded. The baggage was piled high and lashed on top, but there weren't enough seats. The driver had oversold the trip. People started complaining. Arguments ensued, and we feared we'd be thrown out on the street. As it turned out, Mother, Aunt Baji, and three of us children got seats, but Hushang had to ride in a truck with a vile-tempered driver on route to Tehran.

The unpaved roads were dusty, rocky, uneven, and in places washed out or full of potholes. On the first day we passed through Persepolis, where so much of Persian history had played out and was thus an important archaeological site. The driver announced there would be a thirty-minute stop. All of us were eager to explore the remains of what had once been a magnificent palace of ancient Persian kings for two centuries, beginning in 520 B.C. We saw soaring columns supported by stone pillars, and obelisks with exquisite bas-relief carvings of the leaders of the era. We saw the ruins of the royal quarters, council chambers, and audience halls. We would have liked to spend more time, but the bus was ready to continue to Isfahan, the second-largest city in the country with its own landmarks and ancient sites.

In the seventeenth century, Isfahan had served as the capital of Persia. It was known for its art and architecture. The striking part of the city's downtown was a vast square surrounded by a palace, the bazaar, and twin minarets wrapped in shimmering green-and-white tiles with intricate geometric designs. Every evening the square was filled with families and their children, street vendors hawking fruit, snacks, and nuts, and musicians playing popular Persian melodies.

There were plenty of inns, hotels, restaurants, and coffee shops in Isfahan, but not for us. We slept on hard ground under the stars that night. After more stops, mostly caused by mechanical problems, we reached our destination on the third day.

The first sight of Tehran, the big, busy, and bustling capital city, was bewildering. Cars, trucks, and buses crowded the streets, all of them in a race to see who could honk his horn the loudest and longest. As for the pedestrians, more of them were jostling each other on the sidewalks than you'd see in a month on Zand Avenue in Shiraz. The swirling urban chaos was both exciting and intimidating.

Worn out from the trip when we finally arrived, we were eager to see the accommodations Father had found for us. To our dismay, they turned out to consist of two tiny rooms in an old and dingy tenement house on a dark, narrow, and congested alleyway where broken windows seemed to predominate. My stomach tightened and my nose wrinkled at the smells. I saw lines of camels slowly making their way past the house, with bells hanging from their necks clanging endlessly, competing with cars with loud mufflers and street vendors hawking their wares in the noisy neighborhood. I was sure this was the city's foul underbelly. It was a shock to realize that this squalid slum was a part of the nation's capital. I felt as though a hive of bees had gone to war on my chest.

Incredibly, all seven of us lived, ate, and slept in those two rooms for the rest of the summer. There was simply no choice, and the cramped and uncomfortable quarters made us all cranky and irritable. We missed our home with the big backyard in Shiraz and the familiar stars in the night sky. We missed the scent of roses, the Zoroastrians' lush fruit orchard adjacent to our home and their grove of cypress, pomegranate, walnut, and lime trees, and the familiar sights and smells and variety of all the other flowers. We also missed the roosters' cock-a-doodle-doos awakening us at dawn, and our maternal grandfather and his family living with us. I particularly missed my special friends. All of us held on to our temper with an effort.

It did not take long for me to learn about Tehran. The northern part of the city, at an elevation of over four thousand feet, was a great swath of luxury homes, tree-shaded streets, wide boulevards, and elegant parks. Far lower in elevation was south Tehran where we now lived, with narrow streets, belching chimneys, the hovels of the lower classes, and rampant crime. Sandwiched between the north and south sectors was the business district of the city, with shopping areas, government offices, and foreign embassies.

With no friends in town, I had little to do until school started in September, but I dreaded having to attend school in that part of town. Time dragged, with little new happening to change our minds about the unpleasant life to which we were subjected in the capital city.

One day, I came in from running an errand for Mother to find two women, a mother and her daughter, sitting in the yard sobbing uncontrollably. Another woman was trying to calm them, but they were inconsolable. Other tenants came by to see what was happening. It turned out that the older woman was recently widowed. An acquaintance of her late husband's had approached her to invest in his business venture. Still in a state of mourning so soon after her loss, the widow, filled with grief on the one hand and worried about how to support herself and her daughter on the other, invested the meager family savings as the man recommended. Shortly afterwards—in fact, that very morning—he had informed her that all the money was lost. He regretted it, but he assured her it was not his fault.

I felt awful for the poor lady and could sense her helpless outrage and desperation. Even to my untutored mind, it was clear she had been swindled. Her lack of sophistication about money matters had left her wide open to the wiles of a scoundrel. In a society where decent jobs for women were virtually nonexistent, her plight was serious. I agonized over what she could do and whether there were any protections for people like her.

Witnessing this episode turned out to have been a watershed event in the course my career would take in later life.

Chapter Six

Teenage Brother and the Piano Teacher

With straight-arrow parents, you'd hardly expect to read about a family scandal, but with brother Hushang around anything was possible.

Just before school started in September, Father found a rental house for us in a nicer neighborhood, a new subdivision in north Tehran. We would be sharing the house with another family, a widow and her two teenage children. Her late husband had been Father's boss in Shiraz, a kind and likeable fellow. In charge of all the southern provinces for Bank Melli, he had gone on an inspection tour of the branches in the Persian Gulf area. At the time, fierce bandits still roamed the country, making travel hazardous. He was waylaid and captured by roving highwaymen, who treated him with such wanton cruelty that he died from his injuries. His grieving family would now be living with us.

I started sixth grade at a nearby boys' school called Kakh Elementary ("kakh" being the Persian word for "palace"). The student body had been together since first grade. As the newcomer from the provinces, I found no welcoming warmth from anyone, neither the students nor the teachers. In the first week of school, one of the boys tripped me as I was walking down from the second floor. I rolled down several steps and had a painful sprained ankle from the fall. It was my introduction to Kakh Elementary in the capital city; I had to cope with nonstop bullying and got into many fights. When I started a newspaper at the school, I had a brief respite, but it didn't last. Concerned about my plight, brother Barry stopped by the school one day to complain to the principal about the harassment I faced. The principal told me the next day that my brother needed an attitude adjustment himself. So nothing changed.

I was not the only one having problems with life in Tehran. We had moved so Hushang could attend Tehran University after finishing high school, but he never made it. The cost of living was high in the capital, as was the rent on our new house. With World War II still raging, food and other staples were rationed, and we had trouble making ends meet. Hushang had to forgo further education for himself and start working to help support the family. He took a day job in an export-import firm and a night job in a British army camp. Nothing if not adaptable, he also tried to set up his own company for exporting local products to England.

As if all that were not enough to keep him busy, Hushang also applied to become a foreign correspondent for London-based International News Service. Craftily neglecting to mention he was a teenager who hadn't yet finished high school, he received an immediate reply. He got the appointment for which he applied, and INS sent him his press credentials. His first assignment was to interview the king and queen of Iran. Undaunted, Hushang took a photographer with him to the palace and then wrote a piece about Iran's royalty. One of the photos was of a bucolic scene in which the royal couple were having a picnic. A portion of Hushang's writing, together with that photo, appeared in *Newsweek* with his byline.

Not for my brother to think small. I was proud of him, of course, but also dismayed. He was setting an awfully high bar for the rest of us.

Shortly afterwards, Hushang announced he had signed up to take piano lessons. At one time or another, each of us had tried to persuade Father to let us take music lessons. He always said we couldn't afford it. So, Barry and Pary told Hushang they were happy for him, it was great, they were envious, etc. (Once Barry started working and making money, he too would sign up for lessons with the violin.) Outwardly, I joined the parade and wished Hushang well, but I was skeptical. With his busy schedule, his sudden interest in music sounded fishy to me.

My curiosity aroused, I decided to investigate. I wouldn't have pegged myself for a snoop, but this day I learned otherwise. There was an envelope sticking out of Hushang's jacket hanging nearby. Making sure he wasn't around, I quickly lifted it out to read. As I expected, it was addressed to the piano teacher. I knew Hushang would throw a hissy fit if he caught me, but I was committed.

Feeling terribly guilty and breathing hard, I took out the three-page, single-spaced typed letter he had written to the teacher. Unbelievably, my teenage brother was professing undying love in lurid English prose to a woman I was sure was twice his age. Not like that boy to do anything halfway. I was on the second page—and laughing my head off—when he caught me. I gave him my best innocent look, but it didn't work. He was furious.

"Being so nosy," he said all too seriously, punctuating each word by painfully squeezing my arm "will get you in real trouble someday, Cyrus."

Well, okay, but I still thought it was hilarious.

———••———

It should have been foreseeable that by the time Hushang reached his mid-teens, his strong personality would bring him into direct conflict with Father's equally strong precepts. Predictably, in time there were spectacular clashes between them, shattering the tranquility of our home. Family conflicts were becoming a common occurrence.

You know what they say about elephants battling? The other denizens of the forest would do well to stay out of the way, or be trampled.

Chapter Seven

An Elite High School

S till the harassed outsider at school, I was never more relieved than the day sixth grade was over. I had no idea where I'd be going to high school, but that was of small moment. What mattered was that I'd no longer have to put up with the unpleasant atmosphere and the unfriendly kids at Kakh Elementary. Actually, it was not only the other students I wanted to flee from, it was also the unimpressive teachers.

Iran's educational system rewarded scholastic achievement far above sports or music. It had a countrywide system of academic testing for students at the end of elementary school and again at the end of secondary school. At those times, students had to take their finals, not at their own schools and with their own teachers, but at the ministry of education, and the results were published in all the newspapers.

As the day approached when the grades would be announced, the anxiety level was palpable for students and parents alike. If you received failing grades in two subjects, you were *refusé*, which meant you had to repeat a grade, and you were shunned like a leper. The fear of being disgraced as *refusé* hung over all our heads. I was particularly worried, as the teachers at Kakh had generally treated me as though I was brainless. One particular teacher singled me out more than once as an example of a poor student. With that teacher, I'd cringe and try to be invisible each time he turned his eyes in my direction.

The wait to get the results of the finals was sheer torture for me. None of my siblings had ever flunked out. If I were to break the mold and achieve the dreaded status of a *refusé*, Father would not be just disappointed, he'd be furious.

At last the wait was over, and the results were in. I couldn't have been more startled at seeing how I had done. I thought my eyes were deceiving me, and I had to read the results again. It was the most WOW moment of my life. I was ranked second in the nation. Among sixth graders, that is. To compound the irony, I had actually missed being first by a fraction of one percent. Nothing had prepared me for the prospect that I might excel at something, nothing at school, and certainly nothing at home. Anyway, who'd believe that the intellectual performance of sixth graders would be measured with the precision accorded Olympic hundred-meter racers?

Those rankings garnered lots of attention in the press for the top performers, and I received a prize from the Shah at a public event. The prize consisted of three books on Persian history and literature with appropriate inscriptions. The other winners received similar prizes. Instead of the failure I so feared, I had a moment of fame. The same students who had delighted in bullying the provincial newcomer in sixth grade were now suddenly my best friends. That was all right with me, but the real reward came later.

To continue my schooling, Father had his eyes on Alborz High School, located on a magnificent, wooded campus. Set against the bright background of the snow-laden Alborz Mountains, the school had been an American college at one time, founded by the Presbyterian Church in the closing years of the nineteenth century. It was now a boys' school of about 650 students in grades seven through twelve. With its soccer field, running track, volleyball court, gymnastics equipment, chemistry lab, and a large auditorium, Alborz was the envy of all the other high schools. I was worried about admission, and from Father's tone, I could tell he too had some difficulty with the choice. I hesitated to probe, but I did ask whether it was free. He told me the tuition was high but not to worry we'd manage it.

So it was with mixed feelings that I accompanied Father on an afternoon in early September 1944 to enroll at Alborz. The building was crowded with fathers and sons lining up to register. We gave our names and then waited in line for our turn with the registrar, who was seated at a table at the end of a hall. It would be a long wait.

Within a few minutes a man approached Father.

"Sir," he said politely, "the headmaster would like to see you."

Surprised, Father followed the man to another part of the building. He was gone about fifteen minutes. When he came back, he was uncharacteristically ebullient and eager to relate his conversation. The headmaster was pleased that Father had chosen Alborz for me. He assured him that I would receive a vigorous academic education there, and that the teachers were among the best in the nation. As Father was beginning to wonder what all this attention was about, the school principal told him that my academic standing in the sixth-grade finals entitled me to free tuition for the entire duration of high school. Father was pleased that I was being admitted to Alborz, where he knew I'd get a first-rate education. And, of course, he was relieved by this unexpected boon to the family budget.

Alborz was an elite school, ranked as an intellectual institution on par with Eton College in England and Phillips Academy Andover in the U.S. Father, moved as always by the powerful ideal of a great education for each of his children—what he himself sadly lacked—was obviously aware of the school's reputation, why he had picked it for me. Did I feel any gratitude for this chance? Wish I could say yes, but I was a clueless teenager. I did attend Alborz and did my homework, but my heart was not in it.

Like everyone else, I had no choice about my birth, but I knew how I wanted to live my life. In Iran's hierarchical society—and in the equally hierarchical Ansary household—being the youngest and smallest of a brood had never been a picnic. That reality, coupled with Father's admiration of Western culture, continued to arouse in me dreams about life in other lands.

Chapter Eight

Demosthenes and Me

I n 1944, the year I started Alborz, the world was still plunged in war, in Europe as well as in the Pacific. There were camps of English, American, and Russian soldiers in Tehran, but we were unaffected by the actual fighting. Iran was just a way station for the delivery of war matériel by the Allies from the Persian Gulf in the south to the Soviet Union in the north. Unbroken lines of trucks traveled nonstop across Iranian highways, the squash-and-growl of shifting gears by their drivers a constant reminder of the reality of death and destruction in a global conflict, the Second World War.

I spent six days a week in school, as was customary, but my preoccupation was with my evening activities. The alien tongue in which Hushang had been fluent was no longer an unfathomable puzzle as it had been to my four-year-old ears. Luckily, Cambridge University had recently set up a campus in Tehran; it had been growing like a field of wild mushrooms. For those with inquiring minds, it had excellent programs. I signed up for twice-weekly night classes in the Cambridge Lower Secondary program while in seventh grade at Alborz.

Before the year was out, I took the exam, passed it, and was accepted into the Cambridge Proficiency curriculum. By then I was already in eighth grade at Alborz. Most of the students in this advanced program, which took three years to complete, were adults, and almost all of the instructors were accredited Cambridge University professors. It was an intellectually challenging regimen, and I reveled in its depth and variety.

We studied the works of Charles Dickens, George Bernard Shaw, J. B. Priestley, and others, and wrote essays on manifold topics. I was surprised to discover that the curriculum also covered English commercial and financial practices. I heard for the first time about common and preferred shares, bonds and debentures, bailments and commercial contracts, balance sheets and profit-and-loss statements. I was particularly eager to learn this material, as I remembered the episode in the old tenement house in which the poor widow found out she had lost her funds entrusted to a "friend" on the promise of large returns. It was all heady stuff for me, and I yearned to hear more.

At times, the Cambridge campus also put on plays, musicals, chess competitions, and other activities to which the public were invited. The placards announcing these events were always colorful; they were attractively done by hand as there were no machines for the task. I was mesmerized by the calligraphy and decided to take it up. It became a lifetime hobby for me and a source of endless pleasure.

The Cambridge Proficiency course took two evenings a week. I spent another two evenings a week studying French literature at *L'Association des Amis de la Culture Française*. Not knowing where I'd end up abroad, I felt I needed to be fluent in both English and French.

In the meantime, Father was steadily rising in rank at Bank Melli. Shortly after I started Alborz, he found another rental house for us. It had more rooms and a bigger backyard. It was also located near downtown Tehran and convenient to the city's shopping district and government offices.

At home, the daily routine was predictable. Mother and Aunt Baji were the epitome of self-sacrificing Persian women, giving their all for their family. As there was no refrigeration, no shopping centers, and no supermarkets, they had to shop daily all over town for fresh food. There was also no stove, so Mother and Aunt Baji cooked everything on an open fire in the basement. Taking care of a household of seven, including four growing children, meant long days. They both worked eighteen-hour days, seven days a week.

My program of foreign-language studies took place after school, but I followed a regimen of *before*-school activities as well. Tehran was built on the foothills of the Alborz Mountains, a chain that encircled the southern coast of the Caspian Sea and bordered on Iran and Russia. The Caspian is the world's largest inland body of water, best known as a source of sturgeon and caviar.

About halfway between Tehran and the base of the mountain, beyond the northern boundary of the city, were the flashy and cool garden villas of wealthy Tehranis, an area called Shemran. A few miles farther up the slope there was a walled-in piece of raw land, about five acres or so, probably a real estate speculator's private acreage. Located at the end of a trail a quarter of a mile from the main highway, it was invisible to the heavy road traffic. The tract was surrounded by a wall eight feet high, but there was no structure inside, just barren terrain. This arid and soulless acreage played a pivotal role in my morning ritual.

Mother would wake me at 4 a.m. every weekday, the same time she and Aunt Baji started their daily chores. I'd splash water on my face, pull on my shirt and shorts, and with the stars still shining in the predawn sky, I'd set off in the cool air walking north. A solitary street cleaner sweeping the pavement, an occasional teenage boy riding his bike, a stray cat meowing on the steps of a house, a few early-rising Type A's rushing off to their jobs.... These were the common sights at that hour, but the city buses would not start running for a couple of hours yet. It would take me about an hour to get to the walled-in tract, walking uphill all the way. I'd use the time to select a topic to think about. By then the emerging rays of the sun would be almost visible behind the crest of the mountain.

Once there, I'd wait for the ubiquitous speeding trucks to roar past, then cross the highway and walk the short distance to the property. The wall encircling it was built with sand-colored bricks unevenly spaced; it made for an easy climb except when the morning dew caused slippage. I'd scramble to the top, take a moment to check out any passing flocks of sparrows, then start walking around the perimeter of the site. The formidable snow-capped Alborz Mountains were my view to the north, and a dazzling panoramic sight of Tehran was visible to the south.

The air was thin and dry there, and as the pale colors of the dawn broke out fully over the horizon, I'd stand on top of the wall, haughty and proud, delivering a speech on the topic I had selected on the way over. A different one each day. In English. With cars zooming by in the distance and insects trilling nearby, I'd imagine I had an audience of hundreds. My words were like birds taking flight, and I'd use hand gestures, raise and lower my voice for emphasis, and make eye contact with the imaginary people below.

Father had once told me about a famous orator in ancient Athens named Demosthenes who practiced public speaking in his youth by putting stones in his mouth and shouting in the nearby hills. I tried his technique and almost choked. It may have worked for that Greek boy, but it just didn't cut it for this Persian kid.

Anyway, my audience may not have been real, but for me the thrill of delivering an address, even to imaginary people, was real indeed. In an exultant moment, I came up with a grandiose name for that piece of barren ground: I dubbed it my Mound of Oratory.

After my morning speech-making, I'd stop at the bakery to buy fresh bread for Mother on my way home. That was the only part of my morning ritual I did not enjoy. The only bakery in the area, it was always mobbed by early-morning shoppers. The baker never took the customers in order. He'd take care of the adults before getting to me. He'd ask how many loaves each shopper wanted, knead the dough, and slap it into his brick kiln. He'd then have to wait until the bread was ready, before serving the next person. Sometimes he'd make me wait until the shop was empty before serving me, almost making me late for school. Perhaps a handsome tip—really a bribe—would have bought better service, but since the only money I had was to pay for the bread, all I could do was fume and occasionally complain. When I did, the baker would get an unpleasant gleam in his eyes and make me wait even longer. It was humiliating. Ahhh, but someday he'd be sorry…

On the way home, the aroma of the fresh bread was irresistible. Persian bread was called "nan," and the kind I bought came in thin round sheets like large pizzas. I carried them folded over. I'd pinch off pieces and start munching on them as I walked back. By the time I reached home, there was a hole in the middle of each loaf. Mother noticed, of course, but she never mentioned it.

While I was busy at Alborz High School, making early morning speeches, and attending English and French language night classes, Hushang was not exactly sitting still. By 1945 the ground war in Europe was over, and many countries were bursting with optimism about their economic prospects. The export-import firm where Hushang worked decided to expand to England. I suspected that my brother was the one who had planted that idea in his employer's mind. So his boss picked seventeen-year-old Hushang to go to London for two years to open a branch office there. He'd be the first in the family to travel to Europe. Or to ride in an airplane.

We all trooped down to Mehrabad Airport in Tehran to see him off. As the plane prepared to taxi down the runway, the workers tried to remove the wheel chocks, but in the summer heat one of them stuck to the tarmac and would not budge. The pilot revved up the engine to ride over it and the plane took off screaming for the sky, but the blocked wheel came off and went careening down the runway. Would the plane have to make a belly landing at its destination? Would it be safe?

We had a few anxious days until we received a long and newsy letter from Hushang. London was struggling mightily to recover from the ravages of World War II and to rebuild its infrastructure that had been mercilessly bombed by Hitler's Luftwaffe. Shortages remained widespread. There were waiting lists of returning servicemen trying to get into Cambridge and Oxford. Because of the long delays, parents were registering their toddlers on the universities' waiting lists. Hushang registered me for Cambridge. It was a touching gesture, and I thanked him for it. As long shots go, however, this one was quite optimistic for lack of funding, and both of us realized it.

It has been said of collectors—particularly adolescent ones—that they become passionate about the mystical items that capture their fancy. The truth of that aphorism was confirmed by my own pursuit of collectibles.

Some of the boys at school collected stamps as a hobby, some did coins. I wanted to be a collector too, so I looked around for something that would interest me. Father had always shaved with a straight razor, but in Tehran he switched to razor blades. They had not been available in Shiraz. The blades were wrapped individually, and there were colorful brand names and pictures on the small packets. I decided to start a collection of razor blade packets.

I was hooked on my collection all through high school. I had razor-blade covers from Germany, Italy, Japan, U.S., England, France, Egypt, and many other countries. The profiles of their wartime leaders were on the ones made in Germany and Italy. The British covers had either King George VI or the Union Jack, and the Egyptians featured the pyramids. They were all distinct and brightly hued. I begged, borrowed, and bought new ones every chance I had. I was proud of my collection and loved looking at and rearranging the little packets. Once they saw what I was doing, several of my classmates decided to do the same. This made it even more fun, as we began comparing notes and swapping blade covers. We also kept each other informed of new ones as they became available. I lost my razor-blade cover collection in a move. I still regret its loss.

Chapter Nine

A Stab at Currency Arbitrage

With the romance and mystery of foreign lands on my mind, I was a dreamer, long on ambition but broke. Having absorbed Father's attitude toward life and work like a sponge, I was always preoccupied with thoughts of how to fund my education in more nurturing climes. Achieving escape velocity out of the land of my birth, however, had so far proven utterly unattainable.

Still a naive but exuberant teenager, I came up with the idea of canvassing the foreign consulates in Tehran to see if they had any programs for foreigners to study in their countries. Of course they did, but at the students' expense—not what I had in mind. I tried France, Holland, Belgium, Switzerland, and several others to no avail. I would not be deterred, however. If that was not the route to the funding of my education abroad, then perhaps I could pay my own way by getting part-time jobs and saving my earnings.

The kids at Alborz were always asking me for help with their English lessons. *Why not start a school and hold language classes?* That should be a way to pay for a trip abroad, shouldn't it? I bought a piece of plywood and painted "Ansary Language School" on it. After asking Father's permission, I hung it on the front door. Father thought it was a clever idea. I expected some kids to knock. Someone showed up all right, but it wasn't a student. It was brother Barry, my elder by five years, and he was furious. He said I was dishonoring the family name by hanging a sign on the door, and if I didn't take it down, he'd break it.

Barry's objections made no sense to me. How could it be

demeaning to the family to engage in a commercial pursuit, as Barry seemed to believe? From my Cambridge studies, I recalled that in olden times English lords did not soil their hands by working for a living. They often subsisted on patronage from the Crown. But what did that have to do with the Ansary family? *When did we pick up the mores and values of the British aristocracy?* No matter, I just didn't want to get into another argument with my temperamental brother. I knew from experience that a disagreement with Barry would do nothing but raise my blood pressure. He could go from calm to furious in a nanosecond. So I gritted my teeth and took the sign down. I'd have to find another way of getting paying students.

I thought it over and tried a different tack. I passed the word at school that I'd be teaching a class in conversational English for twenty minutes at the lunch break that day. A half-dozen students showed up, and I thanked them for their interest. Someone raised a hand and diffidently asked if I'd be willing to hold another session on the same day the following week. Pleased, I said I'd be glad to.

The next week's session was an eye-opener. The classroom I was using was filled to capacity, and the overflow had to stand in the back. There were quite a few upperclassmen in the group. Aware of the students' need to get home for lunch before returning for the afternoon classes, I tried to limit the session to about twenty minutes, but it ran over.

I did not schedule any more sessions as I already had my answer. There was great demand for English lessons. Of course, what I had done so far was to hold free classes, but I was sure some of the students would be willing to pay for private instruction.

In the next few days, two boys asked if I would tutor them in English. I agreed, at thirty rials (forty cents then) per hour for each. They quickly agreed. When word got around, other students wanted to sign up for private lessons. The father of one of the students recommended me to an army colonel who needed to take an expedited course in English. I agreed, at fifty rials (seventy cents) per hour. A small export-import firm needed someone to translate its English correspondence. I agreed, for thirty rials per page.

A bookstore where I often bought English books and American comic books was owned by a Mr. Artin Skandarian. I was thirteen when I first met him. Iran was home to a large contingent of Christian Armenians whose ancestors traced back to Zoroastrian times. They shared many cultural and religious traditions with the Zoroastrians. I had had many Armenian playmates and friends since childhood. Kindly and middle-aged, Mr. Skandarian was one of the finest men I ever knew. Over time, he and I became friendly, and he'd sometimes let me borrow books without charge. He was actually a citizen of Iraq and spoke only halting Persian. In his youth, he had traveled extensively in Europe. He told me he needed someone to clear his imported English and French books through customs. I agreed at seventy rials ($1.00) per trip.

I got another break soon after. My irrepressible uncle, tall and handsome Mehdi—Mother's lively and energetic younger brother who had always shown a special interest in my upbringing—worked at a remote facility of the ministry of agriculture north of Tehran. He talked with his colleagues there, and forty of them signed up for the monthly English classes. I would charge them a lump sum of 200 rials (almost $3) per month. Spouses of the students could attend at no additional cost. Transportation to the facility would be a problem, but I quickly said I'd do it. This would also give me a chance to see my favorite uncle and his family.

Then I hit the jackpot. Dropping by Mr. Skandarian's bookstore one day, I noticed he seemed troubled. He told me that new government regulations were going to put him out of business. He explained that when he imported books from, say, an English publisher, he'd have to pay for his purchases in pounds sterling. Likewise, importing books from France, he'd have to pay with French francs, and in U.S. dollars for American books. The Iranian government sold foreign currencies at their official rate of exchange, but the new regulations restricted this arrangement to Iranian nationals only. Being a citizen of Iraq, Mr. Skandarian was excluded. His only recourse was to buy what he needed on the open market, but the exchange rate was always much higher than the official rate, sometimes twice as high.

Puzzled, I asked whether he'd mind if I looked into it.

"There isn't much that can be done," he said solemnly, "but go ahead, Cyrus."

I asked Father about Mr. Skandarian's currency problem, and he too was doubtful that anything could be done. "Once a set of regulations is adopted," he remarked, "changing them is often a difficult and prolonged process."

Father had been firm. Still, I thought it wouldn't hurt just to check out what Mr. Skandarian had told me. I already knew where Bank Melli was located on Ferdowsi Avenue, less than two miles from my home. It was also where Iran's Crown Jewels were housed. Father described them as hundreds of diamonds, emeralds, rubies, pearls, and sapphires, worth more than anyone could count. I could only dream about such opulence, but it was great for motivating this child of a modest home.

I decided to start with a visit to Bank Melli. Instead of going straight home from school during the lunch break as I usually did, I caught a bus to Ferdowsi Avenue. I hoped I'd find someone there who had not gone out to lunch. I needn't have worried. There was no receptionist in the large hall in Bank Melli, but there was a line at a teller's window, beyond which there were many people busily working at their desks. I waited my turn and asked the teller if I could talk to someone about buying British pounds. He looked to see how many others were to be processed behind me, then pointed to a door at the other end of the hall and moved on to the next in line. The door to which the man pointed had a small sign that identified it as the "Foreign Exchange Department."

My first afternoon class that day was music, and the teacher was a very nice man. He didn't even question me for showing up late. My mind, however, was not on the first note, it was on foreign exchange regulations. They seemed straightforward. I had learned that anyone could apply to buy foreign currency at the official rate, just as long as you were an Iranian citizen. You'd need to attach a certified copy of your birth certificate to the application. There were monthly limits to the purchase of foreign currencies, but the official rates did not fluctuate. The funds would be paid over to the exporter in the foreign country, not to the purchaser in Iran. I asked if buyers could pool their purchases together, and the man said that, provided everything was legitimate, the bank did not concern itself with a buyer's purpose in obtaining the currency.

I left the bank offices armed with a large stack of blank applications to purchase foreign currency. On the bus back to school, I put together in my mind a list of three of my classmates whom I would enlist in this project with me. I could expand the group to five, but it would be best to keep the circle small for now. I'd assure the others that the bank did not disapprove of what we'd be doing. If this worked, I said to myself, it was worth it to have gone without lunch that day.

I visited Mr. Skandarian's shop after school that evening. He was happy to hear my report. He said he could use at least £20 per month for his book purchases from Britain, similar amounts in dollars for American book purchases, and the same for French imports. He'd pay me a commission of 10 percent of the foreign exchange purchased each month. I figured I'd pay 30 percent of my fee to my friends who participated in this project with me. Mr. Skandarian would pay my commission in rials, which was fine. He gave me the names and addresses of the foreign suppliers he dealt with regularly, and he would give me the cash with which to pay the bank.

The three classmates I approached promptly agreed to the

arrangement. We had to make certified copies of our birth certificates and fill out the application forms. I'd prepare the letters to the foreign exporters in English or French depending on the country, requesting them to credit the amounts to Mr. Skandarian's account.

It was a lot of legwork, but it all went smoothly. Once the process was in place, I would be rolling in dough. A few years of this and I could pay for my own transportation abroad. Besides, there must be other shopkeepers in Tehran in Mr. Skandarian's predicament. I could sign them up too. My schoolwork might suffer, but I'd make up for it once I started attending school abroad. Of course, I'd have to give notice to the students I was now tutoring in English and to the other people I worked for. I wouldn't have time for them.

It all became worthwhile when I showed Father the first commission money I had earned and explained how it had worked out. He kissed me on the forehead and said he was proud of his son. Father was not one to throw around compliments to his children. It meant a lot.

Alas, in less than five weeks my sandcastle came crashing down. The government shut down the whole system. A new edict terminated the issuance of currency at the official rate. Everyone would have to buy foreign money on the open market. A part of me was relieved. My schoolwork was beginning to suffer.

No more financial bonanzas, but my private teaching and other work were thriving. I was having difficulty turning down business. My days were getting longer, and my life was becoming intolerably hectic. I used the school lunch hours and the weekends for tutoring. I had to miss half a day's school each time I went to the customs office for Mr. Skandarian.

After school, I had to catch a bus to get to my evening classes. By the time I'd get home and grab a bite, there was little time for homework or for the translation of the correspondence I had undertaken. Father insisted on lights out at 10 p.m., no exceptions. The frenetic pace, though exhilarating, was causing me to fall behind in my school assignments. Besides, compared with the cost of foreign travel, at the exchange rate of seventy rials to $1, it would take me a couple of centuries to save enough money this way. Clearly, this was not the route to the financing of my education abroad, but I kept on dreaming about the world outside even though I saw no chance of ever getting there.

The Cambridge professors under whom I studied, as much or even more than Father, had managed to plant seeds that were by now in full bloom. My yearning to leave Iran had become a constant ache. I felt claustrophobic in my native land. It was like a loose tooth, to which my thoughts returned, no matter what else was going on.

Chapter Ten

America: The Promised Land

While I was in eighth grade, Alborz ran a school-wide speech contest. Any student could participate and get the opportunity to deliver a speech in Persian to the whole student body in the auditorium. There would be one speaker per week. As it involved public speaking, I'd want to try it. So I was one of six students who chose to participate; the only one from my class. The others were from higher grades.

Hushang happened to be in town and saw the text of my speech on a Friday. He wadded it up and threw it away. He then sat down to write a better speech; he wanted to make sure I'd win the contest. His draft was well written, certainly much better than mine, and I thanked him for it. But when he left, I quickly retrieved my draft and discarded his. I knew that if I won the contest by passing off my brother's creation as my own, I'd feel ashamed of myself. I used my version for the contest.

The faculty was supposed to choose the winner, but when it was over, the school decided not to pick any one student to honor. There was no prize, but a couple of the teachers mentioned they liked my speech. I was thrilled.

In 1946, the U.S. Department of State invited a Tehran University professor to tour the U.S. as part of an initiative to acquaint other nations with postwar American society. The professor sent dispatches to a popular Iranian newspaper under the title "Come with Me to America." Even though he had been detained at Ellis

Island upon arrival in the U.S. because of a mix-up in identification, he was effusive about his experiences on the trip, a substantial part of which he spent at Columbia University.

His portrayal of the American society was bold, graphic, and full of superlatives. He raved about the impressive museums, libraries, and concert halls; the many universities that were citadels of scholarship; the enviable medical facilities. He extolled America's business genius and wrote of department stores that stocked every variety of merchandise. He stressed that he saw no sign of graft or corruption in the country. To top it all off, he saw Americans as generous, hospitable, and friendly.

My eyes lit up as I read the professor's dispatches; they stirred my imagination. Before reading them I had had a vague wanderlust, but the calculus changed afterwards. Father always said university professors were the most trustworthy group anywhere; all I knew was that I was mesmerized by this one. His reports led to an epiphany for me as my goal snapped into focus: America was the end of the rainbow, and I zoomed in on the name like a talisman. It was beckoning to me like the twinkling stars in the skies of Shiraz in my childhood. My pursuit of the Cambridge curriculum made me feel that I was already familiar with British culture, but now I started reading everything I could get my hands on about the American society. I felt exhilarated just thinking about that enchanting land. Father saved the newspapers for me, and I'd read the professor's reports with great eagerness, treasure his descriptions of American life, and wait breathlessly for each new episode.

A few of my classmates at Alborz got the chance to go abroad at their families' expense, to continue their education in England, France, Holland, Canada, or the U.S. How I envied them. They even got a break, as the government permitted the parents to buy foreign currency at the official rate for children studying abroad. My best friend in eighth grade was sent by his family to study in New York. He wrote me often, sent me brochures about American landmarks, and was rhapsodic about his coed school in Yonkers. I had no hope of ever getting there. My father, hard as he worked, could never afford to send me. As quests go, mine continued to be a long shot. Was my longing to travel abroad destined to remain unfulfilled forever?

Soon, I developed an elaborate fantasy about winning a contest and being sent to America. I lived two lives, one in which I tried to act like a normal teenager, the other my all-consuming secret life, which I shared only with my aunt, my favorite uncle's wife. Isn't it a human trait to spin fantasies when goals are unattainable? But do fantasies ever become reality?

In the meantime, I decided to take a bold and unorthodox step toward preparing for my goal of living in America: I'd start *thinking* in English; it appealed to my sense of mission. This would be no idle move, nor would it be easy. Persian was the universal communication medium at home, at school, in offices and stores, and on the only local radio station. What I was proposing would require a special effort. It'd probably create a lag in conversations and set me apart from my contemporaries, who might even think I had become slow-witted. One of my teachers at Alborz liked to lace his lectures with humor. Mentally translating his jokes into English would take all the fun out of them. Perhaps that teacher would think I was humorless or dull.

So be it.

Chapter Eleven

Fantasy Coming True?

I t was early fall of 1948. World War II had been over in Europe for three years, but its ravages of death and destruction would not be forgotten anytime soon. Iran was ruled by a young and enlightened king (more on him later). His father had tried to modernize the country, but the influence of religion was still evident in the presence of many turbaned mullahs whom the public saw as thwarting real progress.

I had just started tenth grade when Father showed me a news item about a major American newspaper, the *New York Herald-Tribune*, planning to convene a forum of high school students from many countries in New York in 1949. The delegates would be selected through a nationwide contest in each country conducted by its education ministry in conjunction with the cultural attaché of the U.S. embassy there. The contestants would be tested for their in-depth knowledge of world affairs, their skill in written communication, and their fluency in English. The winners would be invited to spend three months touring the U.S. and participating in public debates about global affairs.

My fantasy was coming true, I told myself. I could hardly control my excitement.

As the days turned into weeks and the weeks into months with no other news, however, I started getting anxious. I tried to find out anything I could about the program. My first stop was the newspaper office where the blurb had appeared. I spoke with the reporter who had written the piece, but he had no other details. I then went to the ministry of foreign affairs. I was passed from office to office, but no one knew anything. I was beginning to wonder if the initiative would ever materialize. Then one day an Alborz classmate who knew of my interest in the *Herald-Tribune* program told me he had come across some confidential information about it. He was co-captain of the soccer team, a good student, and a good friend. I promised to keep the secret.

"The minister of education has already selected his own son as the delegate." He delivered his bombshell in matter-of-fact tones. "The contest," he added, "even if it were to be held, would be a sham."

As if all that were not enough, he drove the nail home in the coffin of my dream.

"The boy has in fact packed his suitcase," he added, "and is preparing to leave as soon as word comes down from the *Herald-Tribune*."

I was heartbroken.

The following weeks were agonizing for me. I kept brooding over the bit of intelligence my classmate had passed on to me and wondering what I could do if the contest were rigged, as appeared to be the case. In the meantime, there was nothing more in the newspapers, and no press releases out of the ministry of education about the contest.

Weeks passed. I continued my Cambridge Proficiency course, which I'd be completing shortly. I kept up my early-morning speechmaking ritual, albeit sometimes halfheartedly. I also continued my French lessons, but ceased almost all of my outside activities designed to earn money such as tutoring, translating, etc. I did some writing, in Persian, which was published with my byline in a local magazine, but I received no pay for it.

There was no point kidding myself. The goal of continuing my education abroad was becoming more elusive than ever.

Noticing my dispirited mode, Father said, "See what happens when you spend your time reading Captain Marvel comic books instead of good literature?"

So it was all my fault? If he was trying parental humor to cheer me up, it wasn't working.

It was 1949, and I was starting eleventh grade, no closer than ever to continuing my education abroad. I was painfully aware that time was fleeting for me. Then the local papers carried a story about a group of American college students stopping in Tehran for three days. They had already visited Hong Kong, Bangkok, Calcutta, and Delhi. While in Tehran, they were to meet with several local dignitaries and to be hosted by the king at the royal palace. I tried in vain to accompany the group on the rest of their travels. They did in fact take three Iranian university students with them. I consoled myself with the thought that the lucky local kids must have been able to pay their own way.

One morning, shortly after classes started, I was summoned to Dr. Mojtahedi's office. (Some of us had shortened the headmaster's name to Dr. Mo behind his back.) He was a tall man with a full head of brown hair and grey eyes, his face always marked with a serious expression. Students were rarely called into his presence, so I had some trepidation about my summons. *Have I missed too many classes pursuing my outside moneymaking efforts? Am I in line for a reprimand?*

In addition to being our high school principal, Dr. Mo was the most renowned educator in the country. He had been schooled in France and lived on the Alborz campus with his French wife and their ten-year-old son. What he had told my father years earlier was indeed true: He had assembled an outstanding group of teachers at Alborz.

Dr. Mo had only good news for me. He said the minister of education had been asked to nominate a single Iranian student to take part, along with delegates from other countries, in a forum organized by the *New York Herald Tribune* the next spring in New York. Dr. Mo obviously did not realize I knew all about it, but I kept silent. He said the minister would direct each high school to hold its own contest. The winners would then participate in a nationwide contest conducted by the ministry to select the Iranian delegate to the forum. The finalist would be a high school student between fifteen and eighteen years of age who was familiar with the major political and economic issues of the twentieth century and proficient in written and spoken English.

As Dr. Mo spoke, I took a deep breath as my mind was brimming with questions. Was all this a charade cooked up by the minister of education for the sake of appearances, or had he backed off from naming his son as the delegate? In either event, why did Dr. Mo summon me? Was he about to announce an all-Alborz contest to comply with the minister's directive? Was I just being given a heads-up as a courtesy?

Dr. Mo boosted my sagging morale with a final comment. Before calling me in, he said, he had consulted with the vice principal, the dean, and several of my teachers. He said they had voted unanimously to nominate me to represent Alborz in the contest. Dr. Mo said he had already submitted my name to the minister of education.

I was speechless, but the headmaster was not finished. The ministry would hold a series of individual weekly tests to cut down the number of participants. The surviving five would be subjected to more vigorous tests, both written and oral. The minister himself and other government officials would judge the results. Dr. Mo had confidence I'd make the school proud.

And with that, he sent me back to my trigonometry class. Was he kidding? After that kind of news, I should focus on cosines and tangents?

The school vice principal, Mr. Sadre, was a tall, trim, youngish man, brimming with energy and popular with students. He took a special interest in foreign language instruction. I had gotten to know him and liked him. He obviously knew about my conversation with Dr. Mo when he stopped me in the hall the next day. He said all the contestants were required to get a letter from their parents consenting to their travel to America if selected. I promised to get my father to sign one, and I would bring it the next day. I then asked him if a date had been set for the contest. He said the school had not been notified.

Only a few days later, I happened to run into a friend from another school. We stopped to chat.

"By the way, Ansary," he said, "why didn't you participate in the contest to send someone to America? You could have won if you had."

My heart sank. I could not wait to find Mr. Sadre. On Monday I asked him if it was true that the contest had already been held. He knew nothing about it and suggested I should make inquiries at the ministry of education.

There, the next day, I was directed to the vice minister, a Mr. Shamlou, who saw me promptly at two, greeted me in a pleasant tone as I introduced myself and asked what I wanted. He had been my teacher at one time but did not recognize me. Not surprising, that. Nobody at Kakh Elementary had taken me seriously until I aced the sixth-grade nationwide rankings.

When I mentioned to Mr. Shamlou that I had been selected to represent Alborz High School in the *Herald-Tribune* contest, there was a noticeable change in his demeanor. He started talking in a low voice, almost a whisper, as though we were at a funeral. He told me that priority would go to candidates who had already received their high school diplomas.

Emulating his whisper, I asked, "Would the ministry hold a contest?"

"We might."

"Would it be in English?" I persisted.

"No," he answered, "but English may be one of the subjects if a contest were held."

As I took my leave, he repeated what he had whispered earlier: "Remember what I said. Candidates must have their high school diplomas in hand to qualify."

I was stunned. In one decisive stroke, the vice minister had kicked me out of the competition to go to America. I was fuming at the unfairness of it all. On the verge of feeling depressed, I forced myself to think calmly about Shamlou's dramatic pronouncement. "*Wait one darn minute.*" I firmly brought myself under control. What he told me was totally inconsistent with what I knew of the selection process. *Is he trying to discourage me? Is it still true that the minister is grooming his son as the contest winner? Has his son already graduated from high school? If so, wouldn't he be disqualified? And is the vice minister caught in the middle, trying to be a loyal subordinate?*

I rode the bus back to school and went straight into Mr. Sadre's office to report on my meeting with Mr. Shamlou. Mr. Sadre was as puzzled as I was. He had some influence at the ministry, he said, and would try to get to the bottom of it. He then left to report this development to Dr. Mo.

Chapter Twelve

Teenage Espionage

There were always rumors about government corruption, but this would be my first exposure to official hanky-panky. I wouldn't mind losing in a fair contest, but it would be disheartening if I never had a chance.

What to do?

I remembered that Father was always encouraging his children to take charge. He certainly did not believe that the little guy had no recourse, or that we were all helpless cogs in the country's political machinery. Thoughts about Father's approach to life stiffened my spine and I began pondering my options.

I finally decided to write a letter to the people at the *Herald-Tribune*, telling them what was going on and recommending that the American embassy in Tehran oversee the whole process.

That evening I wrote a long letter by hand on ruled, legal-size paper addressed to the "President of the *New York Herald-Tribune*, New York City, U.S.A." I complimented the newspaper for establishing the forum program for high school students from around the world, and expressed confidence that much good was bound to come from it. Unfortunately, I explained, the program was in danger of being sabotaged in Iran, and the process of selection on the merits tainted by the choice of a prominent politician's son as the forum delegate. I urged the *Herald-Tribune* president to take steps to correct such injustice. I finished with "Respectfully yours" and signed my name.

The next day I showed the letter to Mr. Sadre, the dean at school. He approved it, except for the paragraph in which I had accused the minister of education of corruption. Mr. Sadre said using that kind of strong language was not advisable.

He was right. That evening, I reviewed and revised the letter at home.

Now I had to focus on the real problem of writing such a letter. I was under no illusion that a letter from a Persian teenager—one of hundreds of hopeful contestants worldwide—would ever find its way to the head of one of America's leading newspapers. Was there some way I could improve the odds of getting my letter to its target? This was a major dilemma, and I was preoccupied with it for days.

While I was weighing the matter of the letter, we had an unexpected visitor to our history class, an Englishman representing the United Nations. We had a lively discussion with him through his interpreter about the role of the U.N. I caught up with him after class and told him about my frustration with the *Herald-Tribune* contest.

"Well," he said, "I'm not an American, but I'll talk to some people about it."

I assumed he was just being polite. I thanked him and went back to my class.

Still pinning my hopes on the letter, I had to find a way to get it to the right person in America, but who could possibly help me with that? I started reviewing in my mind all the people I knew and all of Father's friends. I quickly realized that I just didn't know people with that kind of high-level standing and clout. It was disheartening to realize that even Father didn't run in the right high-powered circles.

Not giving up, but where could I turn for help?

That night I lost several hours of sleep running over the list again, only to come to the same conclusion as before—that it was a hopeless quest.

Then, in the middle of an algebra class a couple of days later, across my mind flashed a hopeful image—that of the mysterious stranger who often walked by my home at midday.[3] *Could he be an American? Would he know someone in the U.S. embassy?* How could I find out?

The next time I saw the man, acting with more courage than I felt, I was sorely tempted to follow him, but I'd have to be careful. It was widely believed, even among us students, that the Soviet Union was forever agitating to overthrow the Iranian government. Not long before, a Soviet agent had tried to assassinate the Shah. It was crucial for me, therefore, to know who the stranger was I was tailing before attempting to approach him. If he were connected to the Soviet embassy, I'd want to stay as far away from him as possible.

It was early afternoon on a school day. The students had two hours for lunch each day, and everyone went home at noon and returned for classes at 2 p.m. There was no facility for bringing lunch with us to school. If a student decided to stay during the midday break, all he could do for food was to buy a slice of watermelon from a street vendor and some bread at the bakery. He'd be eating bread and watermelon for lunch. I had done that a couple of times over the years at Alborz.

I was on my way back to school from home when the skies darkened unexpectedly, and soon it started raining. Just then I sighted the stranger. I had no umbrella. Normally I wouldn't care; I'd just walk faster, but now? *Should I go right up to him and ask who he was?* That was a ridiculous idea. Even more outrageous would be to tail him like they do in spy stories. I could get caught. I could get in trouble. I just didn't have the moxie.

[3] See Prologue, page 5.

It was now or never, though. Desperate times, I told myself, call for desperate measures. Not quite shaking in my boots but pretty nervous, I made myself as inconspicuous as possible, slinking along with one hand in my pocket, the other covering my books to keep them from getting wet. I tried to avoid looking at my quarry and walked more slowly to stay as far back as possible without losing sight of him. By the time we had gone a dozen or so blocks, I was wet through and through and starting to lose my nerve. On the verge of abandoning this fool's errand, I saw the man turn in to a side street. I quickened my pace and was in time to see him use a key to get into a house. That clearly identified him as a foreigner. An Iranian would knock on the door of his own home to get someone to open it from inside. It was irrelevant to my immediate concerns, but I wondered why Iranians did not similarly use house keys.

I also remembered that in Shiraz our front door never had a lock. It wasn't needed.

Anyway, once the stranger got inside and closed the door behind him, I walked over to take a look. The rain had turned to a soft drizzle by then. I saw no indication that the house was anything other than a residence. Tehran was a city of walls and, in the style of most Iranian homes, this too had a wall around it, beyond which there would usually be a lush Persian garden. As it was meant to do, the wall divided the public and private lives of the occupants, effectively concealing their fountains, pools, and backyards from public view.

My reconnaissance over, I had to rush to school in my thoroughly wet clothes or I'd be late for class.

I tossed and turned that night, trying to come up with a plan. Early the next morning, I walked back to the house. There was no other way to do it, so I steeled myself and knocked on the door—and got ready to bolt in case of trouble. But all that happened was that a tall, thin man with a couple of days' growth of whiskers and a ragged dust coat opened the door and looked questioningly at me. I figured he must be a doorman or a servant. That emboldened me to come right out and ask him whose house this was.

There was no "Who are you?", "Why do you ask?", or "Go away." He did give me an answer but I just wasn't sure what he said. We were speaking Persian, at least I was, but he spoke a dialect that marked him as being from Lorestan, a western province of Iran. I could hardly understand him but thought I detected the words "American embassy" in what he said. Well, that was a surprise. I needed time to think. I thanked him and left.

On the way to school, I tried to make sense of what I'd heard, but I was still puzzled. Could that house be part of the American embassy? It did not look like an office building. If it had been a clandestine operation, the doorman would not have been at all forthcoming. I may have been slow, but I finally worked it out. The man must have meant that the owner of the house had a connection to the American embassy. If so, considering that I had selected him at random from hundreds of pedestrians, this was truly a stroke of luck. I let out a long breath. *Coincidences do happen,* I told myself brightly. But what now? It was easier to think about, I decided, since I now had a real purpose in meeting the owner.

It was nice and sunny the next morning as I went back to the site of my previous reconnaissance. I knocked on the door and didn't even hesitate when the same man appeared. I told him I wanted to see the owner. I spoke with what I hoped was a reasonable imitation of an adult's tone.

"Not in, back tomorrow"—the best I got out of a long sentence. *I am making progress,* I said to myself with a sense of triumph. So far, nobody had dusted off this nosy teenager. Now that I felt I could get in, I'd better be prepared to tell my story properly.

Early the next day, armed with my *Herald-Tribune* letter, I stopped at the house on my way to school. I was eager and curious as I was admitted into the interior courtyard. The garden mimicked a Monet painting—bushes and flowers surrounding a small pool. "What a shame," I thought, "to conceal all this natural beauty behind a high wall." It was like covering up a Rembrandt with brown wrapping paper. The man led me to a small alcove and told me to wait. It was fine with me. I was sure my business would take only a few minutes, and I'd have plenty of time to get to my first class.

Two hours later, I was impatiently fidgeting in the chair when the doorman came by to advise in his inimitable fashion that I should come back the next day. I was, of course, disappointed, but I was more worried about school. I couldn't afford to miss many more classes. I could also not afford to let myself be deterred. I was on a mission. School or no school, I had to run out this string.

That night, as the full moon cast some light into the room, I twisted and turned in bed, nervous but also excited at the prospect of finally meeting the man I had been chasing for days. I needed to work out in my mind the right approach to him. I figured he'd probably direct me to a seat as soon as I entered the room and offer me some tea as was customary in Iranian homes. He'd then give me a chance to introduce myself, and we'd have a nice chat. At that point, he'd want to know how he could help me. I'd give him a rundown on the *Herald-Tribune* program and tell him about my concerns. He'd be shocked, I was sure, about the corruption at the Iranian ministry of education and would probably want to bring into the discussion other high-level embassy personnel, perhaps even the ambassador himself. Assured of success in my fantasy about the encounter, I finally fell asleep with a satisfied smile on my face.

Despite my optimism, I had to bear the frustration of having to wait in the cramped alcove for several hours again the next day before the doorman finally came to lead me to the homeowner. I was glad I had persevered. Exulting at my good fortune at getting this opportunity, I was breathing hard and excitedly rubbing my hands together. I walked into a home office, a room with bookcases paneled in luxurious wood and the floor covered with a large Persian carpet. (I recognized it as a Kerman.) Sitting behind a walnut desk was the man I had followed. He was dressed in a grey suit with a white shirt and a blue striped tie. Then I noticed to my amazement that he was red in the face with obvious anger and impatience, and that he was holding on with both hands to the edge of his desk, In a gruff and truculent voice, and speaking English without checking to see if I understood the language, he bellowed, "**WHAT** DO YOU WANT?"

Having talked myself into expecting a friendly reception from this man, I was stunned. I wondered if I had made a royal nuisance of myself over the past days, ruining my chances of getting any guidance from him. But there was no help for it now. As my favorite Alborz teacher used to say, not every trap catches a bear. Overcome by surprise and guilt, I found a blank hole in my mind where I had stashed the well-prepared explanation for my visit. Shell-shocked and mute with a slack-jawed stare, I could only extend my arm toward him with the letter I had drafted to the *Herald-Tribune* president.

There was clearly some hesitation on his part to accept the paper I was offering him, perhaps expecting that I was asking for charity, or even worse, soliciting support for a political cause with which he as a U.S. foreign service officer had no business being in contact. His face mirroring the play of conflicting emotions, he finally resolved his doubts and gingerly reached for the letter. With another quick glance in my direction, he unfolded the paper and started reading it with genuine surprise on his face.

By the time he finished, he had calmed down, enough to tell me it was a good letter, but that was all. His "goodbye" was the end of all conversation and my unequivocal dismissal.

After all the gnashing of teeth and the interminable waiting for an interview, I bristled at getting a rush-rush three minutes with the gentleman. Feeling baffled and rejected, I got up and shuffled out. Had I accomplished anything? Other than missing time from school, that is? I did not know whom I had met, nor what his position was at the American embassy. If there were a reason to pat myself on the back, I had yet to find it.

But…*he had kept my letter!*

A slender thread, but it was all I had to go on.

Chapter Thirteen

Search for a Mentor

I was not about to expect much from the meeting. I told myself I had probably been wasting my time. Instead of all this cloak-and-dagger nonsense, why hadn't I just gone right to the American embassy and asked to see the press attaché? *Darn good question.* I guess I never imagined it could have been that easy. Okay, why not just try it? All they can do is turn me away, I told myself. I'd then be no worse off than I was already. *Yes, that's what I'll do.*

Two days later, I caught the bus to Ferdowsi Avenue, then walked to the American embassy. A giant U.S. flag on top of a pole at the entrance, its stars and stripes undulating in the breeze, was a harbinger of strength and solidity. For me, it was both inviting and intimidating. Bracing myself, I strode in with my head held high.

"I'd like to see the press attaché," I declared, as though I owned the place.

Unbelievably, it worked.

"Oh, you want to see Mr. Disher," the pretty receptionist said without hesitation and asked if I had an appointment. I did not, I told her, but it was important and I was sure Mr. Disher would want to see me. A couple of other visitors were lined up behind me waiting their turn, so she simply directed me to an office down the hall. I was now committed, but I had no prepared script this time. I'd just wing it. Then, I heard someone say in Persian to my back, "Good to see you again. Come into my office."

Startled, I was sure the voice was not addressing me. I didn't know anyone there. I turned around. It was none other than my mystery man, the object of my reconnaissance, the one whom I had met in his home only two days before. He spoke Persian like a native, without any trace of an accent—a rare accomplishment for an American. I had not expected to run into him but surprised myself by feeling glad to see him. He was at least a familiar face.

"Good morning, Mr. Disher," I said in English.

"No," he said, "I'm Dr. Gurney."

As soon as we were seated, Dr. Gurney cleared up the confusion. He was in charge of cultural relations at the embassy. This time he was quite chatty and amiable. He must have heard me asking to see the press attaché, but he did not remark on it. I told him about my experience at the ministry of education, and the rumors about the selection process. It was why I had written to the *Herald-Tribune* asking it to arrange for the embassy to oversee the contest. Obviously, that was still my burning issue, but he did not address it immediately.

Instead, he asked me about myself. Where was I going to school? Where had I studied English? What did my father do and where did he work? He asked about my siblings, their names, where they went to school, what they did. He was taking notes the entire time. He then asked about any other *Herald-Tribune* contestants I knew or had heard about.

Turning to my concerns, he waved his hand dismissively and assured me I had no reason to worry about the fairness of the contest. He then gave me his phone number and said I was free to call him if I had any other questions.

Speaking with a gravitas that I could tell was genuine, Dr. Gurney had eased my mind and given me fresh hope about the *Herald-Tribune* program. Optimistic again, I asked him about the timing of the conference in New York.

"The student selected should leave Iran at Christmas," he said, "and be back before Noruz"—the Iranian national holiday, which was celebrated on the first day of spring.

He hesitated a moment, then asked, "Do you know what date is Christmas?"

"Of course," I said. "It is the 7th of January."

He smiled. "That is the Russian Christmas," he said. "In European countries, it is the 25th of December."

That was certainly a great meeting. I was deeply glad I had decided to try the embassy.

A couple of days later I took the bus back to the ministry of education to ask Mr. Shamlou the date and time of the first examination. This time, he made no pretense at being courteous. He was downright rude. He nearly shouted that he had already told me I did not qualify for the contest as I had no high school diploma. He then summarily dismissed me. Despite Dr. Gurney's assurances, this decision by the number-two man at the ministry of education seemed final to me. It was more than discouraging; it was depressing.

I had missed several days of school lately and fallen behind in my homework. I had let the fantasy about a trip to America cloud my judgment. It was time to buck up, get real, and focus back on my classes. If I failed even one course, that would be the end of my stay at Alborz. And then where would I be?

.

Chapter Fourteen

Pressures of a Contest

All my self-doubts evaporated the following week. Mr. Sadre pulled me out of class one day to give me the news that quite a few of the *Herald-Tribune* contestants had already been disqualified, and that my own examination was set for November 30 at 2 p.m. That was most reassuring, but I'd have a lot to do to get ready.

Mr. Sadre said he also wanted to share with me the full text of a confidential letter from the ministry of education to Dr. Mo, the Alborz headmaster: The candidates had to possess extensive knowledge of international affairs and current events, not just for their own countries, but globally. They would also have to demonstrate a deep and abiding interest in politics. Each student would be called upon to write a lengthy essay about "The World We Want" and submit a detailed biography. The top-scoring students, probably a dozen or so, would then be sent to the American embassy for the final exam. I thanked Mr. Sadre, picked up my books, and left school to work at home.

The part about an "intense interest in politics" had me worried. Were I to be tested on that, I'd show up as a rank novice. I wouldn't even know how to fake it. As for the essay on "The World We Want," I was sure I'd have no trouble writing one. I knew by heart several quotes from Winston Churchill, Abraham Lincoln, Anthony Eden, and other leaders I could cite. Of course, I assumed that the examination would be conducted in English, but Mr. Sadre was not clear about that. Were it in Persian, I'd have serious competition from the other candidates.

I was early for my session on November 30th, but the other contestants were already waiting. There were twelve of us.

I sat there, fidgety and anxious, for several hours before my turn came. By then my tension quotient was stratospheric. I had noticed no uniformity in the other candidates' time in the examination room. Some finished within minutes; others took half an hour or longer. As I waited, I learned that the tall good-looking boy waiting his turn with the rest of us was the one about whom the rumors were flying—the son of the minister of education. He was dressed in what looked like an expensive suit. In a momentary attack of cynicism, I wondered why he wouldn't just ask Daddy to send him to America.

I was the last candidate called in. My heart was pounding, and I had the butterflies-in-the-belly feeling I often had before finals. As I entered, I saw four examiners standing behind a long table. I noticed that Mr. Shamlou, the vice minister of education, was *not* there. That was fortunate. Then, too, I was glad everyone spoke English. The first examiner introduced himself as the director-general of the Bureau of Higher Education. Next was the deputy minister of education. The third was the minister of education himself, a well-dressed and courteous gentleman. I knew to address him as "Your Excellency."

Then I focused on the fourth examiner. It was none other than Dr. Gurney. He introduced himself as the cultural affairs attaché of the American embassy and showed no sign of recognition as we shook hands.

At first, the interview questions were quite general: "What grade are you in?" "What is your favorite subject at school?" "Do you play any sports?" And so on. Just as I started wondering how they could differentiate among us if they stuck to such innocuous questions, the discussion turned serious.

One or another of the examiners brought up the recent world war, the role of the Allies, the background of the United Nations

Organization, and the prospects for peace in the coming decades. They even pointedly gave me the opportunity of identifying and talking about the current leaders of the major Western nations. It was pretty much what I had expected.

Then the minister, who spoke excellent English, turned to me.

"I want to ask you more about yourself," he said. "Were you born in England, or did you grow up there?"

After years of struggling with English vocabulary and grammar, this was the first time anyone had mistaken me for being English-born. I was almost swept away by the implied compliment, but something about the minister's expression gave me pause. I remembered his own son was one of the contestants. If I had actually spent time in England, I'd probably be disqualified. Gotcha question or not, I'd remain open and respectful.

"No, sir," I replied honestly. "I was born in Shiraz, attended Nemazee and Kakh elementary schools, and have been at Alborz ever since."

I quickly added, "I have never been out of the country."

There being no more questions, we again shook hands all around, and I left. There was no way of speculating about the reactions of the examiners, but I felt satisfied I had done the best I could.

Chapter Fifteen

The Home Stretch

The next morning, I discovered I faced formidable competition in this contest.

As I entered the school, one of Dr. Mo's assistants told me I was to report to the ministry of education right away. I caught the bus there and went to the same office as the day before. There were only three contestants this time. I had not seen the other two before; they had not been part of the previous day's group. But I knew their reputations.

One was a boy I knew only by his last name, Tehrani. I remembered that he had won accolades when he finished eleventh grade the previous year. That made him a senior. He had to be very smart. He was also quite overweight, a rarity in the population.

The other boy was named Enayat. I had heard a lot about him too. He was reputed to have an excellent command of English and a deep grasp of current affairs at the international level. He occasionally wrote knowledgeable articles in a local magazine. It seemed we were scheduled to take the written test together. Tehrani and Enayat would both be formidable competition.

The exam began promptly at 10:30. We were each provided a sheet of paper, on which were written our instructions:

The New York Herald-Tribune Forum for High School Students will be convened once every three years. Write an essay on the benefits you believe will be derived from such a conference. Write a separate essay on what contribution you expect to make personally to the conference. And, lastly, write a biography of yourself. You have one-and-a-half hours.

CYRUS A. ANSARY

Afterwards, the three of us compared notes. They had written longer essays than I. Unhappy with myself, I worried that the brevity of my writing could work against me. As I shuffled on home with slumped shoulders, I had a hollow feeling in my stomach. Once home, however, I had to put the contest out of my mind. I had a physics test the next day, and I had yet to prepare. Before I went to sleep, I remembered that most of the other contestants still did not know they had not made the cut.

At school two days later, I was told to report to the ministry right away. Arriving, I saw only Tehrani and Enayat. *Must be another test*, I thought.

At 11:30 we were told to enter another office one at a time. I was the first. There were two men present, one of whom started asking me questions in Persian. After some conversation, he switched to English. He mispronounced words and had poor sentence structure, but I answered everything politely. Then the door opened, and Dr. Gurney entered. The exam papers from two days before, with the candidates' names blanked out, were lying in a pile on the table. One of the men picked it up and passed it on to Dr. Gurney. I was told to go back into the outer room and wait. Then Tehrani was called in. Enayat was last. We were then told to go home. The winner would be informed by telephone the next morning.

I was certain I had lost. Based on Enayat's description of his essay, his writing had to have been quite impressive. I was having performance anxiety as I got off the bus and shuffled on home. One look at me and Father asked what had happened. I told him how well Enayat had done.

"Aren't you assuming," Father interrupted, "that Enayat was as good at communicating his thoughts in written English as he was in describing them to you in Persian?"

Inability to express himself well in English did not jibe with Enayat's reputation, but I was grateful for Father's encouraging words.

When I received no phone call the next morning, I believed it was all over—a sad end to my cherished fantasy. At school I told my friends that I had failed. Mr. Sadre heard about it, gave me the phone number of a Mr. Payvar at the ministry, and suggested I call him to find out for sure. It was always dicey whether the telephone system worked, or, even if it did, whether the voice at the other end would come through clearly enough.

I made the call from a local store during the lunch break, but predictably the connection was poor. I was blocking my right ear with my hand to hear better with my left ear. It sounded as though Mr. Payvar was asking me to come to the ministry. I rushed back home, changed my clothes, and caught a taxi there. People in Tehran lived or died by the *bus* schedule. A taxi was an extravagance for me; it cost ten times the bus fare. Still, I could not tolerate the interminable waits and the constant stop-and-start delays of a bus at this stage.

It was also a law of nature that buses always pulled away just as you rushed to catch them.

Once at the ministry, I found Mr. Payvar and breathlessly introduced myself.

"I told you to bring your father," he said.

I explained that there had been static on the line and I did not hear him. I asked if I had been selected. He said the contest was down to the three of us but no final decision had been made.

"The minister and Dr. Gurney have yet to confer," he remarked.

Aware of my excitement, Mr. Payvar, whom I had never met before, said, "As soon as we hear, I'll get word to you. I promise. If I have to, I'll send a cyclist to your house. Now give me your home address." He then passed around a bowl of candy to each person in the room and said, "This is hoping that we are celebrating your success in the contest."

With that I trudged back to school to sit for another test for which I was ill prepared.

Chapter Sixteen

Cold-Weather Gear

The next morning, December 6, 1949, I returned to the ministry, only to be told again that no decision had been made. At lunchtime I walked home from school as usual. To my surprise, Father walked in at one o'clock. His office hours were 7 a.m. to 3 p.m., so this was surprising.

Not wasting time on greetings, he turned to Mother and said, "Did you know about your son's ambition to go to America?"

Mother looked mystified. Unaware of my years-long struggle to find a way out of Iran, and uninvolved in the intense and emotional rollercoaster ride of the *Herald-Tribune* contest over the preceding eighteen months, Mother had no context for Father's question, looked perplexed and remained silent. He then went on to explain that an American named Dr. Gurney had called on him at the bank to inform him that his son had won the contest to become a delegate to the New York Herald Tribune Forum for High School Students.

I stood transfixed. It couldn't be. I had won. My elation was far beyond anything I had ever imagined. How do you cope with a fantasy that suddenly becomes reality? I wanted to soar. I wanted to do somersaults. I wanted to sing and dance. I'd be going to the faraway land I had dreamed about for half my life. *Wow! Will there ever be another day for me like today?* I was bursting with joy.

But Father was not finished. Now came the practical issues Dr. Gurney had raised.

After congratulating Father, Dr. Gurney got down to business. The first leg of the journey from Tehran to Basra, Iraq, would be

Father's responsibility to arrange and pay for. The *Herald Tribune* would cover the trip from Basra to New York.

"The same arrangement would apply on the return trip," Father added.

My stomach suddenly turned to ice. Shocked to the core at the idea of a "return trip," I barely managed to ask in a croak, "What did you just say?" I was sure I had heard wrong. I felt a chill deep inside.

"I said the same expense-sharing arrangement would apply on your return," Father repeated, puzzled.

"You can't mean that." I was struggling to hold down my anger, aware that I had never used that tone with him before. But I didn't care. "You can't make me come back. This is the only chance I'll ever have to get a decent education. I want to go to school in America, finish high school, enter college."

I took a deep breath, ready to throw caution to the wind. "I won't do it." I was trying hard to control my feelings.

"Why don't you sit down?" Father had obviously not expected his words to create that level of concern; but he still did not seem offended by my outburst.

He let a minute pass and kept his voice level when he spoke. "I am not the one forcing you to come back. It is a requirement of the *Herald-Tribune* people."

I was unconvinced but struggled to tone down my voice. "Why would they care what I do after the conference is over?"

"Listen, Cyrus. The whole purpose of the trip is to learn about America and share your observations with others in Iran afterwards. Dr. Gurney was quite clear that it would be impossible for you to stay in the U.S. He had me sign an affidavit to that effect. If I had not agreed, you wouldn't be going."

I was crushed. What a letdown. My shoulders sagged. Sorrow had replaced exhilaration. I'd be going to the U.S. for a brief visit only. Once back in Tehran, I'd be no better off than before, with no funds to finance a return trip. I'd have accomplished nothing.

But what choice did I have?

I had jumped in and interrupted Father's report. He had more to say. Concerned about my missing several months of school, he had wisely pointed out to Dr. Gurney that the *Herald-Tribune* trip would cause me to miss so much time of the academic year that I would need to take my eleventh-grade finals in September instead of in June with my classmates. For that, Father explained, "Cyrus would need special dispensation from the ministry of education as well as from Alborz High School." Would Dr. Gurney help with securing the required approvals? He had no objection. Dr. Gurney also said he would be arranging for me to attend Community School (the American school in Tehran) before departing for New York "to familiarize Cyrus with American education."

That day I also learned something about the dominance of legal issues in American interactions. Dr. Gurney had Father sign another document. The gist of it was that the *New York Herald-Tribune* would obtain $10,000 of insurance on my life in the event of my death while a delegate to the Forum, and my parents would waive any claim beyond that amount.

Me, dying in the U.S.? Wasn't that a ridiculous idea?[4]

Dr. Gurney then invited my parents and me to his home for dinner—to the same house where I had first met him. This would be a party in my honor, he told Father, and the guests would include high-level people from the ministry of education and several from the American embassy. As he said goodbye, Dr. Gurney put both hands on Father's shoulders, looked him in the eye, and said in a solemn tone, "God bless you, sir."

For me, there was yet a tendril of another sober thought. *All is not sweetness and light.* Father still had to come up with the money for a portion of the trip. I did not have a suit or decent shirts. I had no overcoat. Never felt I needed one, even in the dead of

---

[4] Not so ridiculous, if I could have peeked into the future.

winter. And what about incidentals during the trip? These expenses required money which the family simply did not have.

Father had always believed in living within one's means. It was one of the fundamental tenets of his beliefs—never to put himself and his family in jeopardy by becoming a borrower, running the risk of landing in the dreaded debtors' prison. Those were the days when a mere default in payment could have that consequence. Going into debt for the first time in his life to make my trip to America a reality was a painful decision for Father, and equally distressing for me. But there was simply no choice. Hearing the love and pride behind Father's support only made it worse. I just didn't know what to say, but I wished it did not have to be. And so Father applied to the bank for a loan to finance my trips to and from Basra, Iraq, and to buy clothes for my stay in the U.S.

There being no stores selling ready-made clothing, Father and I went to Tehran's Grand Bazaar to order an overcoat. As usual, the place buzzed like a kicked beehive. Even though downtown shopping was starting to cut into its business, the bazaar was still mobbed by customers. Hard to believe that its structure spanned eight square miles under cover, with a couple of hundred shops offering every variety of merchandise. Still, Father and I had to order the cloth, the lining, and the tailor's fee at separate locations. The total came to 1,650 rials ($24).

We then had to consider the transportation to Iraq. The cost of a Tehran-Basra ticket by plane was 3,240 rials ($46), which was entirely too much. Barry worried that traveling by train could be dangerous, but I insisted on it. The train ride would cost less than a third of the price of a plane ticket.

The next day at Alborz I made a beeline for Dr. Mo's office to tell him the news. When I entered, I saw that Mr. Sadre was also there. I mentioned that I had been selected as the Forum delegate from Iran. Their reaction was greater than I had ever expected. It wasn't just elation. Dr. Mo, always so cool, so reserved, was on this day openly ebullient, even excited. He said my success was a feather in the cap of the entire school. It was a touching scene. I owed him much and said so. I thanked them both profusely.

I then went in search of my classmate and best friend, Abraham Virdeh, and told him the news. He had accompanied me several years earlier when I made the rounds of foreign consulates in Tehran in pursuit of my fantasy. In those days, he spoke better English than I did. He had played a lot of volleyball, basketball, and tennis in the interim and had placed third in the citywide ping-pong championships. To my regret, however, he had permitted his foreign language skills to slide. He congratulated me and wished me well.

December 7 was the day eight years earlier that Japan had attacked Pearl Harbor in Hawaii, leading the U.S. into World War II. It was also my last day at Alborz, before I was to switch to Community School, the coed school with American teachers. I had tried enrolling there several years earlier, but we couldn't afford the tuition. I was excitedly looking forward to the experience.

Still, there were new frustrations, just to leave Iran. I faced an interminable line at the passport office. Then I was told I needed to obtain a statement certifying that I had no criminal record. For that, I had to go to yet another office as well as the police precinct. I thought I was now past the toughest hassles, but I was not even close.

Even though I was not yet eligible for military conscription, I had to obtain a certificate that I was not dodging the draft. That required several trips to more offices. I had to obtain written permission to carry foreign currency out of the country. I could never get my business done in a single try.

It was heartbreaking to witness such bureaucratic indifference, and it bordered on criminal behavior when so many people on government payroll expected handouts before they'd do their job.

It all served to reaffirm my conviction that I'd never survive, let alone prosper, in that environment. I was barely able to get my passport to the American embassy in time to obtain my visa for entry into the U.S. Dr. Gurney had obviously left instructions, so this part went quickly.

Shortly before my departure, brother Barry surprised me by saying he was arranging to buy $100 worth of traveler's checks for me. That was a month-and-a-half's pay for him. I would not hear of it, but he insisted it had already been arranged.

When I was small, I used to love watching Barry, who was five years older, make things out of wood or metal. To me, he was a genius with his hands. Dismissive of my fondness for him, he always found new and devious ways to torment me and then laugh uproariously at my discomfort. He was the picture of mischief. By the time I got into fifth grade, I had had enough of his harassment. All my pent-up resentments erupted one day as I flew into him and started pummeling away, until Mother separated us. When I calmed down, I regretted my action, but he did not play any more tricks on me.

Ever Buffeted but Never Sunk
The Ansary Family Motto

Now, here he was, buying me these traveler's checks just so I'd have some pocket money in America. I reflected that that was the way of the Ansarys. Lots of arguments and squabbles, but when the chips were down, we were there for each other.

Years later, I would devise The Ansary Family Crest—the picture of a boat under full sail through rough waters. The family motto, penned in Gothic letters underneath, was designed to convey freedom and adventure. It was how I saw the Ansary family dynamics.

Chapter Seventeen

Musings on a Train

It was 1949, and I was embarking on the dream voyage of my life. This was the real thing at last. The night before my departure, I had trouble falling asleep, being so worked up.

By this point Hushang had a new job and was living and working in Tokyo. So Mother, Father, brother Barry, and sister Pary saw me off at the Tehran train station. They were happy for me. I reminded them I was only going on a brief adventure. Just then, unexpectedly, Dr. Gurney showed up. Then a girl came, along with her family, and Dr. Gurney introduced us. I learned that I was not the only delegate to the Herald-Tribune Forum. There had been a concurrent contest to select a girl.

Her name was Mahine. She was of average height, had a round face, brown hair, and fair skin, and was dressed in a simple brown skirt and beige blouse. Her father said Mahine's teenage brother would be traveling with us to Basra, where the family had relatives. There were hugs and goodbyes. As I shook Dr. Gurney's hand, I said "Thank you." It was heartfelt. I meant more than the words could convey; I was absurdly grateful to him. Then the three of us boarded the train for the ride to Ahvaz, the oil capital of Iran.

Mahine and I spent the first hour onboard talking and getting to know each other. She said she was a senior at Jeanne d'Arc, the girls' French high school in Tehran. That was a surprise. I heard her speak English with Dr. Gurney at the station, and she was fluent. So she was trilingual. She seemed a composed and self-effacing Persian teenager.

As the train sped along, I gazed out the window at the spectacular landscape. My first time away from my family, my first train ride, my first view of that part of the country. Away from metropolitan Tehran, the terrain changed dramatically. We passed hills and lowlands, snow-capped mountains and green valleys.

Approaching Ahvaz, we came upon the arid plains of southwestern Iran, a stark and barren vista but also grand and majestic. As the desert sands rolled silent and swift past the window, I remembered that this desolate region was Iran's economic lifeline, and that the world's largest refinery was located nearby in Abadan. I was also reminded that Father had worked in the oil fields of Ahvaz, that my older brother Hushang was born there, and that Mother had cried a lot before getting back to her native Shiraz.

As the wheels of the train clicked away like the ticking of a giant clock, I mused about my great adventure. I thought of the improbable saga of fumbling and bumbling that had brought me together with Dr. Gurney. A comedian Father sometimes quoted would have called it a *mis*step in the right direction. I thought of the many people who had had a part in shaping my life and to whom I owed so much—my parents; my wonderful great-aunt Baji who had reared me; Dr. Mo, the Alborz principal; Professor Yates, my long-term instructor of English literature from the Tehran campus of Cambridge University…so many who had helped me in countless ways. I had to admit I had been most fortunate in life.

Father was, of course, at the top of my list, but then there was another star of that class—Dr. F. Taylor Gurney. He was as solid as a great oak, projecting both strength and wisdom, and yet it was hard to imagine a more nurturing personality. In retrospect, I realized he had been uncommonly effective at getting done what had been a difficult and politically delicate task. It was true, after all, that the minister of education's son was one of the contestants, and that he had the inside track in the competition. So, I was deeply grateful for Dr. Gurney's interest in me and treasured his encouragement and advice. Meeting him had been, well, the inflection point of my life. It was not fate but serendipity that had brought me together with him. He had planted the seed, and I hoped I'd measure up to his expectations. Alas, now that his job was done, I'd probably never see him again.

I was dead wrong. I could not know it then, but Dr. Gurney would remain my mentor, friend, and a dominant force in shaping my life for decades afterwards.

Chapter Eighteen

A Persian Harem?

Flash bulbs began popping as soon as Mahine and I started descending the stairs from our final flight to New York's LaGuardia Airport, where we landed about 6 p.m. on January 5, 1950. A *Herald-Tribune* photographer was recording our arrival. After the eleven-day trip from Tehran, I felt as though I had the cognitive function of a fungus. Thankfully, it passed and I could soon start experiencing the feelings of wide-eyed wonder and delight at having made it to America.

Right off the bat I saw that LaGuardia was several times the size of Tehran's Mehrabad Airport. I mentioned this to the stewardess.

"Everything in the U.S. is supersized," she quipped. "You'll get used to it."

Two host families awaited us at the bottom of the ramp. Mahine went off with hers, and I with mine—Mr. and Mrs. Frisch, a most friendly couple. Their son Bruce, a student at A.B. Davis High School in Mount Vernon, New York, would be guiding me through his classes during the week of my stay with them. His parents wished to tell me about their hometown, but first they wanted to drive me somewhere for dinner straight from the airport.

"Have you ever dined in a self-service restaurant?" Mrs. Frisch wanted to know. When I professed ignorance, she said happily, "We are taking you to one. It's a unique New York experience."

"You'll see," Mr. Frisch added. "It's a fun place."

Soon we arrived in midtown Manhattan. The first impressions came hard and fast. I was goggled-eyed by the majesty of the grand office towers as we arrived at our destination. The restaurant was called Horn & Hardart Automat, and its striking feature was a wall of small windows from which a variety of fast foods was dispensed when you inserted the requisite coins. Obviously popular, it was crowded this night, but Mr. Frisch managed to get us a table.

Other diners were rushing about, but there was no jostling to get to the little windows displaying the food. The new sights and sounds must have been too much for me, as were the unfamiliar food choices. I had to learn new company manners and which fork to use. I ended up with two apple pies and no entrée. My hosts found it amusing. They assumed I had a sweet tooth. Actually, I had never tasted pies before and did not know what they were. I was red to my ear tips.

One bite of the pie and I was done. My hosts couldn't have known that pies were an acquired taste, like caviar. I was embarrassed, but it wouldn't be the last mistake I'd make in the new land I had been so eager to reach.

The next day Bruce Frisch took me with him to A.B. Davis High School. It was a coed school with programs in sports, music, and academics, and great teachers. The students did not have to go home for lunch as there was a large cafeteria with a variety of food choices right there on the premises. I was awed by the school-wide communication system in place in every classroom so the students could hear any announcements.

There was an assembly right after lunch, and I was invited to address the student body. To talk to a live audience would be a thrill, so much better than the imaginary people on whom I had practiced from my cherished Mound of Oratory in Tehran. I was glad to accept.

I spoke of the contest that had brought me to the U.S., of my family, and of Alborz High School. A teacher opened the floor to questions. I expected to be asked about the kind of country Iran was and the role it had played in the war. Speaking of an ancient land like Persia, I was sure the students would be impressed by its history. They might ask about the old rivalry between the Persians and the Greeks, or about Alexander of Macedonia as a conqueror. I'd stick to short answers, but I'd enjoy any give-and-take.

But none of those issues was on the mind of the student who stood up at the back of the auditorium.

"How many wives do you expect to have when you grow up?" he wanted to know.

I remembered a discussion in my eighth-grade history class at Alborz. We were talking about the old kings and their harems, and our teacher said anyone practicing polygamy was permitting fantasy to prevail over reality.

To the boy at A.B. Davis High I answered without thinking—a bad habit to get into. "One," I blurted, "preferably, a warm and outgoing American girl." *Did I just say that?* That thought hadn't even been conscious before. To cover up my embarrassment, I quickly added I didn't know anyone in Tehran with more than one wife.

"One wife at a time, that is," I explained.

"Dating among boys and girls is not widespread," I said. "It is still frowned upon in some quarters." There was no time to elaborate, as the bell rang ending the assembly.

The next day, the school principal took me to lunch at the Kiwanis Club. He explained that there were several such clubs in most American cities and they performed a number of civic functions in their communities. It was another new experience for me. The president of the club shook my hand and asked if I'd mind saying a few words after the conclusion of their scheduled program. Mind? I'd pay for the privilege. I spoke briefly about the Forum program and took a few questions, thoroughly enjoying the repartee.

Back in school, I continued attending classes with my host Bruce. The teachers could not have been more dedicated. The only unusual moment occurred after history class one day. Chatting with me afterwards, the teacher called me Darius. I was Cyrus, I corrected him mildly.

"Well, you and I both know you have Anglicized your name," he said with a conspiratorial wink, "but we know it is really Darius, don't we?"

If he were pulling my leg, I wanted to be a good sport about it. I laughingly winked back and thanked him for keeping my secret. I decided not to mention that Cyrus, Darius, and Xerxes were all kings of the ancient Persian Empire. Cyrus seized power in 550 B.C. to establish a dynasty based, for the first time in recorded history, on social justice and respect for individual rights. Darius, his successor, expanded the Persian Empire far into Africa and Asia. He also built a dazzling new capital outside Shiraz, where I was born. Xerxes was mentioned in the Old Testament for saving the Jews from genocide.

The *Herald-Tribune* program required the delegates to spend only a week at a time at each location we were assigned. So after Mount Vernon came Hastings-on-the-Hudson, New York. I asked my host family there if I could take a day off to meet with fellow delegates at the *Herald-Tribune* offices in Manhattan. Surprisingly, the family were so concerned about my safety they insisted that my student host and his mother would have to accompany me. I told my host I had traveled in several large cities on the way to the U.S. without any escorts and had had no trouble navigating there, but my host was adamant that it was risky to have me walking alone in New York City streets. Not wanting to be the cause of my host missing school, I decided to postpone the visit.

Next, at Briarcliff High School in Briarcliff Manor, New York, my host was the captain of the football team. He was big, bluff, easy-going, and in great shape physically. He had a steady girl-friend, also a senior. With him I was totally relaxed, and we had a great time together. I took advantage of my week there to look for someone to help with my pronunciation.

I didn't want to continue speaking English with a clipped Cambridge accent, don't you know?

I settled on a girl in the English class who was both outgoing and a good student. I asked her if she'd be willing to tutor me. She was puzzled until I told her what I wanted. She seemed fascinated but tried to talk me out of it. She said she liked how I talked, then giggled and said my accent had sex appeal. Not what I wanted to hear. I wouldn't be swayed. She finally relented, and spent an hour every day after school listening to me talk, and correcting my pronunciation.

She helped a lot, but the tutoring unnerved her boyfriend.

The final stop was Princeton High School in Princeton Junction, New Jersey. My host took me on a tour of Princeton University nearby. He was planning to apply there after graduation and encouraged me to do the same. I thanked him, but there was no way to know what would be in store for me once I returned to Tehran.

By the time I had completed my four-week tour of the high schools, I felt like a new person. I was far more at ease with mealtime etiquette and mingling with boys my age. But I was still awkward around girls. As for speaking to groups, I found American audiences quick to laugh at my attempts at humor, quick to overlook my gaffes, and quick to applaud. All of it gave me new confidence.

Chapter Nineteen

Aerial Decompression

As Forum delegates, all of us were burning with curiosity about the genesis of the project that had brought us together. We grabbed any chance we could to meet at the *Herald-Tribune* offices at 230 W. 41st Street in mid-Manhattan. We wanted to get to know the staff and learn about the background of the Forum.

We soon learned that Helen Rogers Reid, president of the *New York Herald-Tribune,* an eminent daily at the time, was an early American trailblazer. She could afford to indulge her consuming passion—striking a blow for world peace. In a moment of high optimism, she devised a program of bringing together a generation of "future world leaders" while still in their teens, encouraging lasting friendships among them, and indoctrinating them in international amity before their minds were contaminated by ethnic prejudices and national animosities.

With World War II still fresh in everyone's mind in 1945, Helen Reid hired a young war correspondent named Helen Waller to flesh out the concept, line up collaborating resources, and roll out the program. Thus was born the New York Herald Tribune World Forum for High School Students.

We quickly recognized that Helen Waller was the project's operational founder. Still in her early thirties, she was of medium height, with light brown hair and an attractive face. She was passionate about the initiative she and Helen Reid had launched and dedicated to its success.

We learned that it took Waller more than three years to secure the requisite approvals, establish the delegate selection process in each country, line up airline transportation to the U.S., choose volunteer families as hosts to the delegates, arrange for tours in the country, and finally organize the Forum itself with prominent speakers and panelists. The 1950 Forum at the Waldorf-Astoria Hotel would be the first assemblage of such magnitude in television history.

———···———

The next phase of the program called for us to tour the United States. We were eager to see more of America and to mingle with the populace. We'd visit Tennessee, Texas, Oklahoma, and California, and meet with political and community leaders there.

For travels around the U.S., Helen had commandeered two C-47s and crews belonging to the Civil Air Patrol, the civilian auxiliary of the U.S. Air Force. All of us piled into the planes, and we took off from Mitchell Field on Long Island. Accompanying us were several representatives of various U.S. government offices.

I was eager to spend time with my fellow delegates, to explore their ethnic and national diversity and their views about America's role in the world. I used the first leg of the trip to get to know as many of them as I could. Spotting a microphone on an empty seat, I picked it up and was excited to find it was live. Here was my chance to record the others' impressions of our visit and learn of their plans after the Forum.

I started moving down the aisle, interviewing each of my fellow delegates. All of them, boys and girls alike, were talkative, lively, expansive, and full of their own opinions. As the plane sped toward Knoxville and the TVA, I continued my self-appointed research. The interviews were later broadcast over the Voice of America, and I was pleased to receive a copy of the audiotape in the mail for myself.

On the leg of the flight from Knoxville to Dallas, we came within a hair's breadth of having a fatal accident. The C-47 was a troop-and-cargo carrier, a utilitarian military plane stripped of anything nonessential, dubbed the "gooney bird" in World War II. It was not equipped with any passenger safety features (e.g., seat belts), nor did it have the sharp gleaming functionality of my previous airplane experience, TWA's *Star of New York,* the Lockheed Constellation I'd flown from Basra to New York.

Heading into Dallas, I happened to be sitting alone in the first row of the plane, immersed in a fascinating magazine article about an immigrant to America who rose from modest means to reach great renown, a man named Andrew Carnegie. *Would I ever be a similar immigrant here? Could I duplicate this man's success in America?* Deep in thought, I was utterly unprepared for the calamity that suddenly engulfed us.

We were flying at about ten thousand feet when, as I turned the page in the magazine, the plane hit an air pocket and my elbow inadvertently nudged a harmless-looking handle protruding a couple of inches from the bulkhead. I had seen no label by the handle when I took my seat, and no *Warning* or *Caution* sign anywhere near my seat, but instantly a large escape hatch blew open into space. It was as though the universe had exploded all around me with terrifying suddenness. The plane began to buffet and the rush of wind filled the cabin with an ear-splitting WHOOSH. The cut of air hit my face like sharp knives as the craft shuddered with rapid earthquake-like tremors. I thought the wings would shake loose from their rivets. The plane gave a violent lurch, the starboard wing dropped precipitously, and the nose went into a steep descent as I glimpsed with horror the rapidly diminishing distance to the ground. Inside the cabin, mayhem erupted. Papers, magazines, books, handbags, clothing, and anything else loose careened round and round like objects in a tornado. The sound of rushing air was deafening, and the ensuing chaos frightfully disorienting.

We went from calm-and-routine to deadly emergency in milli-seconds. The passengers had to get a death grip on their seats, or they'd be yanked off. My horrified brain was paralyzed, and I stopped breathing, certain I was going to die.

By pure chance, the captain had just stepped out of the cockpit and was passing by my seat the instant the hatch blew. Moving with almost superhuman reflexes that could only have been honed in combat, he grabbed and physically lifted me out of my seat and hurled me forcefully down the aisle—saving my life. A second later and I would have been sucked out into space.

The highly trained crew also reacted instantaneously, wordlessly jumping into action. While the copilot was struggling to regain control of the aircraft, two crewmen braced themselves against the bulkhead and grabbed hold of each of the captain's ankles as he thrust his head, torso, and arms out into space. As the hatch kept swinging violently on its hinges, the captain tried but for several heart-stopping moments failed to catch it. Again and again he tried. With what seemed like his last ounce of strength he was finally able to grab hold of the hatch, forcefully slam it back in, and quickly close and lock it in place. To our enormous relief, the plane then stabilized.

The outcome could easily have been different. I had come within a hair's breadth of losing my life. I felt tied up in knots. Afterwards, if the captain had directed a look of disappointment my way, he would have destroyed my self-confidence forever. But he never did. Obviously, he did not blame me for what happened. When I tried to thank him, he patted me on the shoulder, smiled, and said he was glad I was all right. Then he pointed to the hatch and whispered with a conspiratorial wink, "We'll get that fixed." Only a short time later, the plane made a feather-soft landing at Love Field in Dallas.

I later learned that the mishap on the plane was called a force-ful decompression. Whatever. It was an experience I could readily forgo. I was not in a hurry to get to the Kingdom of Heaven.

After everything had returned to normal, I thought briefly about the agreement my father had signed in Tehran, waiving his right to make a claim in excess of $10,000 in the event of my death while a Forum delegate. If I had in fact died in this accident, nothing on earth could have persuaded my father to accept *any money* for his son's demise. To him, to profit from the death of a child would be a monstrous application of moral turpitude.

I would have preferred it if everyone forgot the episode, but I knew no one would. Certainly not the other delegates, nor the brave captain and crew. And if they needed a reminder of it, the incident became the subject of a two-column article the next morning in the *Dallas Morning News* under the headline "Frisky Cyrus Bit Cautious—Gets Lost, Stumps Experts."

I wondered where the reporter had gotten his information.

While still on the tour in Dallas and Tulsa, we had the opportunity of meeting with many business and civic leaders. One with whom I was particularly impressed was George McGhee, the oilman who had helped shape the American petroleum policy after World War II. We spent several hours talking with him about global economic issues.

Many meetings and discussion groups later, we headed back to New York. It had been a lively and memorable tour of the U.S. For me, it was equally stimulating to be with my bright and energetic fellow delegates from so many different ethnic and cultural backgrounds. Insatiable intellectual curiosity was the common characteristic of them all. I thought Sabam, the delegate from Indonesia, was destined for high office. The Burmese delegate, Yadana, was a genuine princess. She was tall, elegant, and stunning, and men were attracted to her in droves wherever we went. The male delegate from Israel was a puzzle, he was much older than the rest of us, in his late 20's or early 30's and clearly not a high school student. The rumor was that he was in state security. Eddie, the boy from Malaysia, was super-bright and super-ambitious. He was already planning to attend Yale for his undergraduate degree. The girl from Egypt, Bella, was well-spoken and knowledgeable about world affairs. She and I once had a long conversation about American culture. We were both enthusiastic about life in the U.S., but she preferred living in Egypt where she had roots, while I could not wait to escape from mine. She mentioned she was a little uncomfortable with the boy/girl freedoms in America. I reminded her that in societies where gender segregation was strictly enforced, women were allowed few rights and had little say about their lives. She looked thoughtful but didn't comment.

During the tour, a most unlikely liaison developed between two of the delegates. Hamed, the boy from Egypt, was tall, affable, and a true extrovert. Ada, the girl from Israel, on the other hand, was quiet, soft-spoken, and reserved. She did not mingle much.

No two people could have been more different, and yet we saw them together throughout the tour. They seemed inseparable. By the time we were back in New York, anyone could see the flames of love in their countenance. Ada now laughed a lot, was far more animated than before, and freely mingled with the other delegates. Ironically, Hamed and Ada were demonstrating the validity of the thesis underlying the Forum, namely, that kids from different backgrounds could learn to get along before their minds were infused with ethnic hostilities.

Hamed confided in me with a huge innocent grin that he and Ada were planning to elope and get married. They were both sixteen, but he was a big boy and could pass for eighteen. It was an exciting scenario. Who snitched on them I never knew, but someone did. The Forum office in turn informed their parents, and both kids were unceremoniously yanked out of the program and put on separate planes back to their countries. Reality had set in, and the lovers were being separated, probably never to see each other again. Actually, while those two youngsters were falling in love, their two countries were not exactly enamored of each other. At the time, in fact, a state of hostility existed between Egypt and Israel.

I didn't get to say goodbye to Ada or even see her before she left, but I did see the bluff and ebullient Hamed. With a shattered look about him, he was openly tearful—sobbing, in fact—as he got into the car to be driven to the airport for the trip to Alexandria, Egypt. For me, it was a truly touching scene. *They did not have to handle it that way.*

Chapter Twenty

Call for a Miracle

A very different matter was on my mind as our group toured
California, Texas, and other states, seeing the sights and
meeting with various local leaders.

I was preoccupied with the urgent problem of how to extend
my stay in the U.S. There were many obstacles to worry about,
the most important being the affidavit Father had signed in Tehran at the urging of Dr. Gurney. The *Herald-Tribune* people were
determined that, once the Forum was over, the delegates would
immediately return home and recount the American story to their
countrymen and women. Since the U.S. embassy in Tehran had
been involved in this process, I was also afraid that trying to extend
my U.S. visa would run into a brick wall at the Immigration Service. And, of course, raising money for living and school expenses
would also be big issues for me.

I had no wish to violate Father's commitment nor the Forum's
rules, but I was equally determined to get an American education.
If I had to go back to Tehran, I was desperately afraid that financing a return trip to the U.S. would be as hopeless this time as it
had been before. What to do?

I kept coming up with glimmers of some promising solutions,
only to find that, upon examination, they dissolved like snow in
sunshine. I felt that I needed a miracle to solve these conflicting
imperatives.

All of us delegates were on our way back to New York where
we'd participate in the televised Forum, and that would be the

end of our stay in America. I could see myself having to fly out to Tehran within days. There would be precious little time to get anything done.

It was literally as our flight was about to make a touchdown at LaGuardia that the urgency of the situation caused my creative juices to kick in finally. All the disparate pieces came together and the solution to this mind-boggling dilemma hit me with full force as though it were an epiphany:

A man named Hank Miller was the key to my predicament, the only one who could help solve everything for me.

A tall (6' 6") New Yorker in his early forties with a fluent speaking style and a friendly manner, Hank worked for the Voice of America, the arm of the U.S. government that broadcast radio programs to various countries in their own language. (I had heard its Persian-language programs on a friend's short-wave radio back in Tehran.)

I had met Hank on several occasions as part of our *Herald-Tribune* activities. He showed special interest when he heard me interviewing some of my fellow delegates. From him I learned that VOA was always looking for new programs for its foreign-language broadcasts.

This was crucial information for me.

As the plane landed on the tarmac I knew what I had to do: The minute I got to midtown, I'd call Hank's office to make an appointment for myself. I'd then present to him a proposal I had worked out in my mind: Would VOA be interested in my hosting ten weekly fifteen-minute programs, in Persian, about my experiences in the U.S., to be broadcast live to audiences in Iran? I'd also mention a few interesting vignettes as previews of what I'd say on the air, just to engage Hank in a discussion of content.

I was convinced this would be a natural fit for VOA, too enticing an opportunity for it to pass up.

Were my proposal accepted, the *Herald-Tribune* goal of getting the word out in Iran about the U.S. society would be fully accomplished. Instead of making a few speeches to small groups in Tehran, I'd be extending my reach to far larger Iranian audiences through the VOA broadcasts. Once the program was in place, Helen Waller could not possibly object to this initiative being undertaken by an arm of the U.S. government. And to keep the American embassy in Tehran in the loop, I'd also write Dr. Gurney to explain what I had worked out.

I was cheerful and confident about my plan, and excited to start putting it all in place.

As I was about to call Hank Miller's office for the appointment, I got an urgent summons to Helen Waller's office at the *Herald-Tribune* near Times Square. I thought nothing of it, but I was curious about what had suddenly come up. I rushed over.

When I showed up, Helen had no greeting for me, nor any word of welcome. No probing about the tour, or any discussion of how it could be improved upon in the future. I had barely walked in when she stood up and abruptly handed me an envelope. Puzzled, I looked at her in wordless inquiry. She just issued a warning that I was to return to Iran immediately after the Forum was over.

"There will be no exceptions," she proclaimed in stern tones.

This was not the Forum director I had come to know and love, all smiles and maternal warmth. Confused, I had no idea what this was about until I opened the envelope and read the telegram inside. It was from brother Hushang in Tokyo. It read:

"Expected your cable immediately upon arrival. Terribly disappointed. No wonder thrilling sightseeing causes forgetfulness. Investigate possibility of obtaining scholarship. Airmail details. Alternatively estimate monthly expenses for continued stay. Awaiting detailed weekly letters. Hushang."

Obviously, the cable had set off alarm bells at the Forum office. I quickly intervened to calm Helen.

"I certainly can see why you'd be disturbed by this telegram," I said to her in my softest voice. "It does require explanation. It was sent by one of my brothers. The Ansarys are a family of seven and we live in Tehran, Iran, as you know, except that one of my brothers, the one who sent this cable, lives thousands of miles away in Tokyo, Japan. I haven't seen him in quite a while. He feels isolated and misses his family. Whenever there is any news from home, such as my being selected to represent Iran in the Herald-Tribune Forum, he likes to get involved. He feels that without his keen intellect to help, the rest of us could not successfully navigate life's daily issues.

"Problem, of course, is that, living so far away from us, he may act before he has the full picture. He has no idea, for example, of the ground rules for participating in the Herald-Tribune Forum. The rest of us have learned to humor him. After all, his heart is in the right place.

"So, Mrs. Waller, there is really no need to be concerned about this telegram."

"That is all right then," She announced, and I started to relax.

"And, oh incidentally," she added after a pause, with a gleam in her eyes I had not seen before, "we have made a reservation for you on TWA for your return trip home and will be driving you to LaGuardia on Thursday morning."

I stood dumbfounded. What I was witnessing were the forlorn ashes of my meticulously-laid plans for extending my stay in America.

And I wasn't sure who was more to blame for this tragedy, this sad end to my cherished strategy: Helen Waller for invading my privacy and reading my mail, or Hushang Ansary for treating me as a brainless five-year-old whose nose had to be wiped.

In a fit of pique after I left Helen Waller's office, I drafted a blistering reply to Hushang's cable:

"Your ill-advised telegram infuriated Herald-Tribune and de-
molished my careful plans for extending my U.S. stay STOP
Now having to fly to Tehran on Thursday STOP letter follows
STOP Cyrus"

By the time I reached the Western Union offices, however, I
had cooled down and couldn't bring myself to send it. My brother
never learned how much trouble he had caused.

The World Youth Forum opened to a packed house in the ballroom of the Waldorf Astoria Hotel in New York City on Saturday, March 4, 1950. Many national and international figures
spoke about "The World We Want." As the delegates, we were
conspicuous on the stage, but the day really belonged to several
prominent leaders—the President of the United Nations General
Assembly, Carlos P. Romulo; another top- ranking U.N. director,
Ralph Bunche; a U.S. senator from Connecticut, Brien McMahon;
and other luminaries.

Still glum about having to return to Iran so quickly after the
Forum was over, I moved into the International House, a favorite
stopping place in Manhattan for the international student community, for the brief interval before my scheduled TWA flight.
To show I had no hard feelings, I called up Helen Waller to say
goodbye. She invited me to share the cheese-and-crackers lunch
that was her usual fare, eaten at her desk. It would be a first for
me; her office had always been a mob scene while the Forum was
ongoing. I happily accepted.

As usual, the Forum program was on Helen's mind during
lunch, and she was picking my brain. I hadn't fully formulated
my impressions of the trip, but I didn't mind sharing with her my
off-the-top-of-the-head thoughts.

From my world history classes at Alborz I had walked away with the conviction that through the centuries, from Genghis Khan to Caesar Augustus down to the Spanish conquest of Latin America, the stronger countries at times had unleashed their military might to conquer other lands, often their neighbors, primarily with the goal of imposing their own language, customs, and values on the vanquished people.

Ever the presumptuous teenager, I told Helen the U.S. was alone in world history to have no need of armies to achieve the same results. People all over the planet were already clamoring to come to America, to speak the language, and to emulate the customs, institutions, and social mores of Americans. Must be a first ever.

"I'm so glad to hear you say that, Cyrus." Helen beamed. "Tells me we are right on track at the Forum."

She took another bite of a cracker and then with great enthusiasm began talking about her expanded plans for the next year's Forum, and she was as voluble and entertaining as she had been before the recent brouhaha.

I was back in Tehran shortly afterwards. As Dr. Gurney had predicted, I was in time to celebrate Noruz, the Persian New Year, on March 21, 1950. The U.S. trip had been a pretty incredible experience, leaving me exhilarated and as determined as ever to travel out of Iran again, not just to complete my education but to live permanently in the U.S.

Several months after the Forum was over, my Malaysian friend Eddie wrote from Yale asking me to join him there to do our undergraduate work together.

I wished.

Chapter Twenty-One

Looking Young for My Age

It was late Spring in 1950, and the world was still laboring to overcome the effects of the all-too-recent global conflict. Germany was being rebuilt with help from a great American initiative known as the Marshall Plan. The war with Japan had ended in 1945, but the peace treaty with that country was yet to be signed.

Like much of the world, Iran was in upheaval. There was talk of nationalizing the oil industry, until then an exclusive British concession. Enraged, London was threatening Tehran with "agonizing reprisals" if Iran proceeded. And predictably, the Soviets saw any turmoil in Iran as helpful to their strategic goal of installing a communist regime there.

As for me, I was faring no better than the government. Back from my *Herald-Tribune* trip for less than ten weeks, I was having a hard time. While I was away, my parents had separated, and I had no idea what had triggered it. Brother Barry, feeling the toxic atmosphere of our parents' separation, got into an argument with his boss and quit his job. Brother Hushang, working in Tokyo as a consultant to a major Japanese company, was trying to cope with the family problems long-distance. Sister Pary had just graduated from the best girls' school in the country, but her prospects for funding a college education were not too bright. All of us were having money problems. I was back to picking up odd jobs but earning little. There were no summer classes to attend but I was preparing to take my eleventh-grade finals in September, as Father had arranged for me several months earlier through Dr. Gurney.

Thursday, June 1, 1950, was a pleasant sunny and mild day in Tehran. As usual there was a light breeze blowing from the mountains. Around 11 o'clock that morning, I happened to be walking along Ferdowsi Avenue, a major artery in the city's central business district. Predictably, the daytime traffic was heavy and the sidewalks were crowded with well-dressed pedestrians, but there were no curbside peddlers in this part of town.

The imposing façade of the Central Bank on the other side of the street reminded me of my foray into a teenager's version of currency arbitrage not so many years before. It had been fun while it lasted. I was half a block away from the vibrant commercial hub of the city, with loads of stores, restaurants, cafés, delis, and movie theaters. I was headed for the largest English language bookstore in Tehran, hoping it had received the latest American magazines.

Ever since getting back from the Herald-Tribune Forum, I was always wracking my brain for ideas on how to raise money for a return trip to the U.S. I couldn't bear the thought of going back to tutoring students and picking up odd jobs. Even though my prospects were grim, I refused to believe that my recent *Herald-Tribune* trip had been a one-and-done experience. As I saw it, my financial black hole stood in the way of a brand-new life. *Darn it, but I'm out of options.* Then I reminded myself that Father had not raised his children to give up when things seemed hopeless. I just needed to mount a whole new campaign to get on the road to solvency.

Deep in thought, I didn't realize I had just passed the gates of the American embassy. Belatedly a thought the size of a planet hit me. Why not go in to see if they had a job for a classy guy? Correction, a poorly dressed classy guy. I was wearing a short-sleeve sport shirt and khaki slacks. One does not apply for a job at the bastion of formal attire and silk neckties of the U.S. Foreign Service dressed as though I was meeting my teenage buddies. I should go home, come back wearing a shirt and tie and my best—and only—suit.

But wait, I thought. *Why not go in now and see if I can get an appointment for another day?*

Yes, that is what I'll do.

I rushed in before I could have second thoughts, but my first sight of the reception desk was of two U.S. Marines. With stern no-nonsense bearings, they looked intimidating. I was filled with self-doubt. I slowed down my headlong rush, not sure why I shouldn't just turn around and get out of there. A moment's reflection, however, made me realize that the embassy had chosen to replace the comely receptionist I had seen before with military personnel on account of the riots in the streets. I firmly told myself not to freak out. The Marines were now eying me as I approached. They looked alert and fit. Their nametags identified them as Shallue and O'Donnell. They had stripes on their sleeves, but military rank was unfamiliar to me. In a casual tone, Shallue said, "Yes?" I wanted to apply for a job, I told him. He didn't even blink and directed me to a Mr. Stuart, the administrative officer, in a nearby office.

I let out the breath I hadn't realized I was holding. I was past the first hurdle, but I had no idea what would come next.

Still unsure of myself, I walked over to the office Shallue suggested and came upon a fellow in a tan summer suit with an open countenance and a friendly expression.

"Are you looking for me?" he asked, seated behind a small desk. "I'm Mr. Stuart."

"Hi," feeling encouraged, I said enthusiastically. "I'm Cy Ansary. The guard out front directed me to you. I'm looking for a job."

Mr. Stuart looked puzzled.

"How old are you?" he asked.

I was about to blurt out that I was sixteen, but stopped myself just in time.

"I'm twenty-one," I muttered sheepishly, unable to look him in the face.

"You look young for your age," he remarked with an amused glint in his eyes, obviously not fooled. *He'll be showing me the door now.*

Instead, he brightened up. "It happens we have an opening coming up, but you have to be fluent in English."

He peered at me appraisingly. "Are you?"

"Well…" I hesitated. "I sometimes get my gerunds and participles mixed up."

Not cool, being a wise-ass when looking for work. I was surprised at myself, but I couldn't help it. I figured his question had been rhetorical. I mean, hadn't we been chatting in English all along?

Mr. Stuart looked momentarily nonplussed, then his lips curled as he grinned, made a deprecating gesture with his hand like "Go on," and said, "Okay, you'll do."

He paused for a breath, then told me to come back Monday morning at nine o'clock.

I left realizing I hadn't asked what the job was. It didn't matter. I'd grab it, even if it was janitorial work. I figured they'd be interviewing me on Monday, and I'd start working on Tuesday. How lucky can a guy get? I'd just waltzed in off the street, and here I was with a job interview lined up. I was walking on air the whole time.

I showed up early at the embassy on Monday morning to find wooden chairs with wide arms, such as those used in schools, set up all over the building. What had been the large reception area was now filled with hordes of people. There were still more people sitting in the other hallways and corridors. Barely an inch of unoccupied space was left anywhere.

There were probably forty or fifty people there, all applying for the job, *my job*. And whatever the job was, it was obviously not a youth-oriented position. These applicants were adults, many middle-aged; I'd have to compete with people who had years of experience. I recognized one of my own Cambridge instructors among the applicants. What chance did I have against such people? Besides, this was obviously not an interview process. We were going to be tested, in writing.

Okay, in for a penny, etc.… What did I have to lose?

A staff member directed me to an empty seat in a back hallway and pointed to a white ruled pad on the seat arm that she said contained the instructions for the applicants. The embassy, it read, was recruiting a candidate to work with other local staff attached to the political section. The person selected would have to demonstrate a working knowledge of foreign affairs, international and regional relations, and recent American and Iranian history. He'd also need to have full familiarity with the jargon and terminology applicable to such work, in English and Persian.

The instructions then set out the day's assignment: To write an essay in English about the role played by the United States in the Middle East after World War II. The papers would be collected at 1 p.m. The applicants would be asked to return at nine o'clock the following morning as the testing would continue for four days.

The next day's topic for our essay was to discuss the current political and economic environment in Iran. The third day, we were handed several essays in Persian that we were to translate into English. The fourth day, the essays were in English, and we were to translate them into Persian. As the testing continued through the five days, I noticed the number of applicants was dwindling. At the end, only five of us remained. We were told there would be a typing test the following Monday and oral interviews for each of us.

I had a long weekend to learn to type. We had a broken-down old portable Underwood at home, a real hunk of junk, that Hushang had used years earlier for writing dispatches to International News Service. I had used it occasionally with a two-fingered hunt-and-peck method of typing. If you tried to type fast, the typebars would jam, creating a typing error, and you'd have to separate the keys manually, smudging the paper and your fingers. The use of that machine was not much of an improvement over the stone tablets of ancient Persia. I had three days to teach myself touch typing, using all ten fingers. The hours passed in a blur. Worked up and energized, I got by on catnaps the whole time.

The typing test on Monday was a timed copying of news articles from unnamed American publications. Afterwards, each of us was ushered into the office of a Dr. Saleh. I was the third to go in. He was an amiable Iranian with a ready smile and a professorial manner, but I did not know his title. He spoke English with me and asked about my background. When I mentioned my *Herald-Tribune* experience, he seemed to light up.

"Oh, then you must know Dr. Gurney," he said.

I told him I did. He asked me to describe the essay I had written for the contest. And then, without further comment, he thanked me, we shook hands, and I returned to the waiting room.

At the end of the day, I was told to come back the next day. I assumed the others were similarly informed.

I had no clue what was in store for those of us left standing. The pruning process had been brutal, eliminating fully ninety percent of the applicants so far. That I had survived the ordeal to this point was nothing short of a miracle, but how long could I continue counting on the auspicious hand of luck?

Mindful of the hopelessness of my financial situation, I was keenly aware I had no other prospects if this one did not work out. I'd be doomed to spend the rest of my days in a society I could barely tolerate. The Herald-Tribune trip already seemed a lifetime ago. Engulfed in uncertainty about my chances at the embassy and pretty nervous, I tossed and turned the whole night.

Exhausted and bleary-eyed in the morning, I looked around as I crawled out of bed. I checked myself out in the tiny handheld mirror we had at home. I still did not shave, had no need to. I just got dressed, but it was early for my appointment at the embassy. It was a pleasant sunny day, so I started walking toward Ferdowsi Avenue, a couple of miles away.

When I arrived at the embassy, the receptionist said Mr. Stuart wanted to see me. I headed for his office, but he wasn't in. I sat in a chair to wait, but when the minutes turned to thirty, then to forty-five, I started feeling like a potted plant as my foreboding grew. Obviously, Mr. Stuart wanted to give me the bad news himself. He was a nice guy, so he'd sugarcoat it. "We'll of course keep your application on file, etc." By the time an hour had passed, I had no doubts. I was about to tell the receptionist that I had to leave and to let Mr. Stuart know I'd be in touch, when he came running in. He was full of apologies. He'd been upstairs in a high-level meeting in the ambassador's office.

He didn't really have to apologize to me. An out-of-work teenager didn't rate such courtesies, but wasn't he a nice guy to be so considerate?

Settling behind his desk, he reached into a drawer and extracted a thin file and said, "Well, let's get to it." *Here it comes.*

The political section of the embassy, he said, had a wide area of responsibility, including noting developments as they occur, regionally and internationally. The local staff was an important adjunct to the primary role of the political section. "You must have noticed that aspect of the work from the essays you had to write," he said. There had been a large number of applicants for the job, he added, and many were deemed well qualified, but the U.S. Foreign Service was exceptionally careful in its recruitment.

I was listening with all my mind, but so far what Mr. Stuart was telling me could end either way. Then he began talking about the embassy's retirement program, and I gulped as I sat up in the chair, my heart racing.

"Have you reached a decision about…?"

He didn't let me finish. "Didn't I tell you?" A smile spread across his face as he continued, "You won over all the others, Cy. Congratulations."

I flushed, closing my eyes and folding my hands. I was trying to calm myself but I wanted to whoop and holler. Feeling giddy, I swallowed and started breathing again, but I did not trust myself to speak. It would be unseemly for a grown man—well, a grown teenager—to lose his cool. Mr. Stuart must have noticed, for he remained silent, giving me a chance to compose myself. It took a moment, but then a feeling of joyful serenity came over me.

Mr. Stuart became all business then and gave me a brief description of the work each member of the section performed, which would be quite varied depending on need. He told me that Dr. Saleh managed the local staff, and that he reported to the Deputy Chief of Mission. My immediate supervisor would be a Mr. Vaziri-Tabar. Mr. Stuart also said there were hiring formalities to complete, and that the personnel officer would review them with me.

As I'd be working for the U.S. government, he explained, I'd require top security clearance, which would involve filling out reams of forms and undergoing an investigation. Once the process was completed, I'd be put on a salary, and he explained in some detail the annual leave and retirement policies of the Foreign Service for my level. I paid little attention to all that. I had no plans to take any leave, nor to retire anytime soon. He added that there would be various deductions from my pay, and he would itemize them for me. He wrote down the gross amount of my salary, the total deductions, and the net pay on a sheet of paper. He then passed the paper to me, and I suddenly sat bolt upright as my eyes almost popped out of their sockets. It was a sinful amount of money. My net pay after deductions was several times my father's monthly salary after working at the bank for thirty years.

I suspected I had misunderstood, or that perhaps Mr. Stuart had made a mistake. *I'd better check.* I thanked him for the generous monthly salary. He was amused.

"No, Cy," he said. "That's your pay every two weeks."

My stunned reaction must have made me look like a country yokel, for my mouth was hanging open. My immediate thought was of Aunt Baji, my great aunt who had raised me. She always said I was born under the right star. I mean, how lucky can a person be? Against all odds I had been selected to represent Iran in the Herald-Tribune Forum. I had miraculously escaped meeting my maker in the airplane mishap on the way to Dallas. And now I had won over dozens of older, more seasoned applicants to get this fantastic job.

I was overcome with pride and pleasure—utterly ecstatic. I thought I should thank my parents, to whom I owed everything.

With that kind of pay, I quickly figured, I'd have enough money for a return trip to the U.S. in no time. I asked Mr. Stuart if it were possible to save my salary and have it paid to me in the U.S. He said perhaps some of it could be arranged that way. He'd check. He then repeated that, as I'd be working for the U.S. government, there'd be miles of paperwork involved.

Daisy at the embassy's accounting department gave me a stack of forms to fill out the next day, all of which I carefully and truthfully completed, including my correct date of birth. I was terribly worried that I could be rejected by reason of age, but to my unabashed relief no one mentioned it. Daisy then sent me to a Mrs. Euglale in the personnel office, where I raised my right hand and swore that I'd not engage in any activity against the U.S. government. Back to Daisy, who explained the rules for working at the embassy. I was so eager I didn't want to wait. I told her I was ready to start the next day, without pay, until the paperwork was processed and I got on the payroll.

I was so excited I was afraid I'd pop. Instead of going back to Alborz High School in the fall for twelfth grade, I'd now be working fulltime in this new dream job.

Chapter Twenty-Two

CIA Station Chief and Me

Having never imagined myself on the world stage, it was now exhilarating to have the opportunity not only to tackle the important work of writing about the latest geopolitical developments, but to get paid a previously inconceivable sum to do it. The embassy was a serious and stimulating environment, and the Foreign Service staff uniformly bright and well educated. I was elated and pumped up by my work and found it immensely satisfying. My colleagues quickly helped me find my niche. I made friends with the staff in other sections and was fortunate to have two helpful bosses.

I learned to take quick lunch breaks at a nearby café, where I ate open-face caviar sandwiches—Melba toast with a thin layer of caviar from the Caspian Sea—for fifteen cents each, oblivious of the fact that they'd be quite expensive in the U.S. I liked what I did and started putting in long hours, including on weekends. The embassy hours were rather odd to conform with the Iranian weekend, which was Friday. So we worked on Saturdays but were off Fridays and Sundays.

After a few weeks, I started a newsletter at the embassy. I'd prepare a digest of the current news, add brief analyses of political developments, and send them around to various offices. There being no English-language newspaper in Tehran, the newsletter became popular, generating a daily buzz at the embassy and the offices of the U.S. Information Agency. I felt genuine pleasure in the feedback I received about it.

While at the embassy, I thought I might as well put in my

application for immigration to the U.S. I figured by the time I was ready to go, my turn would have come up to get a permanent resident visa. But that turned out to be pure wishful thinking. The lady in the consular section told me that people who had signed up twenty years earlier were still waiting their turn.

The news of my working at the U.S. embassy quickly got around to my former classmates at Community School and Alborz. They were excited for me, and eager to show it. I had quite a few teenage visitors at the office, never imagining I was thus arousing suspicion in some quarters.

I also often worked on Sundays, trying to get my work done without distraction. On one of those days, while putting the finishing touches to the next issue of my newsletter, I had a visit from an embassy higher-up. A tall distinguished-looking man impeccably dressed in a dark blue suit and striped tie, he introduced himself, then said he had been trying to find a certain Persian-language magazine. Did I happen to have a copy? I did not. Would I mind canvassing the other offices to see if they had a copy? It was an unusual request, more suitable for the secretary I assumed he had, but I wasn't going to argue with a superior. I couldn't find the magazine, so after about fifteen minutes I went back to my office—the gentleman was still there—and told him I could not find what he wanted.

"That's perfectly all right," he said. Then he just left.

The episode had me puzzled. Several days later, a colleague confided in me that the man who had visited me on Sunday was the CIA station chief in Tehran.

It dawned on me then that by putting in long hours at work and having a stream of visitors I had triggered CIA scrutiny. So when the spy chief visited me, his purpose must have been to see what I was doing in the office on a Sunday. If he had read the paper that was in my typewriter, he'd have recognized that the newsletter I was working on commanded wide circulation at the embassy, and that he himself was on the distribution list.

My immediate supervisor, whom everyone called VT (for Vaziri-Tabar, his last name), had an engineering degree from the University of Birmingham in England. I liked him as a colleague and also had great respect for his professional skills. One day, he and I were having lunch and talking about our section chief, Dr. Saleh, whom we both liked and admired. The conversation then turned to my work at the embassy.

"The newsletter you started has been well received," VT remarked. "It obviously fills a need."

"I'm not trying to create a literary masterpiece," I quipped. "It is strictly news and analysis."

With sudden inspiration, I asked, "Do you think such a product might have commercial value?"

Intrigued, VT volunteered that "there may well be a potential market for it among all the foreign diplomats and expats in Tehran."

VT and I excitedly started making plans to go into the newsletter publishing business and to attempt a mass mailing to test the market in Tehran.

Over the following three weeks, VT and I met after hours in his home and put together the first issue of a commercial newsletter. We also laboriously compiled a list for our mass mailing. Everything was ready to go, but just before pulling the trigger, I had another visit from the same gentleman from upstairs.

Apparently, he had not stopped looking over my shoulder since his last visit. He quickly put a stop to our budding commercial venture. Even though VT and I had done everything on our own time, without using any embassy resources, I probably should have realized we needed clearance from our superiors for such an undertaking. Now I knew better.

Chapter Twenty-Three

A Golden Goodbye

By the time the cold winter months turned to pleasant spring days in Tehran, I was ready to return to the U.S. After working at the embassy for a year, I had saved just enough to pay my way, but that was about it. I'd have to find work quickly once there.

Did I realize there was risk in what I was planning? Of course not. What could possibly go wrong? Calculating risk was not in this teenager's DNA. What I thought about were all the exciting adventures that awaited me in America, a future more glorious than any my mind could visualize.

The wife of the agricultural attaché at the embassy heard about my plans to finish high school in the States and stopped by several times to chat about R. L. Paschal High School in Fort Worth, Texas, her alma mater. She persuaded me to apply to Paschal. I wrote to the school and attached my Alborz transcripts. I received a quick reply accepting me as a senior for the fall semester of 1951. I showed the letter to the folks in the consular section of the embassy and they approved a student visa for entry to the U.S.

In early June, as I prepared for my trip, political events in Iran were taking unexpected turns. The prime minister succeeded in mustering the votes in parliament to nationalize the Anglo-Iranian Oil Company, a move that would result in much higher revenue for the national treasury. It could have been a cause for celebration, but international oil interests took a hand and riots erupted in the streets of Tehran demanding the prime minister's ouster.

Happily, political developments had no bearing on my plans. I was focused on my own future: I just knew that life in America would never be boring.

It was finally time to go. My passport and visa were in order, and I had bought my ticket to fly to Naples, Italy, and a berth on a ship bound for New York from there. It was hard to contain my excitement. Mother, Father, Barry, Pary, and several friends came to the airport to see me off, but my parents were hardly rejoicing at my departure. In a sad tone, Father predicted that once I was out of the country, they'd never see me again. He was right to be concerned. In the Ansary clan, being the lowliest of the children had never been a piece of cake. Besides, distances were long, international travel was expensive, and I would be a poor foreign student in America. Nevertheless, I promised I'd be back as often as I could.

Still despondent, Father took off his gold family ring on which was engraved "Ansary" in Persian script. I knew it was precious, being the only memento he had of his own father. Amazingly, he had hung on to it through all the struggles of his years as an orphan. He put the ring in my hand. Tearful and overcome by emotion, he whispered, "Cyrus, you are now the guardian of the Ansary legacy."

Deeply moved, I assured him I'd cherish the ring all my life. For years I had dreamed of leaving the land of my birth, perhaps forever, but now that it was becoming a reality I had a lump in my throat. I walked out of the terminal and took the few steps to board the plane. When I turned to look back and wave, the obvious sorrow of my family tugged at my heartstrings.

The plane, a small commercial Douglas DC-3, flew from Tehran to Cairo, arriving at 5 p.m. on July 8, 1950. My seatmate was a serious middle-aged English diplomat, and he seemed quite worked up about the recent parliamentary vote in Iran nationalizing the oil industry.

"The Iranians better watch out," he said frankly. "We'll take over the country," as he made a gesture like tearing a sheet of paper in half, "and divide up the territory between ourselves and the Soviets."

Taking him seriously, I assumed he was speaking for the British government, but why was he directing his bluster at me? It was a bit heavy going when I was on a high about my trip back to the U.S. The plane was not full, and I took advantage of a lull in the conversation to switch seats.

My new seatmate was more fun. He was an Iranian boy named Javad. We were about the same age and quickly became friends, chatting merrily for the rest of the trip to Cairo. We were both scheduled for a four-day layover.

After landing, Javad and I decided to go sightseeing and walk along the Nile River. With a population of 2.5 million, Cairo was more than twice the size of Tehran. Fawzia, the beautiful sister of Egypt's King Farouq, had at one time been married to the Shah of Iran, and I wanted to explore her homeland.

Then I thought of my friends, the Herald-Tribune Forum delegates from Egypt, Bella and Hamed. I had gotten to know them well in the States and wanted to try to find them, say hello, and reminisce about the Forum. I'd start with Bella. *But wait,* I brought myself up short. *This is Egypt, a Muslim country. Contact between boys and girls could be forbidden. I might not even be allowed to see her.* I decided to try anyway, but my search for her the next day was halfhearted. Javad went with me.

Cairo was an unfamiliar city, but after wending our way through several areas we finally located her street and then her house. I knocked. Bella herself opened the door. The minute she saw me, her eyes got wide, she broke into a huge smile and wrapped me in a powerful hug. I was overwhelmed. With brown hair and big brown eyes set in a round face, Bella was gracious not only to me but to Javad as well.

Then she pulled me along to meet her mother and an older married sister, both most welcoming. Actually, they seemed to know all about me, which was a pleasant surprise. Her sister, married to a university professor, sat and talked with me at length. Another sister had died a year earlier and I could see the anguish in Bella's eyes about it. She was still wearing black. Bella apologized for her father being at work and unable to meet me. She volunteered with obvious pride that he was the inspector-general of the Egyptian ministry of education. She offered to show us around Cairo. It was wonderful to see that the bond formed as Herald-Tribune Forum delegates still held.

Before starting out, I asked Bella if I could also see Hamed, the male Forum delegate from Egypt. She said he lived in Alexandria, about 150 miles from Cairo on the Cairo-Alexandria Freeway. I was sorry to miss him. I was eager to find out if he had recovered from his doomed love affair with Ada, the Israeli delegate.

Bella started us off by taking Javad and me to the Andalus, Cairo's botanical garden. Hidden behind high walls to protect its peaceful setting, the Andalus had colorful terraces and secluded sitting areas surrounded by fountains and soaring palms. Dating back to 1929, it was built on the banks of the Nile. It encompassed several ponds, splendid flowers, shrubs and trees, and relics of ancient statues. It was an oasis of calm at the core of a busy city.

Next we went to the Pyramids. I was awestruck by the triangular planes of the pharaohs' five-thousand-year-old tombs but couldn't help wondering about their history. *How many years, how much money, and how many lives did it take to build these monoliths?* Unaware of my thoughts, Bella pointed out that thieves had plundered the contents of the Pyramids, including the gold and jewels buried in the pharaohs' sarcophagi, and that the outer casings of white limestone were later pillaged for building new forts and mosques.

"This was before Egypt enacted laws," Bella said, "intended to safeguard our country's heirlooms."

I could see that tourists were having their pictures taken inside the Pyramids or while riding camels with the Pyramids in the background. I missed these opportunities, but they were not free and I had to be frugal. Nor would I want Bella to spend money on me. So we did not enter the tombs but instead caught the tram to leave the area.

On the tram, another passenger, an Egyptian youth, asked Bella in Arabic where I was from. She told him about me and he switched to English. His name was Behjat and he had just graduated with a business degree from Cairo University. An engaging fellow, he invited us to see his school, and we happily accepted. He then gave us a tour of his alma mater, which he described as Egypt's premier public university and one of the largest in Africa. It had been built on the European model, he told us proudly, accepting female students as early as 1928. And in a country best known for its religious symbols and minarets, the university instead showcased a most imposing landmark, a clock tower designed by an unnamed European architect.

Behjat next took us to Cairo's Zoological Garden, the first such facility built in the Middle East, he recounted proudly, and with eighty thousand acres, the second largest zoo in the world. I had never been to a zoo before, and was fascinated by the great variety of animal life. Behjat then gave me his address, and we shook hands like old friends as we parted.

Afterwards Bella took us on a tour of the city. We noticed that Americans had brought their own brand of ice cream to Egypt. It was called the "Americienne." We stopped at a café to try it; it was delicious. We next went to an exhibition of Egyptian rugs. Having grown up in a country known for its carpets, I examined these for their texture, weave, and design. They were splendid, colorful, and all hand-knotted.

On the way back, I asked Bella about the tram we were riding and how it operated. "Come with me," she said. We walked to the front of the tram, and she spoke with the driver in Arabic. She said he'd show me how to drive it. He explained everything, stopped and started it a couple of times, and even put it in reverse. I had a fun ride and thanked him in English, then made a circle with my right hand over my face in what I had noticed was the Egyptian gesture of gratitude.

The three of us trooped down to a theater to see an Egyptian movie in Technicolor. It was a love story, and Bella translated the dialogue. That night Javad, Bella and I had dinner at a local restaurant and lemonades at a café on the banks of the Nile River.

As they say, all good things etc.... I had enjoyed myself immensely in Cairo, and Bella had done everything she could to make it a pleasant visit. But it was time to say goodbye. Javad and I were flying out to Italy the next day.

With a long face, Bella gave me a lingering hug, shook hands with Javad, and wished me well in the Texas high school to which I was headed. She had made my stay a memorable one. I was truly delighted to have had a chance to see my fellow delegate and told her so. I also asked her to thank her family on my behalf for their gracious hospitality and for permitting their daughter to shepherd two foreign visitors around Cairo. This brought a smile to her face. She then asked me to be sure to give her best wishes to Helen Waller and the staff at the Forum office. I solemnly promised I'd let Mrs. Waller know.

I was very much taken by Cairo. The promenades along the Nile were always crowded with people walking and children playing, and there was much laughter and socializing. The Egyptians, I decided, were extraordinarily hospitable and friendly to guests in their country, and my concerns about the strict segregation of boys and girls there seemed to have been overblown. I had an unbidden—and irreverent—thought: It would help Egypt's image if the people redesigned their national costumes and lost the fez.

Silly of me, wasn't it, to think the whole world should dress in Western garb?

Chapter Twenty-Four

A Forceful Entry

The view of the Nile River meandering through the Egyptian countryside was spectacular upon takeoff from Cairo in the early morning hours. Then, arriving in Naples, I was treated to the equally impressive sight of Mt. Vesuvius and the blue waters of the Gulf of Naples. At Capodichino Airport the friendly but harried customs officer asked me with a hopeful glint in his eyes if I had any cigarettes—apparently scarce items in Italy then. I would have been glad to give him all I had, but I didn't smoke.

There was so much I wanted to explore in historic Naples, but the museums and cathedrals would have to wait. The money issues came first; I had to be frugal. I was no better off in Italy than I had been in Egypt.

There had been one other Iranian on the plane from Cairo. He was an Armenian named Sarkis, and he was older than Javad and me, perhaps in his mid- or late twenties. He had a job lined up at Ford Motor Company and was moving to Dearborn, Michigan. After landing in Naples, the three of us—Javad, Sarkis, and I—discussed lodging and found out we had one thing in common: We were all cash-strapped travelers. We decided it would make sense to pool our resources.

The three of us went to town in search of the lowest-priced accommodations we could find. We ended up at a small inn on Piazza Garibaldi, where we were each assigned a cot in a dormitory-style room for 700 lire per day. The official exchange rate was 620 lire per U.S. dollar, so we would be paying the equivalent of about 35 cents a day each. We put up our suitcases, then went grocery shopping. We each bought a hundred grams of salami for 90 lire, and bread for 25 lire. It was like 18 cents in dollars, and it took care of breakfast, lunch, and dinner for each of us.

I knew that Naples was known as the only city in the world that housed hundreds of churches as well as several museums, but I had not known about the Neapolitan passion for music. Our room overlooked the piazza, where at 7:00 p.m. a festive crowd started gathering to talk, sing, and dance right under our window. It was most entertaining, and a pleasant introduction to a fun-loving Italian city.

Naples had special appeal for me. It had retained its historic charm unsullied by busloads of tourists. With its Mediterranean climate, friendly people, and location on the Gulf of Naples, it was ideal for an interlude on this trip.

Javad was staying on in Europe, but Sarkis and I were on our way to the U.S. and needed to check on our arrangements. Both of us had paid in Tehran for our tickets to travel by ship to New York. When we went to the office of the cruise line, however, we were in for a shock: There were hundreds of people crowding the pavement, all jostling to get through the narrow front door of the company.

Who were these people, I wondered? They did not appear to be dull-witted ruffians. And yet the idea of properly queuing up British fashion had apparently never occurred to them.

It was only a few short years after World War II and millions of people from all over the world, counting on Americans' readiness to give humanitarian aid to the homeless, were trying to get into the U.S. The scene at the cruise line was unimaginably chaotic, even on the days when we arrived at the crack of dawn. To our chagrin, there was never any thinning of the crowd. We learned that these were *displaced persons*, who had no passports, tickets, or money. They obviously could not afford to pay their way. Nevertheless, they were not about to step aside politely for us. After days of fruitless jostling, trying to get to someone at the shipping office to claim our tickets, Sarkis and I became seriously concerned about our predicament. We were beginning to feel like ants in a giant anthill.

The travel agent in Tehran had assured me there'd be no hitch getting my ticket in Naples. All I had to do was to show up at the shipping company. He obviously had no idea what an insurmountable task that would be. Even though I had already paid my fare, it looked as though I'd soon be left out in the cold. I had loved my time in this pleasant and picturesque city, but I was churning with anxiety that my money would soon be running out and I'd be stuck in Italy.

Sarkis was in the same boat, so to speak.

At the end of our ropes, he and I huddled one evening to talk over our options. We spent a couple of hours batting ideas back and forth. We felt we were left with few options. In the end, we were both in accord that gently trying to inch our way forward through the sea of people had been demonstrably futile. We needed to get serious and revise our tactics. It was now clear that nice-and-polite didn't cut it. Sarkis was the first to spell it out: Desperate measures were called for. Much as we both hated to think of it, we had to bull our way through and get to someone in charge to claim our berths, no matter what. There was no other choice.

The next morning, we were there at five o'clock with stiffened resolve, but still fearing the worst. The wall of people was already in place. Sarkis and I maneuvered around and zoomed in on a group of men whose dispersion might give us our best start at pushing through. We got in position behind them.

"Shall we?" With more nerve than I felt, I whispered conspiratorially through clenched teeth.

"Let's do it." Sarkis set his jaw and yelled back in his loudest baritone.

Like a man possessed, he put his head down and his right shoulder up and charged into the thick cluster of people blocking us, and I followed.

The white-knuckle details of that day's events are painfully etched in my memory. No one was willing to let us through. We had to push, wrestle with, and savagely shove the people for hours before we slowly whittled down the crowd and plowed a path through for ourselves. It was a hell-for-leather struggle, an ugly scene, and a close call. I had multiple cuts, some still bleeding, and torn clothing. My ribs hurt, and I felt a bruise in the vicinity of my left kidney. Sarkis was spitting blood, had a badly bruised face and a cut lip, his pants were ripped, and his shirt was barely hanging on. That was as much as I could see of his injuries, but he told me he had taken a punch to his right ear and was worried about a ruptured eardrum. *Is he hurt more than he is letting on?* I was concerned about my new friend, but we'd take careful inventory later. In the meantime, we were utterly exhausted. As for the ones we had plowed through, I was certain their injuries were no worse than our own. Even so, we had created more than a few enemies. I consoled myself with the thought that it had been their choice; they could have permitted us through in the first place.

It was midafternoon by the time we reached one of the company employees. The aches and pains remained but normal breathing returned. Unexpectedly, a new problem surfaced: The harassed and overwhelmed shipping clerk—a thin and intense-looking middle-aged man—saw everyone as a displaced person and was skeptical that we had confirmed bookings. His expression was a clear warning that we didn't belong there.

We had had enough. It was again time to take a stand. Sarkis physically threatened the man before he'd take us seriously. Finally, he reluctantly dug out our records, satisfied himself that we had already paid, and issued us our tickets. It had been a long battle, accompanied by worry and fear, but we had won. My breath rushed out between my teeth as relief washed over me and as Sarkis forced a thin smile.

As for the crowd, it was still there in full force when we finally left.

We were lucky, because the ship on which we were supposed to sail, the SS *Conte Biancamano,* was scheduled to sail for New York at eight o'clock the very next morning. It had taken us three weeks, but Sarkis and I had our coveted berths—in steerage with 658 other passengers. Mine was an upper among 330 double bunks.

On the way out the door of the shipping line, I picked up a brochure about the ship. I read tantalizing descriptions of an exquisitely furnished lounge and dining room with Persian rugs and works by famous Italian artists. There was also a movie theater as well as a card room, several bars, etc. The *Conte Biancamano* would be carrying 1,810 passengers and a crew of 500. Never having been on a ship before, I was impressed. Once on board, however, I learned that as a passenger in steerage (now renamed tourist class), I was not permitted to visit those elegant sections.

The voyage was nevertheless most pleasant for me, and the spaghetti bolognese tasted heavenly to someone who had been subsisting on a ration of bread and salami. I tried not to look as if I were half starved in the dining room. The sea was smooth much of the time, but when turbulence came, many got sick, causing a bad smell in some of the corridors. I always thought I had a delicate stomach, but surprisingly remained unaffected by the storm. I was perfectly content throughout the trip, eagerly chatting and making friends with my fellow passengers from diverse nationalities and backgrounds and learning about their destinations and plans for the U.S. I also enjoyed relaxing on a deck chair with a book while soaking up the sunshine, or just watching the endless mosaic of ocean waves and whitecaps. The dolphins riding the waves were a beautiful sight. I did not know what awaited me in the States, but I felt calm, optimistic, and eager to get there.

A flock of noisy seagulls heralded our approach to the New York harbor. By then I was no longer the gaunt, undernourished, and anxious teenager who had boarded the ocean liner ten days earlier. My first sight of the Statue of Liberty was electrifying. The journey was over, and I reveled in the feel of coming to the end of the rainbow as we docked. With a lighthearted bounce to my step, I disembarked, then rode and walked with Sarkis to the Greyhound terminal, north of Penn Station on 33rd Street, carrying our suitcases. We shook hands warmly, promised to keep in touch, and parted. He caught the Detroit bus, and I the one for Dallas, where I'd switch to another for Fort Worth.

It was August 10, 1951. After a series of cascading random events and lucky breaks, I had achieved the dream of my life and was now back in the good old U.S. of A. I only had a little money left, but in my exhilarated mood, I was sure it was enough to carry me until I got a job in Fort Worth. Anticipated joy, as the saying goes, is the greatest joy. Everything was wonderful. History awaited me.

I took a deep breath and prepared to start what I just knew would be an exciting new life.

Today, Pier 84 New York.... Tomorrow, the stars!

Chapter Twenty-Five

Baptism by Fire

I t was not exactly the stars that awaited me in Fort Worth. Rather, I was in for one of the most painful cauldrons of sensation and emotion of my young life.

The bus left me at the Greyhound depot in downtown Fort Worth. First I had to arrange for a roof over my head. Figuring that the YMCA was the cheapest place to stay, I looked up the address, picked up my suitcase, and started walking.

The Y was a four-story brick-and-stone building at the corner of Fifth and Lamar Streets. Inside, the check-in counter faced the front door. A cigarette machine, a Coca-Cola dispenser, and a phone booth were lined up along the gray wall of the lobby. On the right, a sign warned:

When You Use Swear Words,
You Are Showing Your Limitation.

Most of the people hanging around were wearing cowboy hats. The thin clerk at the reception desk had a heart-shaped tattoo on his arm honoring one named Penny. All business, he said he had a room on the fourth floor for $7 a week and that there was no elevator. He added that the bathroom and showers were communal and down the hall from the room. *Is he trying to discourage me?* There was an indoor pool in the building, he said, and surprisingly added that I wouldn't need swimming trunks to use it. He wrote down the number of the pay phone in the lobby and said if I were to get a call, whoever was at the desk would take a message if he was not too busy. And, oh, the rent was payable in advance, and there would be no exceptions.

I walked up to my room. It had gray walls and just enough space for a single bed, a small brown dresser, a tiny desk, and a chair. But nothing could mar the unabridged joy I felt. I unpacked and shoved my suitcase under the bed. Next I had to figure out my upcoming expenses. I'd need to pay for meals, books, stationery, supplies, bus fare to school and work, and incidentals. Adding them up, I figured I'd have to earn at least $30 a week. Unfortunately, after buying sandwiches and soft drinks over three days on the bus, I had little money left. Not wanting to waste any time, I went out and bought a newspaper and started scanning the want ads. One caught my eye. A laundry/drycleaner on the other side of town needed part-time help.

The next day I caught a bus for the thirty-minute ride to the laundry. It was a small store with several racks for customer orders. A short middle-aged woman with a pale face and streaks of gray hair was working through her receipts. She looked up without curiosity as I approached. I said I was applying for the job advertised in the paper. She pointed to a small man in a gray shirt with rolled-up sleeves busily operating the noisy washing machines in the back.

"He'll be with you," she said as she went back to her work, "when he gets a break."

I looked around for a place to wait, but there were no chairs. While customers came and went, I just hung around, trying not to think of the mind-numbing tedium of that work. Half an hour or so later, the man in the gray shirt hastily walked over. He said he had been running the ad for a couple of days and already had seven applicants. He'd make a decision soon.

"Could I leave my name and phone number?" I asked, but he had already turned away.

No luck there, but it was all right. *There'll be other jobs.*

Undaunted, I sauntered out to catch the bus back to the Y. It was a warm day under a cloudless sky on this my first time in Fort Worth. The sunshine reflected off the shop windows, casting dappled light. The sidewalks were positively pullulating with pedestrians. I noticed there were no foreign cars, but lots of Fords and Chevys in the street. I was gawking at the high-rise buildings and the shoppers at a nearby department store as I reached the intersection.

The traffic light was red and all of us pedestrians, including an African-American youth, stopped at the curb. After a short wait, the light turned green, and we started forward almost in lockstep to cross the street. Half a step ahead of me, the young black man stepped off the curb just as a car careening around the corner from the left at high speed ran the red light and struck him. The lad was catapulted upward several feet, and his body arced in the air as though he were doing a back dive from a high platform. He landed on his side on the hood of the car with a loud thud, only to roll off soundlessly onto the concrete, unconscious. That I had missed being hit myself was a miracle. Stunned by what had just happened, I was frightened, in shock almost, and breathing hard. That reckless driver, I swore to myself, deserved whatever punishment awaited him.

Hesitantly, I stepped over to take a look at the crumpled form on the ground. I wished I could help. *That boy wasn't much older than me.* I was muttering under my breath. *He didn't deserve this.* I didn't know him, but found myself grieving for the tragically ruined young life and struggling to control my feelings. I looked up to see several people converging on a tall policeman in blue on the opposite sidewalk. *Good, he'll be getting solid eyewitness accounts,* I reassured myself. There couldn't be any question about how the accident happened. Still, I thought I should give him my own description of the scene as well, and he'd want my name and address.

I walked over, and the officer turned to me after he finished with two others, but as soon as I started telling him what I had witnessed, he scowled and cut me off. He said he had just been talking to several witnesses and they were all quite sure that the driver had a green light, and the boy was walking against the light. In a tone that smacked of less concern than I would have expected for the tragedy that had just happened on his beat, he cut me off again when I tried to protest, then dismissed me with a warning against perjuring myself.

I knew that bystanders were not always attentive witnesses to events, but what was happening here smacked of design and intent, not carelessness.

I shook my head to clear the pounding in my ears. It was my deep anguish for the youthful victim of the accident that wrenched so powerfully at the moment. I was now convinced that there would be no justice for him, and that the perpetrator of this crime would escape punishment. I felt emotionally bruised. My mouth was dry, and feelings of confusion swirled in my mind. How could I regain the calm and peace that had suddenly fled from my universe? Would I have to give up the comfortable principles with which I had always viewed life just to be accepted into the society here?

Kindness, generosity, and charity had been the hallmarks of the Americans I had met as a *Herald-Tribune* delegate, in Texas and everywhere else. What I saw in this incident, however, was the willingness of so many people—and so readily—to bear false witness against a black youth hardly worn down by life's cares. There was no way I could reconcile these stark contradictions. It was my introduction to the pivotal role that skin color seemed to play in the social system of the country. In a momentary fit of pique, I asked myself if I had been living in fantasyland, making up fairy tales about America.

With a last look at the inert form of the victim's broken body still on the ground, I started to walk away, aware that there was as yet no sign of an ambulance for him.

The sun was still shining but not for me. The image of the boy being flung into the air by the rushing driver was seared on my mind. If that lad survived, he'd have so many broken bones and internal injuries, his would be a lifetime of agony and misery.

The incident was an unbearable glimpse into the dark side of society, a heartbreaking introduction to my new life in America, and an unwelcome first step for me on the road of lost innocence.

Chapter Twenty-Six

Life's Ennobling Pain

F eeling as though I was teetering on the edge of a bottomless pit after the accident, I still couldn't permit myself to be deterred in my job search. I had to get a grip, hunker down, and follow every lead. Over the following days, I checked in with dozens of small businesses but struck out with every one of them. Desperately short of money, I tried to shake off the feeling of depression as my gut tightened each time I got another rejection, all the while watching with dread and resignation my meager funds disappearing little by little every day.

Despite the low wages for these jobs, there were always more applicants looking for work than there were openings. I was finding to my chagrin that steady unskilled work was scarce. I was not one of those who thrive on dire calamities, particularly my own. Taking stock of my situation, I knew that staying at the Y cost $7 a week, payable in advance. As the desk clerk had made clear, if I couldn't pay, I'd be out on the street. And I suspected that the Fort Worth police did not look kindly upon vagrants in their town—a thought that added a knife-like frisson of fear to my near-panicky state of mind. There was yet another unavoidable problem—bus fare. Looking for a job all over town required public transportation. Even at twenty-five cents a run, it was a big hit to my miniscule cache of funds.

For the second time since embarking on this journey, my anxiety level was growing with each passing day. I was back to my special diet, Naples style. With no income, I was subsisting on a couple of small rolls most days. I had not realized that rugged individualism, for which Americans are admired, included an introductory regimen of near starvation. I was almost getting used to the abdominal discomfort of going to bed hungry, trying to forget that when I'd wake up in the morning the same miserable cycle would repeat itself. *Miles to go before I eat.* Hardly in a mood to chuckle, I had involuntarily paraphrased Robert Frost's poem.

Isn't one supposed to get used to the gnawing pangs of hunger after a while? I recalled that India's Mahatma Gandhi had once fasted for several weeks, but how does one think of capital-letter issues with a gurgling stomach? I remembered that Father had come out of his childhood adversity with a will of iron. Too bad I hadn't inherited that trait. I felt that I was really screwed. For me, nighttime sleep was my only solace from the unbearable gloom of the day.

> *I was in a vast desert. Sand as far as the eye could see. With the fierce heat of the noonday sun high in the sky, I was on the verge of exhaustion. My lips were chapped, and my tongue was parched. There was no shelter anywhere, and no hope. I was stumbling along, desperately trying to find water. Suddenly, I glimpsed a river in the distance. With my last ounce of strength, I ran and jumped in, but there was only sand, and it was now in my mouth, nose, and ears.*
>
> *In utter despair, I had expended my last breath on a mirage.*

My eyelids twitched as I woke up with a start, feeling like I had surfaced from a deep pit. I had collapsed on my narrow bed face down. My head throbbed, and I felt as though stonemasons were cracking granite inside my skull. Sitting up in bed I dried my eyes with the back of my hand, unsure for a moment where I was. I looked around. I was in my small dark YMCA room, soaked in sweat and swallowing shallow gulps of air and coughing. I eased out of the tangled sheets and padded over to the bathroom down the hall. I was stiff all over, and the glare of fluorescence stabbed my eyes painfully. I felt drained and leaned against the sink to steady myself. I blew my nose, splashed cold water on my face and patted it dry. It was an eerie feeling seeing my startled, unsteady image in the mirror. I didn't want to look again. Hollow-eyed with sunken cheeks and sporting a perpetually worried face, I had downshifted into the most frazzled-looking foreign student anybody had ever seen. The reality of my desperate situation had hit hard, and its crushing weight felt as though I had gone beyond the limit of my endurance.

It was easy to fall into self-pity. Ahead of me was a long bleak road, a lonely and friendless existence. My self-confidence in tatters, I saw myself as a marionette in the hands of pitiless capricious gods, not just a foreigner, maybe even a freak.

Loaded with a tsunami of anxiety, I felt as though the world was closing in on me. Hope for a better life had gotten me out of my native land, but what happened to the happily-ever-after scenario I had promised myself in the U.S.? Had I naively conjured up in my mind a beautiful land of whistling kids with fishing poles? Was it all a cruel joke? Starvation and depression were high prices to pay for what was supposed to be a noble march to my future. Interlaced with these thoughts was intense loneliness. *Why am I here? This sucks big time.* My good sense almost eluded me as I reached for the answer. I gave a shudder and tried to shake off the negative thoughts. Despite my unenviable situation of the moment, I firmly told myself it was my karma that had brought me to the Land of My Dreams, and I wouldn't want to be anywhere else.

I tried to convince myself that this misery was my tuition for the glorious days ahead. It is always best, I told myself, to experience life's hardships early in one's youth. *It'll be over soon.* Father's cool voice rose from deep within my mind to reassure me that this adversity was the price we pay for achieving the promise of growth that has always flowed within ourselves. He had never lost the fire in his soul, but for me, unfortunately, the sense of defeat and the empty stomach drowned out my self-directed pep talks. Why would anyone hire a teenager who looked so beaten down? Someone was bound to take notice and respond, I kept telling myself.

And, believe it or not, that is exactly what happened the next day.

A men's clothing store owner, to whom I applied for a job, said he had already picked someone else. But then he was nice enough to take a moment to chat. He had a piece of advice for me. He said store owners like himself who needed temporary or part-time help often posted the jobs on the bulletin boards of the local schools. That had never occurred to me, but it certainly made sense. I thanked him profusely and decided to test this new lead immediately at Paschal High School. I should have thought of going there anyway, just in case I needed to do more to complete my enrollment.

With renewed hope, I raced to catch the bus to Paschal. The school turned out to be a large four-story red brick building, but there was no bulletin board in the main hallway. *Where should I look?* Even though it was the summer vacation, I hoped someone may be around to direct me. As it turned out, the principal himself, Mr. O. D. Wyatt, was working. When I knocked on his door and introduced myself, I was bowled over by his warm reception. He had been expecting me, he said. He asked about my trip and how I was doing since arriving in Fort Worth. I hesitated to burden him with my problems, but he seemed genuinely interested, so I told him about the imperative of finding a job and the difficulties I had so far encountered. He held up his index finger, asking me to wait a moment, his eyes clouding with thought. He then asked if I could come back the next afternoon. He might have something for me then.

The Paschal principal had brightened my day, but I was loath to slip into optimism as yet.

When I returned the next day, Mr. Wyatt was in a meeting, but his office door was open. As soon as he saw me, he stood up to hand me a note with a name and an address.

"Go see this lady," he said. "She'll fix you up."

His promise was more than I had expected. I was pathetically grateful to him.

Obviously Mr. Wyatt had gone to bat for me. A short and compact gentleman, he was totally dedicated to his students as I soon found out. A true educator, he never met a student he didn't like. His motto was emblazoned in bold letters on a placard behind him in his office:

**Every morning as I awake,
I thank the Lord I have students to educate.**

I had a giddy moment to reflect on the ray of hope Mr. Wyatt's note held for me before I sprinted crazily down the street to catch a bus, and then another, to get to Montgomery Ward Department Store, the name on Mr. Wyatt's note. I had trouble keeping my voice steady as I breathlessly presented myself to the personnel manager on the eighth floor. A trickle of sweat was running down my back and I had a tight knot in my stomach, fearful that this lead would also fizzle. The lady said yes, there was a part-time job in the warehouse, stocking merchandise and delivering packages at ninety-six cents an hour. Was I interested? My heart slamming hard in my chest, I barely managed a "yes." I wanted to say more, a lot more, but this lady was not the right person on whom to unburden myself.

"Would I be able to put in about 30 hours a week?" I asked, forcing myself to focus on the practical issues. She said that could be arranged.

"When can I start?" She said I could start the next day.

Wow! I had finally landed a job. In less than twenty-four hours, I had gone from my earlier lassitude of joblessness to the heady feeling of being productively employed. I had been bloodied by my ordeal of hunger and deprivation, but I felt proud to have been unbowed. Still, I wouldn't want to make that kind of life my everyday reality. In some corner of my mind, I kept wondering what would have happened if Mr. Wyatt hadn't come to my aid. I hated to think of the possibilities, none of them good. My mind kept going over the pain and humiliation I had experienced when nobody would hire me. This job was manual labor, so what? It was a last-minute thing, but luck was with me. At thirty hours a week, my net pay would be just enough to keep me out of the poorhouse. To say I was jubilant would not do justice to my exultant mood. I felt as though a huge burden had been lifted from my shoulders.

But then the personnel lady casually dropped her bombshell. The payroll, she said, was always a week behind. It was company policy designed to keep hourly workers from just walking off the job after payday. My stomach clenched, and I swallowed hard. She must have noticed that my shoulders had suddenly sagged, for she asked after a barely perceptible pause if I still wanted the job.

Are you kidding me? Hell, lady, my whole future depends on this job. Of course I want the damn job. That was what I thought. "Yes," delivered humbly with downcast eyes and a frayed edge to my voice was what I said.

I'd never walk out on a job without giving plenty of notice to my employer, but the policy the personnel manager had mentioned would play havoc with my life at that point. It meant I'd have to get by on my cash for two more weeks before receiving a paycheck. Asking for an advance on my pay was crossing a line I had never crossed before. My head whirling, I kept quiet. There simply was no alternative for me.

I started working the next day, but it was touch-and-go to make my puny stash last. I did pay for my room at the Y, but having to save my last couple of dollars for bus fare, I could not even afford to buy the daily bun I had subsisted on. I had to fast for the last three days. By then, it was getting hard just to maintain a grand sense of myself as I shuffled around in a haze of apathy. My brain had turned to absorbent cotton, and my limbs moved with the spontaneity of a rusting mechanical robot. These last few weeks, just to stay alive was a triumph, but hunger did not show on the outside. I had not had a full meal in weeks, and the last morsel of food—a single piece of bread- had passed my mouth almost seventy hours ago.

No one had ever been happier to see a payday. It was my moment of redemption, and I almost wept with joy. Fortunately, the company paid its workers in cash, as I did not have a bank account. Within minutes I made a beeline for Ted's Diner across the street from the Y. The aroma of Ted's fresh-baked French bread was pure heaven to me. I felt overwhelming relief, and laughter came more easily than it had in weeks.

So I had a paying job, my earlier languor was starting to disappear, but I was not out of the woods yet. Those in the U.S. on a student visa required approval to work even part-time, and I was not about to violate the terms of my stay. I had to file an application on a form provided by the Immigration & Naturalization Service and secure the endorsement of both my employer and the school. Fortunately, it all went off without a hitch, but the process had to be repeated every six months.

After the first hectic weeks at work, I was starting to adjust to my stay in Fort Worth. It helped that I could swim laps in the Y pool several days a week, often early in the mornings. I sensed a tentative return of my self-confidence.

It was now time to examine my life in light of my primal experience in Texas. The torment of recent weeks wracked me, and I gasped as I reviewed them in my mind. It had been a cathartic experience, a drastic comedown from the hubris I felt for untethering myself from the land of my birth. Whether I was now a better, tougher, or more resilient person remained to be seen. I recalled Father's conviction that "suffering ennobles," but I found nothing noble about poverty and hunger. Quite the opposite. At the same time, somewhere in my soul I felt that God must love the naive and the innocent, of which I had been one in spades.

This new society was wondrous, but navigating through its shoals and pitfalls was taking a while longer than I had allowed. Throughout my recent ordeal, I never said "Why *me?*" Nor did it ever occur to me that I had been rejected by so many employers because I was foreign-born. At the same time, I firmly rejected the notion that deprivation would be normal fare for me in America. Then, too, I recognized another reality: To achieve my goal of being an educated person, I'd have to endure many more years of schooling. Was I destined to live on the edge of poverty for all that time? I needed a better plan, or I'd be condemned to the same pitiful lifestyle for a long time.

I'd rather chew glass.

I had to take out insurance against this kind of ordeal… but how? I should have some idea of how to get away from such drudgery and trauma, some kind of plan, but I was drawing a blank.

The quandary bothered me for weeks. It kept bugging me even as I toted the heavy loads over my head in the Montgomery Ward warehouse after school, but nothing occurred to me. I thought browsing in magazines and newspapers might trigger an idea, so I started spending Sundays at the Fort Worth Public Library conveniently located near the Y. I researched the job markets in the major cities. I devoured the want ads. I figured something might catch my eye. My research confirmed an important point though, one I had already learned in my short stay in Fort Worth: The pool of applicants for unskilled jobs was big, and the pay abysmally low. Add to the mix the requirement of working only part-time, and you increased the scarcity factor immeasurably.

I felt the glimmer of an idea but the tantalizing answer kept eluding my grasp. I couldn't understand why it was taking me so long to come up with the solution. I was groping toward a concept, but there was a cascade of possibilities and they were hard to pin down. I took a deep breath, sat up straight, and spelled it out for myself. If looking for unskilled work was the problem, why not develop a skill that was in great demand?

Like what, for instance?

Now that I knew what to look for, I rushed frantically but hopefully through dozens of newspapers from various cities in the library, searching the want-ads. It did not take long; in fact, by the very next day they had led me to an answer that was both acceptable and not difficult to achieve. My slap-to-the-forehead moment came when I noticed that many newspapers listed scores of jobs for stenographers, part-time and full-time, male or female. So simple an idea was a dazzling solution to my quest. That is right, stenos. They seemed to enjoy outsized popularity in the U.S. They were in demand in the courts, in businesses, in law offices, and in the government. And when I called a few of the jobs advertised, I found out that the hourly pay could run as high as an eye-popping five times my pay at the warehouse. Why didn't I think of it before? I already knew how to type (courtesy of the U.S. embassy in Tehran), and learning shorthand couldn't be rocket science, *could it*? I felt kind of proud of the insight I had achieved in my research.

And then doubt set in. *Wait one darn minute. I didn't come all this way to America to become a professional steno.* I needed to bring myself under control. *Pipe down, Ansary. Stenography is a respected and honorable profession.* I also reminded myself that the skill would come in mighty handy in taking notes if I ever made it to college.

It then turned out that stenographers were not all created equal. Some used stenotype machines and achieved speeds in excess of two hundred words per minute. Others took shorthand at slower speeds but fast enough for ordinary dictation.

I was now on a roll; I'd be studying stenography. The jobs that paid the highest rates went to those proficient in stenotype. I looked into stenotype classes but decided that developing the requisite speed for court and conference reporting would take too long for my purposes. Even for regular shorthand, there were different systems. I looked into the prevailing Pitman and Gregg disciplines. The former method was popular in Britain, but the latter was used more in the U.S. So I chose Gregg, and signed up for classes. Of course, I'd have to continue juggling my time between the demands of work and school. I just hoped my grades would not suffer.

It is amazing what pathways dogged research can open up for you. It had brought purpose to my life at that point. I was now convinced my destiny in America would be fulfilled. I just had to finish my education, and my day would arrive.

———••—

The first day of school at Paschal began with a noisy student assembly. After my recent adventures, I permitted myself a moment of contentment at being back in an American high school. Mr. Wyatt quieted the auditorium and said he wanted to introduce a new student. He had everybody's attention now. He talked about me, and everyone applauded when I stood up. It turned out that the previous year, Mr. Wyatt had read my letter to the student body, the one from Tehran in which I applied for admission and mentioned the alumna who had recommended Paschal. The school had no foreign students, and there had been skepticism that I'd show up. So I received a warm welcome.

Some kids came over afterwards to say hello. One of the boys said his name was D. B. Martin and wanted to know if I played chess. I had grown up playing chess. Everyone in my family played the game. Father was not a particularly skilled player, but my favorite uncle was. You could become addicted to chess. It was a game of strategic planning.

"I do," I told D. B. Martin.

"Okay, let's play a game," he said.

I looked around for a chess set and a board. He said, "We don't need a board. I am moving my queen pawn to queen four. What do you do?"

I blinked. "You mean you want to play on a mental board?" I asked.

"Of course," he said, as though that was routine.

D. B. Martin had a phenomenal memory and could indeed play without a board. That was beyond me. I could not keep up with him all the way, but it was fun trying.

D. B. and I became good friends. He'd drop in on me at the Y on Sundays, and we'd play chess in the recreation room. He took chess seriously. He was always reading about the gambits great players had used to win major tournaments. I was not that into the game, but D. B.'s stories were always interesting.

The teachers at Paschal were dedicated and outstanding, as was the principal, Mr. Wyatt. One day, one of the teachers talked about the prospect of admitting black students to the school, which was then all white. To the classroom, it seemed farfetched. The Supreme Court's decision in *Brown v. Board of Education*—holding that racial segregation in public schools was unconstitutional—was still in the future.

Chapter Twenty-Seven

Teenage Foibles

S tocking merchandise in hot, stuffy, and cramped quarters was not great fun. I couldn't help but think wistfully about my work at the American embassy in Tehran. It had been intellectually demanding, with opportunities to gain new knowledge almost every day. The memories brought a smile to my face. In contrast, the stifling grunt work I did in the cavernous warehouse of the company my coworkers called Monkey Ward was hardly conducive to deep thoughts about global affairs and watershed events.

Things, however, soon changed for the better—not to an inspirational degree but at least to a more pleasant level. My supervisor gave me a pair of roller skates—an activity I loved—and asked me to pick up a ticket at the hydraulic tube station at the far corner of the floor, then skate to the warehouse to pick up the merchandise, attach the ticket to it and drop it down the chute, all within five minutes. There were several other high school students doing the same work, and more of us on other floors. We were a grungy crew called "hotshot" boys and girls. It sounded cool. I was assigned to the seventh floor.

As we flew down the aisles holding big merchandise over our heads, we became adept at jumping over unexpected obstacles, such as two-wheelers left carelessly across intersections. Most often stacks of orders awaited as we rushed back to the hydraulic station, but occasionally there were no orders from the catalog department. We then had to mop the floors, dust the shelves, rearrange the merchandise, and help take inventory. My talents, if I had any, ran far from the chores with which I was tasked. I had thought the unaccustomed manual labor would be difficult, but I acclimated quickly. I was more malleable than I knew.

My part-time job gave me the opportunity of making a couple of good friends. One was Joe Claunch, a high school senior like me but attending Arlington High School, a Paschal rival. Joe was a big and brawny eighteen-year-old, and he frequently let me use his car. Trouble was it kept stalling at awkward moments, twice in the middle of the busiest intersection in the city.

Joe's girlfriend was pretty and outgoing, but Joe wouldn't tolerate other boys talking to her. He'd unapologetically challenge them to a fight. So their relationship was rocky and turbulent. When his girlfriend was mad at him, he was particularly hard to live with. On one of those occasions, our supervisor at Montgomery Ward, a man named Bill, got on Joe's wrong side by telling him he wasn't doing his job. Not one to tolerate criticism, Joe was glad to find a target for his anger that day. He told Bill he'd be waiting for him outside after work.

Bill, in his late twenties, was big and muscular with a prominent Adam's apple. Joe confided in me that when Bill showed up outside after work, he planned on tricking him by offering to shake hands and be friends. As soon as Bill put out his hand, Joe planned on punching him out.

I waited with Joe on the lawn outside Montgomery Ward at quitting time. I had expected Joe to be nervous about the upcoming confrontation, but he actually seemed excited by the prospect. We didn't have long to wait. Bill came out shortly afterwards and casually sauntered over to where Joe was waiting. Joe immediately tried to pull his trick, but Bill wasn't fooled. As soon as Joe put out his hand, Bill hit him with a solid uppercut to the jaw. If that was meant to discourage Joe, it didn't work. It only infuriated him, and he started pummeling Bill. They exchanged blows for a full fifteen minutes, and Joe eventually got the upper hand. Bill was now stumbling after each of Joe's blows, visibly tiring and bleeding profusely. With a last powerful blow to the face, Joe knocked Bill down, and he didn't get up. The fight was over.

The whole scene felt eerily unreal. A lowly hourly worker challenging his boss over a mild performance-related reprimand, and then beating him up with impunity, was shocking to me. In some other countries, Joe would probably have been hauled away in handcuffs. The amazing part was that in Fort Worth Joe wasn't even fired. Bill missed work for three weeks, and when he came back he was still all bandaged up.

Besides Joe Claunch, I had a friend whose name was Nelson Robertson, Jr., and he was from Austin. He was a graduate of the University of Texas. He had applied for a civil service position after college, and was waiting in Fort Worth for the result. In the meantime, he too lived at the Y and had an administrative job at Montgomery Ward. Nelson, his teenage cousin Morris John, and I became good friends. Nelson persuaded us to try golf and target practice with handguns. He also invited me to spend Thanksgiving and Christmas with his parents in Austin. His sisters, both unmarried, were also University of Texas grads. Nelson's girlfriend lived and worked in Dallas, but I never met her. My own brothers being far away, Nelson became like an older brother to me. He was also the first person to introduce me to economic concepts—his own undergraduate major. Unexpectedly, he also had an unending repertoire of jokes, many of which I would come to repeat to others over the years.

———•••———

Once I was properly settled in Fort Worth, I decided to call Stanley Marcus, president of the Neiman-Marcus Department Store in Dallas. I had met him and his family in my days as a *Her-*

ald-Tribune delegate. When I let him know I was in Fort Worth, I received a warm greeting, and he invited me to dinner and asked me to meet him at the office. I caught the Greyhound bus to Dallas and then walked to the store, the only Neiman-Marcus in the country at the time.

Stanley, still in his forties but losing his hair, greeted me warmly and gave me a tour of the store. He became quite animated as he talked about his retailing philosophy; he planned on incorporating it in a book someday. As an example of his business practices, he cited the case of a local lawyer who bought a pair of tassel shoes at the store and returned them eight months later contending they were unsatisfactory. The salesclerk noticed the shoes were scruffy and the heels worn down. Nevertheless, the customer received an immediate refund, no questions asked. I was amazed at this unorthodox retailing approach but looking around at the crowd of shoppers in the store, I could see that Stanley's method was obviously successful.[5]

We drove to the Marcus home at No. 1 Nonesuch Road in Dallas. I was delighted to see his family again. His wife, Billie, a very gracious lady, and their three children, Jerrie, Wendy, and Richard. It was a wonderful dinner and I had a fun evening.

Stanley Marcus became one of America's most celebrated twentieth-century retailers. Knowing him was a seminal event in my young life.

Several weeks later I received a message at the Y from a Mr. Lillard Hill. When I called back, he introduced himself as a television commentator. He said he had heard about me as a former *Herald-Tribune* delegate now a high school student in Fort Worth.

---

[5] Characteristically, Stanley Marcus remembered our conversation almost a quarter-century later and sent me an autographed copy of his book hot off the press. It was titled *Minding the Store: A Memoir*, published in 1974.

He was intrigued, he said, and wanted to interview me on his program. I was glad to accept, and we worked out a script for four fifteen-minute sessions to be aired live on Sundays. He was taking me through my life story, so it was a no-brainer.

Lillard was short, with sandy-colored hair and a pronounced limp from childhood polio in Oklahoma. As you would expect of someone who makes his living by talking, Lillard's delivery was easy, smooth, and without hesitation. The TV station where he worked was owned by the local newspaper, *The Star-Telegram*. Once I started appearing on his program, I became something of a minor local celebrity but continued working in the warehouse for ninety-six cents an hour. It was a most therapeutic reality check.

———•••———

Months passed.

I was still living at the YMCA and working after school and on Saturdays to make ends meet. Homework and shorthand practice added to my weekly scramble to put in thirty hours a week at the warehouse. At times when I would be late for work I had no choice but to ask the other hotshot boys and girls to cover for me.

I still had my tiny room at the Y with the bathroom down the hall, the communal showers, and the only telephone downstairs at the main desk. Nothing had changed. Living for months in a hotel could be a drag, and the Y was the epitome of a barebones one. It also attracted many transient men, not always the kind you'd invite home to meet the family.

After a day of school and work, I usually had dinner by myself at about 9 or 9:30 at night at Ted's Diner across the street from the Y for 60 cents plus 10 cents tip. I devoured my meal before Ted closed up at 10. The long hours at work made it difficult for me to make friends at school. I had started out being an honor student at Paschal in the first few months, but by the second semester, my schoolwork was falling behind. My life followed a predictable pattern, not exactly what I had expected. I was still filled with love for the new land I already called home, but I was starting to lose my characteristic zest and ebullience and experiencing periodic bouts of neediness, even fragility.

Having always attended all-boys' schools in a country where dating was frowned upon, I was unacquainted with the realities of gender interactions. My brief exposure to a coed environment during the Forum period had done little to prepare me for the complexities of that arena. Being both an innocent and a romantic, I soon learned, was a surefire recipe for making addlebrained assumptions about girls.

As it turned out, I was not the only transfer student in twelfth grade at Paschal. There was one other. Her name was Ann Fink, and she had come from a high school in Odessa, a center of oil activity in West Texas south of the panhandle. A petite outgoing brunette with few special interests, she had no close friends at Paschal. She lived with her mother and three younger brothers. Her father had remarried and lived in Brooklyn, New York, and did not keep in touch with his children. To support her family, Ann's mother worked as a waitress in downtown Fort Worth. Ann found her home life unbearable and was as eager to start anew as I was. Being the only newcomers among the Paschal seniors, we gravitated to each other. We began dating and, amazingly, somehow found ourselves talking about marriage.

As graduation approached, I thought about college, but there was no formal guidance office at Paschal. The morning after graduation, the clerk at the Y knocked on my door and said I had a visitor. I went down to find a gray-haired woman who introduced herself as a vice president at Texas Wesleyan College in Fort Worth. She wanted to buy me breakfast, an invitation I readily accepted. Over the bowls of corn flakes we both ordered, she said she was a fan of Lillard Hill's television program and had watched my Sunday appearances. She said TWC was prepared to offer me a full scholarship. It would also provide my books. I was elated. It was a stroke of good fortune.

When I told Nelson and a few other friends that Ann and I were talking marriage, they were aghast. Had I taken leave of my senses? I was too young to make that kind of commitment. My Texas friends were not alone. Far away in Japan, Hushang sent an urgent telegram telling me to fly to Tokyo immediately. Similar objections followed from my parents and other family members.

Was I aware of the seriousness of this decision at eighteen? Had I assessed its effect on my future? The truth is I had thought about none of those things. I was focused instead on getting out of the Y, having a home life, and socializing with friends. All of my pent-up anxieties, hopes, and fears of the recent events came together in a desperate decision to proceed, heedless of the avalanche of objections.

Ann and I were married in a brief ceremony by Dr. Foote, the pastor of the First Methodist Church of Fort Worth, in July 1952. We were both eighteen. Nelson relented and served as my best man. Afterwards, we rented a one-room garage apartment within walking distance of Texas Wesleyan College, and I was ecstatic to be moving out of the Y. Ann got a job as a telephone operator, and I started college and continued working the same number of hours in the warehouse.

Chapter Twenty-Eight

Practicing Law Without a License

I had to paint my face as though I belonged to an Indian tribe. I also had to tolerate being paddled and hazed by the upperclassmen. This was called "hell week" and marked the start of the freshman year at Texas Wesleyan College. I went on to be appointed the associate editor of the college newspaper. I wrote op-ed pieces that drew attention on the campus. Before long, however, I realized that I would prefer a more rigorous academic environment.

After a semester at Texas Wesleyan, I transferred to American University in Washington, D.C. The tuition was $250 per semester, and I could take as many courses as I wanted. Ann was excited by the move, and we packed our meager belongings and hopped on the train in January 1953 for the two-day ride from Fort Worth to the nation's capital.

With its world-class museums, the Supreme Court's imposing façade, and the magnificent Washington Monument and Lincoln Memorial, the first sight of Washington was mesmerizing. I couldn't wait to go jogging along the gravel path around the National Mall.

We checked into a rooming house on Washington Circle near downtown and started looking for work. Ann interviewed at GEICO and was promptly hired in the underwriting department. I started looking for part-time work as a test of my new stenography skills. I found out I now had my pick of part-time jobs in Washington. There was great demand for male stenos, a shortage of qualified applicants, and far higher pay than manual-labor wages in a warehouse.

I'd never have to subsist on a starvation diet again while going to school.

A woman who lived on a hilltop overlooking the Potomac River in Virginia happened to have a room for rent in her basement. Ann and I signed up for a year. The house was a couple of miles from American University, and I'd climb a muddy embankment to walk to the campus.

Living on a hill overlooking the Potomac was an opportunity to do some fishing. In the spring the river teemed with herring and shad and sometimes perch. I loved working my way down to catch some. I particularly enjoyed the feel of a fish in my hand struggling to break free just before I'd release it back into the water. The river was deceptively smooth, but I was warned about becoming careless and slipping down as the undertow was deadly.

At American University, I chose economics as my major—a tribute to the guidance of my friend Nelson Robertson. Full-time students carried four or five courses per semester. Eager to get through my undergraduate work as quickly as possible, I signed up for six courses during my first semester, and planned to enroll in two summer sessions. I'd repeat the same schedule the following year, allowing me to graduate at an accelerated pace. I also arranged to work twenty to thirty hours per week at a temp agency.

Then I was blown away by an opportunity to take flying lessons. A television personality and aviation enthusiast by the name of Arthur Godfrey made flying scholarships available at AU. I remembered the first time I had ever seen an airplane: I was a fourth grader in Abadeh. A small plane was flying over the school, and the entire student body and teachers poured out of the classes to marvel at the aerial machine passing overhead.

I submitted my application for an Arthur Godfrey scholarship to the dean's office at school. Shortly afterwards, I was notified that Mr. Godfrey had picked me as one of the three recipients of his awards. Don't ask me "How come?" because no explanation accompanied it. I was of course excited, but I had no idea that the very first time I was to solo I'd get in trouble.

For flying lessons I went to a small airport in Virginia. To avoid this new activity interfering with my school and work schedules, I signed up for lessons on weekends. Having had no previous experience with flight instruction, I did not find it surprising, as I should have, that there were no introductory classes and lectures on the ground. At the airport, an instructor led me to a single-engine plane, a Piper Cub J-3. We climbed in and he quickly pointed out the controls to me and someone on the ground gave the propeller a spin, as there was no means of doing so from the cockpit. The engine literally ignited with a sudden burst of power, and we were taxiing down the runway within minutes of my taking my seat. Then the plane picked up speed and we were airborne. I tried to relax but I was all keyed up. I took a deep breath while the instructor kept up a barrage of instructions as I was trying to get the feel of the controls. Soon we began flying loops around the runway practicing takeoffs and landings, but I was too tense to be enjoying myself. Incidentally, I never had the same instructor twice.

After the requisite eight hours of instruction, there came a time for me to solo. I filed a flight plan at the school and plotted a straight line to the airport in Annapolis, Maryland. No one at the school objected or raised any issues. The plane I was to fly that day was pointed out to me, I got in the cockpit, someone gave me a spin, and I took off. It was a sunny day with virtually no wind. Steadying at two thousand feet, I jiggled the joystick and reveled at the feel of the plane as the wings responded to my hand. I began checking off the familiar landmarks: "Oh, there is the Pentagon." I pulled back on the joystick and banked steeply to get a closer look. Then a few minutes later, "Ah, there is the White House." And so on. I was following my flight plan and felt I was doing fine.

Immersed in the pleasure of the moment, I was not immediately aware that I was no longer alone in the sky. Two other planes were flying in close formation with me, one on each side. Yet a third plane was flying loops around me, over and under. Were we playing tag? It looked like great fun, and I wanted to let the other pilots know how much I was enjoying the game. Laughing, I kept waving to them—they were that close. Then I noticed they weren't waving back.

Soon I sighted the Annapolis airport and dropped down for a landing as the wheels touched the tarmac and rolled down the runway. Several small planes were tied up at one end and I taxied there, stopped, and turned off the engine. The minute I stepped down from the old Piper Cub, two grim-faced men who had apparently been waiting rushed over to intercept me. They turned out to be federal agents, and they seemed outraged about something and started yelling the moment they were near. I had no idea what was going on but finally zeroed in on the words "restricted airspace." It was the first time I'd ever heard the term, but it immediately made sense. The open skies weren't quite as open as I had imagined. Flying at such low altitudes over the Pentagon and the White House was a bigtime violation of the air traffic rules. Feeling like a complete idiot, I was falling all over myself apologizing for my aviation naïveté. I explained that I was a college freshman, described the Arthur Godfrey scholarship, and mentioned that my few hours of flying had included no instruction about restricted zones in the air. They seemed to relax at that point, and left after they told me they'd have a talk with the man running the airport school.

After they were gone, I got one of the airport personnel to initial my flight log and help me plot a different route for my return flight. The rest of the trip passed uneventfully.

Way back as an eighth grader in Tehran, I had promised myself that life in the U.S. would never be boring.

I wasn't far off, was I?

———•••———

Earlier, in fact soon after arriving in Washington, I happened to run into Tom Shallue in downtown one day. With light brown hair and a Midwestern accent reminiscent of his Wisconsin roots, Tom was a friendly face from my past. He and Paul O'Donnell were the two Marines sitting on guard duty at the American embassy in Tehran that fateful day when I barged in unannounced to apply for a job. It seemed like eons ago, but only eighteen months had passed.

Tom was in civilian clothes, but you could not miss the erect military bearing. Never expecting to see each other again, our greeting was warm and friendly. We were both talking at once, trying to catch up. He told me that he and Paul O'Donnell had married two of the Iranian girls working in the consular section of the embassy, Seda and Odette. I remembered them both. They were attractive, bright, outgoing, brown-haired Persian women. After leaving Tehran, both couples had chosen to live in Washington, D.C. Paul remained in the Marine Corps, while Tom gave up the military life and began working at IBM.

A couple of months later, Tom hesitantly asked if I could help with a problem. The couple lived frugally in a tiny apartment in southeast Washington. Seda, his wife, had only one luxury item she cherished, a magnificent white mink coat her father had given her as a wedding present in Tehran. She had stored it for the summer at a well-known Washington department store. When she retrieved it in the fall, she was distressed to find that her beautiful coat was moth-eaten and ruined. She was in tears when she called the store to report the damage, but she received no sympathy, nor even an apology, only denial. Could she prove that the coat was not already ruined when she stored it? Could she produce a receipt for the original purchase? Did she have witnesses to the condition of the garment just before storage? Unbelievably, the store was stonewalling. The back-and-forth continued for months, with no recompense and no offer of settlement.

Hearing the story, I could not help but remember my conversation with Stanley Marcus and his retailing philosophy—a vastly different approach from the one practiced by this department store in Washington, D.C.

The Shallues finally turned to me. Could I please intervene on their behalf?

Who, me? Granted, my ambition was to study law after graduation, but at the time I was a lowly college freshman. In the uncertain world in which this still-poor foreign student lived, there was no certainty I'd ever make it to law school. At best, it was years in the future. It was like asking a first-year pre-med student to perform appendectomy on a patient.

But how could I refuse?

I told the AU law school librarian the story. He referred me to some cases which I read carefully. I remembered from my Cambridge courses in Tehran that when one puts an item in storage, the arrangement is called a bailment. Then figuring it was best to go right to the top, I got the name of the president of the department store and boldly drafted a letter to him. I described the problem, attached a copy of both sides of the original storage ticket, and referred to the law on bailment in the District of Columbia. I threw in a brief reference to the reputation of the store for honesty and good service, and asked if the president would personally intervene and settle the matter. I had Seda sign it, and sent it off.

Four weeks later, the Shallues invited me to dinner at their apartment. They wanted to show off a brand-new mink coat the store had given them to replace the damaged one. They were effusive in their thanks, and Seda gave me a bottle of scotch with a tag that read,

May all your cases be as successful.

I was sure nothing would ever match the satisfaction I felt at this outcome.[6]

Tom Shallue and Paul O'Donnell became two of my closest friends in Washington as well as the role models for my later decision to join the Marine Corps. Tom kept up with my studies, went to the airport to watch me learn to fly, and attended my graduation from college. Later, he'd drive me to the train station on my way to Parris Island.

I finished the requirements for a Bachelor of Science degree in economics at year-end 1954, with graduation in January 1955. To my delight and relief, my eagerness to finish college as quickly as possible had worked. It had taken only two-and-a-half years after finishing Paschal High.

———•••———

When I was ten, I happened to walk by Father one day as he sat reading a book. I figured if I distracted him, he might want to go for a walk with me.

"What are you reading?" I wanted to know.

"Reading about Abraham Lincoln."

"Never heard of him," I proclaimed with what I thought was just the right note of disdain. After all, what I was after was his time with me, not somebody in a book.

---

[6] The bottle of scotch, still unopened, sits prominently on a shelf in my study at home.

"Why," Father answered with awe in his voice, "he was a LAWYER."

Perhaps that was the moment law became a revered profession in my impressionable mind and my career path became fixed in stone.

Eleven years after that incident, I applied to Columbia Law School for admission in September 1955. I was told to take the Law School Admission Test. This was news to me. With no idea what I was in for, I sat for the test at a Washington, D.C., site. Used to writing essays on exams, I was unfamiliar with the multiple-choice and true/false questions on the test. Shortly afterwards Columbia University advised that I was accepted to the law school, offered me a full scholarship, paid for my law books, and gave me $2,000 of low-cost loans. It was manna from heaven.

I moved to New York and began working part-time while attending law school, but because of the demanding curriculum, I restricted myself to twenty hours per week of outside work. In addition to paying well, my job as a temp brought me into contact with several successful corporate executives. One of them was Arde Bulova, president of Bulova Watch Co., for whom I worked for several weeks. He offered me a full-time job if I'd quit school. Once my training period was over, he said, I'd be a vice president of the company. I had a similar offer from the U.S. manager of Atlas Copco, a Swedish industrial group, several months later. I was not tempted by either offer. I was determined to be a lawyer. Besides, my professional aspirations did not include working for others. Father, who had always worked for large organizations, had drilled into me the wisdom of being my own boss.

———••——

By the mid 1950's, Hushang had established his own export-import firm in Tokyo. The enterprising Japanese were then busily engaged in rebuilding their country after the devastation of World War II, and asset prices were skyrocketing. Hushang quickly became successful. He underwrote the expenses of the rest of the family to travel from Iran to the U.S. for a family reunion. It took place in the summer of 1956, after my first year of law school. Barry rented a sorority house at Occidental College in the Eagle Rock section of Los Angeles for three months and all of us including Father and Mother, still separated, descended on it, but Ann decided to stay in New York.

It was wonderful being together again. I got a summer job in a direct-mail advertising company in North Hollywood, and Barry got one in the Auto Club of Southern California in downtown L.A. He also enrolled in the business school at the University of Southern California. Pary got a job at a bank and enrolled as an undergraduate at L.A. State College.

Book II

A Hopeful Professional?

Not failure but low aim is a crime.

—James Russell Lowell

Prologue

Amoment of reflection…
In the galaxy of first-rate teachers assembled at Paschal, my high school in Fort Worth, one was a superstar. Her name was Miss Mixon, and she taught modern American history. She was short and heavyset, with curly jet-black hair cascading down the sides of a broad sympatico face. On me she had a transformative influence. I had always thought history was not a particularly exciting field, but Miss Mixon's enthusiasm for her subject was infectious. She made the characters jump off the page and come alive. You felt you knew them, understood their motivations, and recognized their impact on contemporary society.

We spent a week in her class covering the U.S. business scene in the nineteenth century. When she mentioned Andrew Carnegie, the Scottish immigrant who was deep into steel manufacturing, I was suddenly transported back to the near-fatal accident on the plane between Knoxville and Dallas when I was a *Herald-Tribune* delegate. By pure chance it was Carnegie I had been reading about—and wishing I too could own a company in the U.S.—at the very moment the plane went into a nosedive.

I brought my attention back to Miss Mixon with an effort. She was into the good stuff and I needed to hear. She was talking about the wild-west atmosphere that prevailed in that century, and the swashbuckling free-for-all actions of those early businessmen. There was a fight over control of Erie Railroad in 1867 that I found fascinating but also quite troubling. It pitted two tough and pugnacious characters named Jim Fisk and Jay Gould against a third, Cornelius Vanderbilt. I recoiled at the lawless behavior of the parties and the hostile nature of that takeover. I knew that countries marshalled their armies to conquer territory, but taking over a corporate entity? I had never heard of it. *But why did it have to be a hostile act?*

And so it was Miss Mixon who unwittingly planted in my mind the seeds of acquiring companies. The idea took on a life of its own as I read more about the subject in college and law school. By then my focus in reading material alternated between articles and books about famous lawyers on the one hand, and famous financiers on the other. Clarence Darrow, Louis Nizer, and Edward Bennett Williams on the one hand, and Jim Ling, Roy Little, and Tex Thornton on the other.

I had started out believing that trials would be my life's work, and that I'd be arguing cases before juries all over the country, but with the passage of time I began to see law and finance as a formidable combination.

Chapter Twenty-Nine

Thrill of a First Trial

The grind of law school was finally behind me, and I received my degree from Columbia University in June 1958. Military service was obligatory, and my student deferment had run out. Still impressed by my Marine friends at the American embassy in Tehran, I signed up right after graduation to serve in the U.S. Marine Corps Reserve for six years.

Boot camp was in the sprawling six-thousand-acre swampy grounds of Parris Island, South Carolina. Shortly before my arrival, five recruits had tragically died there during a night march in April. The press accounts placed the blame squarely on the drill instructor, who had been drinking heavily before leading his platoon on the fateful midnight excursion. So I wasn't sure what to expect.

Training on the island lasted four months. There was a lot of yelling and harassment of the recruits. Others may have cringed, but to my surprise I had no trouble taking it all in stride. The rough treatment I had received years earlier at Kakh Elementary in Tehran turned out to have been great preparation for life in Parris Island U.S.A. At the end, all of us in my platoon were in the best shape of our lives. We had grown from a ragtag mob of awkward young men to a proud unit of the U.S. Marine Corps. The day before graduation, the drill instructor, a twenty-six-year-old regular Marine from Upper Marlboro, Maryland, took us on a five-a.m. run around the perimeter of the island. At one point, the road ran alongside a sharp drop-off on our right. Calling cadence, he yelled, "By the rank flank," the order for the platoon to execute a right turn. To complete the order, he'd have to yell, "March." Had he done so, we would have had to go off the cliff. Interested only in showcasing our discipline, the drill instructor of course never completed the order.

After graduation, we began advanced combat training at Camp Lejeune, a huge 250-square-mile base in Jacksonville, North Carolina. We had more time to ourselves there than we ever had had as raw recruits in boot camp. The occasion reminded me of the summers after my eighth and ninth grades at Alborz. A classmate and I were into hypnosis and spent our vacations studying hypnotic intervention. We read about it, then looked among our friends for willing subjects and practiced hypnotizing them. I had forgotten about it until my time at Lejeune. I started entertaining my fellow Marines by hypnotizing some volunteers in the squad bay. I'd have them perform a few antics while in a trance and leave post-hypnotic suggestions which were hilarious to the others.

Also at Lejeune, one of the guys got in trouble during furlough and I spent an hour preparing him for Captain's Mast, a non-judicial procedure for minor offences. He got off without punishment.

At twenty-three, I was the oldest Marine in the platoon. Several had finished college but none had a graduate degree. Another Marine, Bud Grebb, started calling me Doc and the name stuck. I recognized it as a sop to my advanced age rather than any perceived wisdom. Bud even sketched me as a Marine bulldog. (He would later become a high school athletic coach in Pittsburgh.)

In the middle of a combat exercise at Lejeune one day I unexpectedly received a piece of extraordinary news. If I showed up at the federal courthouse in Manhattan and raised my right hand, I could

take the oath of U.S. citizenship. My sympathetic company com-
mander arranged a three-day pass. I bought a ticket on a Trailways
bus to Manhattan and presented myself at the courthouse.

The clerk of the court, noticing that I was in uniform and
learning that I was on a brief furlough, was particularly solicitous.
When he found out that I had finished Columbia Law School, he
laughingly said I wouldn't need to bother with the constitutional
law test required for citizenship. He said I'd be taking my oath in
the judge's chambers, after which he congratulated me as I took
my leave.

It was a moment of boundless joy. I didn't know how the naturalization process worked for others, but mine was thrilling. It
had taken exactly eight years after my stint as a *Herald-Tribune*
delegate to become an American citizen. The occasion called for
a spectacular celebration. I felt like laughing and leaping like an
ecstatic gazelle, but I could only do the dancing and singing on the
inside. I had to catch the next bus for the twenty-hour ride back
to Jacksonville, North Carolina, or I'd be AWOL.

In time, I completed the active duty part of my Marine training
with a heady feeling of accomplishment before switching to reserve
duty. I was glad to have chosen the Marine Corps. It had been a
rigorous regimen and an exhilarating, confidence-building experience. It was where you learned to rise to the occasion or perish in
the attempt.

———···———

By New Year's Day 1960 I was on a high. The career path on which
I had embarked so long ago was finally a reality: I was ensconced
back in Washington, had finished a clerkship with a lawyer who
soon became a federal judge, taken and passed separate bar exams
in Maryland and Virginia, and been admitted to the D.C. bar by
reciprocity. If there had to be an obligatory "hard knocks" period

that preceded a fulfilling life, I was confident I was well past the worst. The days of stomach-churning hunger and humiliating penury had already receded into distant memories. I could not recall ever feeling so good about my life after leaving Shiraz. *"Now I have a future,"* I said to myself with immense satisfaction. Still in my mid-twenties, I was ready to hang out my own shingle, earn a decent living, have children. Instinctively, I knew I'd be going from survival to comfort.

Going into law practice for myself defied the advice of many friends who believed I was committing professional hara-kiri.

"All the worthwhile clients," they would say, "are already locked in with their lawyers."

I told my friends that being independent was the reason I had gone to law school, and I just knew the world would soon beat a path to my door. I was putting on a brave front. I had another incentive. At Columbia, many of my classmates were from prominent American families and were shoo-ins for recruitment by the most prestigious firms. I, on the other hand, still self-conscious about my beginnings, felt I didn't stand a chance with the elite white-shoe law firms.

I landed my first case before I had an office. I was shaking with excitement, even though it was a divorce case. There were a few lawyers in town who specialized in family law, but adventures in divorceland were not quite what I had gone to law school for. Leery of the intense emotional aspects of a broken marriage, I was concerned that handling divorces could be almost as draining for the lawyers as for the couples. Besides, while alimony, child support, and visitation questions were vital issues for the parties, the suits were not known for being precedent-setting or involving complex legal issues. Nevertheless, when a friend asked me to take the case and said it would be a contested trial, I couldn't resist. Chuck Richey, the federal judge for whom I had clerked, used to say that every lawyer needed *some* trial experience. But without an office, how was I going to handle the actual work—preparing my witnesses, doing research, drafting pleadings, etc.?

Luckily, an accountant friend offered me free desk space in his downtown office, long enough for me to handle this first case.

My client was the husband in the lawsuit—I'll call him Gus. He was about thirty, of medium height, trim, and athletic. He seemed low-key, understated, and strait-laced. His wife—I'll call her Grace—was demanding custody of their three children, substantial alimony and child support, and limited visitation rights for Gus. I was aware that judges often favored mothers with small children in divorce cases. Gus was worried that if the court were to award Grace the alimony and child support she sought, he wouldn't have enough to live on. Momentarily reminded of my own days of poverty and hunger, I found myself sympathetic to Gus's concerns. As for visitation rights, Gus went into fits over Grace's attempt at severely restricting him from seeing his kids.

As the interview progressed, Gus seemed to grow more ill at ease and less talkative, which I attributed to his distress at being in this predicament. After getting the basic facts about the parties and the children, I asked him what had brought on the breakup. He said he couldn't point to anything special: There had been some tensions and quarrels about money, the children, the house, but no blowups.

Something about the interview bothered me but I couldn't pin it down. Before bringing the session to a close I wanted to settle on my fee. From conversations with fellow members of the bar, I had garnered a pretty good sense of the fees for these types of cases. I asked Gus for a retainer at the lowest end of the range. Gus asked to pay it in six monthly instalments. Considering that the payments Grace demanded in her suit would leave Gus with little money for legal fees, I was taking a chance, but I agreed.

In the meantime, Tom Shallue found me an office a block from the White House. The Washington office of an aerospace company had some unneeded space to sublease. Tom arranged a meeting and recommended me. So now I had my own office. The building was full of other professionals, with some of whom I soon became friends. A special feature was a unique parking arrangement. As a tenant, I'd drive up a winding ramp to my own floor, park, and let myself into the office with a key. Mine was on the seventh floor. It was a most convenient system, the only one in the city.

Earlier, on a Saturday morning, a group of us newly-minted members of the bar had crowded into a room at the Mayflower Hotel in downtown Washington to hear from Edward Bennett Williams, then the most celebrated trial lawyer in the country. As a speaker, he had the reputation of being a spellbinder, and you could have heard a pin drop for the entire three hours he was speaking. His subject was trial strategy and I had a lot of takeaways from his presentation. One of his most poignant points was that a lawyer should do his own investigation of the facts of a case, and then present each piece of evidence at the trial with the meticulous care of an architect designing a skyscraper.

Gus's case kept nagging at me. The interview with him had produced little ammunition for the defense in a contested trial. A thought kept gnawing at me at night as I reviewed in my mind the facts of the case before going to sleep. Why not do some digging around, as Ed Williams had recommended, reconnoiter the area where Gus and Grace lived, see what I could dredge up. Every scrap of new information could be helpful.

I drove into their immediate neighborhood in mid-week. Theirs was a small stucco house with a relatively large front yard on a quiet side street. I thought perhaps I could get a better feel for the case if I talked to some of the neighbors. I might pick up some helpful information.

I could have never imagined how helpful.

I spent that and several other mornings knocking on doors. I introduced myself and mentioned whom I represented. About half a dozen wives invited me in. They were eager to talk about Grace.

I wanted to try this case—my first case, my first trial—and I was counting the days. I spent hours in the Federal Bar Library drafting memoranda on questions of law that might arise. I then reviewed the testimony of the neighbors with each of them and prepared them for cross-examination by the opposing counsel.

When the time came for Gus's own review, I found myself in a quandary. Unsure of how he might react to what I had uncovered, I decided to play it safe and mention nothing to him about it ahead of the trial. I therefore prepared him separately from my other witnesses. As for the cross-examination of Grace, I deferred any decision about how I'd handle her. I also prepared several versions of the court order I could present to the judge at the end of the proceedings.

I was consumed by the fervor of this first trial. If it is true that in trial work luck follows preparation, then I was ready, eager, and fully alive.

The courtroom was long and narrow with a 24-foot-high ceiling. In the corridor outside there was a line of straight-back chairs near the door to accommodate any witnesses called to testify before their turn came. Inside the courtroom there was a raised platform behind which was the state seal, and a leather chair for the judge. Draped in a black robe, he was a man in his fifties with graying hair, a pleasant manner, and wrinkles at the corners of his dark eyes.

Softly clearing his throat on this day, he banged his gavel as all conversation ceased, and then called the case.

Surprisingly, the courtroom was packed. My opposing counsel stood up, scowled in Gus's direction, and called Grace as his lead witness. Petite and blond, she was demure and soft spoken as she testified, and dabbed at her eyes from time to time when she made her case for the custody of the children. She presented herself as a hardworking and devoted mother. She only wanted what was right for her children and was determined to give them the best upbringing possible. Limited visitation rights for the father were psychologically important to assure a conflict-free environment for the children, as her doctor had advised. She repeated these assertions several times.

Her attorney then carefully guided her through testimony about the alimony and child support payments she was seeking. She spelled out her own and her children's financial needs after the divorce. Her mother also testified on her behalf, confirming Grace's testimony of being a devoted parent. To bolster her daughter's financial requirements, Grace's mother also talked about how frugal her daughter was in running her family's household. A psychologist was the source of some testimony in support of Grace's attempt at limiting Gus's contact with the children.

Without the intelligence I had gained from visits to my client's neighborhood, I'd have been aggressively cross-examining Grace and her witnesses, hoping to gain concessions that would persuade the court to reduce her demands. It would have been tough slogging, with small return on effort. Fortunately, I had done my homework. It would soon be time to find out if it was going to pay off. I was a hot caldron, a racehorse at the starting gate, but I had to keep a tight rein on my emotions until the right moment to show my hand.

My cross-examination of Grace must have seemed strange to the judge. Instead of trying to poke holes in her testimony, I gave her successive opportunities to stress what a faithful and devoted wife and mother she was. I must have come across as a rank amateur. I also adopted a risky strategy of not inquiring into the amounts of support Grace wanted. Nor did I cross-examine her mother or the psychologist. If what I was trying to accomplish worked, alimony and child support for Grace would no longer be issues in the case, nor would visitation rights for Gus.

By this point, I could not have blamed the judge if he thought I had been somehow persuaded to turn the trial into an uncontested case. I was sure the spectators must have wondered about my competence, if not my sanity. As for Gus, without any knowledge of my carefully orchestrated trial strategy, he was becoming increasingly edgy and fidgety in his seat. I was concerned he might be on the verge of an outburst about being saddled with incompetent counsel.

Finally, it was the respondent's turn. No one would be expecting the explosive 90-degree turn I was about to inject into the proceedings. But it was time to pull the rabbit out of the hat, to reveal what I had carefully concealed, even from Gus. Especially from Gus. Instead of using him as my lead witness, I called a neighboring wife to take the stand. I knew she'd be understated, low-key, and a credibly objective observer. I had also judged that she'd show conviction and determination when faced with the inevitable assault from the opposing counsel.

Once on the stand, my witness rose to the task beautifully. In low and subdued tones, she described several instances of Grace's behavior she had personally observed. Two or three times a week, after Gus left for work, a man would furtively sidle up to the house and Grace would quickly let him in. Not always the same man. She would then push her small children out the front door into the yard by themselves and close the door. There were times when the kids were left out in pouring rain, and on occasion in the middle of a snowstorm, even when one of the kids was suffering from a cold or the flu. The man would stay two or three hours at a time. This charade would sometimes occur in the afternoon, and the man of the moment would duck out the back door as Gus was coming in through the front after work.

Being a mother herself, my witness conveyed helpless outrage at Grace's treatment of her own children and at her daytime visitors. Her testimony was interrupted repeatedly by loud and angry objections from Grace's lawyer. Amazingly, the judge never lost his patience while overruling all of counsel's objections. They also caused quite a stir in the courtroom, and the judge had to bang his gavel to quiet the audience.

From the corner of my eye, I was watching Gus's reaction to the shocking revelations about his wife. He looked like his brain was on fire. Breathing hard, he was compulsively twisting and turning in his seat, obviously restraining himself with great effort. His eyes were reduced to dagger-like slits, and his face was beet-red. I walked over to the counsel table, ostensibly to check on my trial notes. I gently squeezed Gus's arm several times to reassure and calm him. I also permitted myself a momentary feeling of satisfaction at having kept him in the dark about Grace's behavior. If I hadn't, I might now be defending him in a criminal case instead of one for divorce.

It was then time for the cross-examination of my witness by Grace's counsel. He looked angry, was clearly wound up, and ready to charge into battle. Under the assumption that he could shake her up and discredit her testimony, he went at her with such ferocity that the judge, with no prompting from me, repeatedly cautioned him against badgering the witness. Stone-faced and brutally adversarial, counsel spent himself trying but he never made a dent. Quite the contrary, all he accomplished was to confirm the accuracy of my witness's recollections and her veracity. In my view, he had made a tactical error and risked losing whatever sympathy the judge may have felt for his client at the start of the trial.

Then came my second witness, another neighbor whose observations closely matched my first witness's, even though they covered different occasions. The cross-examination by Grace's counsel took less time and was less truculent. By the time I put on my third witness, the mosaic had fully formed, and the opposing counsel's demeanor spoke loudly of the hopelessness he felt for his case. He had his head in his hands, leaning on the counsel table. He looked shell-shocked. Perhaps it had all been a surprise to him (as he later confirmed).

In answer to a question from the judge, I replied that I had four more witnesses to put on: Three other neighbors and the respondent himself. The judge said that unless either party objected, the court was ready to rule. There was no objection.

The court order showed the judge's shock at Grace's behavior. The turn of his mouth betraying his distaste, he awarded full custody to the husband and no alimony to the wife. Deemed unfit to have charge of small children, Grace was permanently barred from visitation with them.

I put on a brave face when people came up to congratulate me on my handling of the case. Now that the battle was over, reality had set in. In my mind, there was no cause to celebrate. There was no victory here, and no happy ending. Nobody had won, least of all those children. The trauma of those kids' lives did not end with the court's decree.

The case only served to strengthen my resolve not to handle domestic relations matters. The story obviously got around, however. I was suddenly the go-to divorce lawyer. Not a role I cherished or pursued. And for several years afterwards, I continued receiving calls from a series of lawyers representing Grace who wanted to break the trial court's order. I referred all of them to Gus's new counsel.

In time I took on new partners and associates, and the practice became known as Ansary Kirkpatrick and Rosse. I spent a large portion of my time trying cases in the courts of D.C., Virginia, and Maryland, and occasionally in other states. It turned out that if you liked people and wanted to be helpful, getting clients was not an overwhelming process.

Other clients soon followed, including several embassies, an interesting group of psychoanalysts, various government officials and civil service employees, and scores of businesses. Law practice, I found out, opened a panoramic view of human foibles and heroics, and fascinating peeks into people's most intimate thoughts and emotions. And if that were not sufficient reward, clients tended to treat their lawyer with the respect, even the fondness, they reserved for their favorite grade-school teacher. When one of my clients had a success, he or she would sometimes present me with a keepsake to celebrate, which I displayed in a prominent place in my office. Such mementos and the variety of cases stirred my enthusiasm.

A particular reminder of my beginnings was a client whom I held in special esteem, the scion of the Iranian philanthropist for whom my school in Shiraz was named. After making a fortune with his father in the Far East before World War II, he had moved to the United States and bought a mansion on four acres of land in Bethesda, a fashionable Washington, D.C., suburb, where he entertained lavishly every Sunday. I was a frequent guest at his parties.

Chapter Thirty

Sequel to a Cherished Institution

A wise man keeps his friendships in good repair. That is a paraphrase of something Samuel Johnson once said and I have always been glad I took his advice to heart.

Late one night, soon after I started practicing law, there was a knock on the door of my small rental apartment in Arlington, a suburb of Washington. I opened it to find Johan Holst and Judith Perry, two former *Herald-Tribune* delegates, standing there hand-in-hand with big smiles. Johan, tall, handsome, and super bright, had been the male delegate from Norway, and was now a grad student at Columbia University. Judy, talented, beautiful, and outgoing, had been the female Canadian delegate, now working at the Herald-Tribune Forum office in New York.

Seeing them was an unexpected pleasure. Just like Johan to show up unannounced late at night. "Come in, come in," I said, standing aside. They didn't move. Instead, Johan announced with a huge smile that they wanted me to marry them. I didn't even know they were dating. Surprised and delighted, I said I wasn't sure lawyers were authorized to perform marriage ceremonies, but I knew someone who was. They spent the night in my apartment talking and catching up far into the hour. The next day I took care of all the requirements for a marriage license, and then asked a Methodist minister friend to perform the ceremony. I was the best man for Johan and had another friend stand in as the second witness. We celebrated with a great dinner the next evening before they took off for New York.

Johan Holst received a master's in International Relations soon after at Columbia University, then worked for five years at the Hudson Institute, a respected U.S. think-tank, before returning with Judy to Norway. By then, they had four lovely children. He joined the government and had a meteoric rise, ending up as Norway's foreign minister. We had many visits together each time he came to the U.S. He took it as his cause to try bringing about peace between Israel and the Palestinians. He worked tirelessly for months to create what became known as the Oslo Accords signed in 1993–94—an effort that exhausted him and led to sickness and his premature death. Acclaim for his groundbreaking efforts for Middle East peace poured out from Yitzhak Rabin, prime minister of Israel; Warren Christopher, U.S. secretary of state; and many other national leaders. One of the world's great twentieth-century statesmen and a wonderful friend, Johan Holst died in 1994. He was fifty-six.

The *Herald-Tribune* program for high school students produced more than eight hundred alumni throughout the world, including many other luminaries. It was a rich and unforgettable experience. True to Helen Waller's vision, we the former delegates bonded and kept in touch over the years. In 1960, a group of us organized an alumni organization called the World Forum Association, which was headquartered in my office in Washington, D.C. Johan Holst was its first president. It later morphed into the World Youth Forum. Annual meetings have been held in various cities around the world—Berlin, London, Paris, Tokyo, Johannesburg, New York, Oslo, Rio de Janeiro, Washington, Rome, etc. The organization's newsletter, *The Delegate*, was started by Gerry Thompson (1960 delegate from Rhodesia) and has been in continuous publication ever since.

Helen Waller had a monthly television program interviewing former delegates on CBS in freewheeling discussions of geopolitical issues. She invited me to participate in two of her panels.

Not long afterwards, in 1961, Helen and her husband Ted went mountain climbing in Chamonix, France. In a tragic accident, Helen was struck by a falling rock and was killed. She was deeply mourned by all her former delegates.

The *Herald-Tribune* higher-ups gamely tried to keep Helen's brainchild going, but the innovative spark had gone out of the program. It died as the newspaper itself began losing readership. Ted Waller was by then the chairman of The Grolier Society, the publisher of a popular encyclopedia. He and I met frequently for lunch or dinner in Washington or New York to talk about Helen and her alumni delegates, and issues of global concern that had been Helen's passion in life. We both missed her greatly, as did all her former delegates.

Chapter Thirty-One

Thrill of an Acquisition

M y first acquisition was a large thrill, and it happened in 1960 by pure chance.

During a weekend Marine Corps Reserve exercise I was paired up in a foxhole with another Marine I had not met before. We had a few minutes to introduce ourselves before the war games began.

"What do you do in civilian life?" I was making conversation.

"I'm an AHC."

The acronym was unfamiliar to me. "Do you belong to a professional association?"

"Oh yes," he replied with some pride. "It is called the American Society of Architectural Hardware Consultants."

I didn't know how much time we had to talk. "If you should need a speaker for your convention," I was taking a stab in the dark, "let me know."

Even in combat attire, I had not forgotten to bring my calling cards. I gave him one. Excited to be a brand-new lawyer, I was making like Johnny Appleseed, passing my cards around whenever I could.

We were interrupted a few minutes later, and I did not see him again.

I had forgotten the conversation a month later when I received a call from a man in Santa Rosa, California, who introduced himself as the president of the American Society of Architectural Hardware Consultants. We had a nice chat, and he asked if I'd be willing to deliver the keynote address at their annual convention scheduled in the fall in Chicago. It would be a first for me. I eagerly accepted.

"We are expecting more than 600 people," he added.

Once I came back down to earth, I realized I had no clue what I'd say that could possibly interest people in a wholly unfamiliar field.

Fortunately, the Library of Congress, a short cab ride from my office, was the repository of information on every subject imaginable. Over the following weeks, I spent several afternoons in the reading room, boning up on the latest developments in the industry. In the end I prepared an hour-long presentation titled "Trends in the Hardware Industry: A Lawyer's View."

The day I was to deliver the speech I showed up at the appointed hour in the grand ballroom of the Pierre Hotel in Chicago—only to find it empty. Not a soul in the place. I must have gotten the date wrong, but no, it was the right day. I was really fretting, until belatedly I realized I had blundered. In my youthful eagerness to get started on the big event of my career, I had overlooked the time change. *Could have happened to anybody,* I sheepishly mumbled under my breath.

Fortunately, everything else went perfectly. My hour-long address appeared to be well received, and I thoroughly enjoyed the experience.

Among the calls afterwards from some of the attendees, one was from the owner of a small manufacturing company in Washington, D.C. His name was Leonard, and he invited me to lunch in Georgetown, a popular spot in the city.

It turned out to be a long lunch, three and a half hours. Leonard was an affable older gentleman, bald, muscular, and genial in manner. I judged he was hardworking and dedicated to his company. I quickly learned he already had a lawyer, not why he had called. Instead, he wanted to chat about his business, which was fine with me. I was genuinely interested as it fed into my curiosity about the demands of running a plant. He told me his company had been established sixty years earlier by his stepfather. It manufactured hardware for doors and was a union shop. After about a couple of hours of this conversation, he was fully relaxed and started to unburden himself. He was 62 years old, he said with a sigh, and tired of the daily battles. What he'd love to do more than anything was to spend his remaining days traveling the world with his wife. While he still could, he added.

The next thing I knew we were talking about my buying his company, and discussing price and terms. He was willing to accept a down payment, with the balance to be paid over twelve years. If I agreed, he'd have his lawyer draft the contract, and we'd be in business.

Determined to slow down this headlong rush into buying a company, I told him I'd need a lot of information before giving him an answer. He said he'd open his books and give me access to his people.

Some quick due diligence convinced me there was room for operational improvements in Leonard's company. I had to scramble to borrow the money for the down payment, which took several weeks. His lawyer then sent over the documents. We got together in his office to sign and close, and Leonard gave me the keys to the building with an obvious sigh of relief. In the annals of corporate acquisitions, this had to rate as one of the fastest transactions ever, but the idea of owning a company, even a small one, had my juices flowing. I could not wait to put into practice some of my own operating ideas.

Over the following months, I put in new procedures including a cost accounting system and an inventory control system. I then elevated two of the employees to oversee the company on the day-to-day basis, and I agreed to give them ten percent of the annual profits as a bonus. I also set up a reporting system so I could keep abreast of any operational issues.

The plant became profitable quickly, and I paid off the balance of the sale price in two years—ten years ahead of schedule. I looked upon the company as a base while I sought more substantial operations. Five years later, having moved on to other businesses, I turned the company over to the two men who had been running it for me. They were tearful when I gave them the keys and signed over the stock. I knew I'd be criticized for giving things away, but I felt those two deserved it. They had been loyal and worked tirelessly for me, and I gave them much of the credit for the success of the company.

Several years later, the men to whom I had given the company decided to retire. My chief financial officer helped them find a buyer, and my general counsel guided the sale.

Leonard, the previous owner, sent me occasional cards from various ports and cities abroad. He and his wife were doing what they loved.

Chapter Thirty-Two

Taste of Dealmaking

This is the story of how a screened porch in a dilapidated tenement house became a bank and changed the path of my career.

It was the summer of 1961. Earlier, John F. Kennedy had been inaugurated President. The Korean conflict was over, and the Vietnam War had not yet started. I was still active in the Marine Corps Reserve but hadn't been called up. One of my clients (I'll call him Dick) was the prototypical young-man-in-a-hurry. Short and pudgy, with sandy-colored hair and a florid complexion, Dick had inherited a couple of retail stores and was eager to prove himself by expanding their market. He had his eyes on a piece of ground in northern Virginia, about a mile from George Washington's Mount Vernon, and retained me to get it rezoned for a new store.

I boned up on Virginia law, then drove out to the property and began calling on the neighbors to give them notice of the rezoning application. One of the houses looked familiar. It was a two-story brick colonial with six tall columns across the front and topped with a cupola. I introduced myself to the thin elderly lady who opened the door and explained my purpose.

"You'll be pleased with what will be happening on that vacant lot." I was pointing to the empty ground nearby and brimming with enthusiasm, giving her a full complement of white teeth with all the ardor of a devoted Fuller brush salesman. "There'll soon be a nice new store there and...."

She didn't let me finish. "You mean you're putting a commercial establishment right next door to my home?"

Her face mirroring her displeasure, she did not hesitate to express her strong opposition before I could say anything. "That's never going to happen if I have anything to say about it," she announced.

The finality of her tone left no room for discussion. I could tell she was about to slam the door in my face. Her fury made me pity all those who made their living as door-to-door salesmen, but there was no time for social commentary. I had to talk fast to intervene.

"If you don't mind my asking," I hesitated a moment to collect my thoughts, "how did you happen to build a house that resembles George Washington's plantation?"

She brightened considerably and offered to give me a tour. Her late husband had been an admirer of the first President, she explained, and had built their house as a replica of Mount Vernon. She now made her living by renting out rooms. Once inside, I noticed that the property was severely run-down but it had a very inviting feature in a large and airy screened-in porch.

"This would make an attractive office," I remarked, thinking it was a nice throwaway line.

Puzzled, she asked, "What kind of office?"

I hadn't planned on being pinned down but remembering my disastrous childhood attempt at organizing a bank, I blurted out, "Why, a bank!"

Amazingly, she took me seriously. Her face took on a thoughtful look as she asked, "Why don't you take that up with my son?"

Wait a minute. I was just making conversation. I'm a brand-new lawyer. I don't own a bank. I was wondering how to break the news to her when I noticed she almost had the look of a drowning person reaching for a lifeline. I had inadvertently given her hope. My mouth had gotten me into trouble, not for the first time. I couldn't break the news to her and back out now.

"I'll be glad to talk with your son," I replied with more bravado than I felt.

"He is a colonel in the Army and has just finished a tour of duty as a military advisor to the government of Iran," she volunteered as she wrote down for me her son's name and phone number at the Pentagon. Then, with a mischievous smile, she asked to sign the form for the rezoning application.

As she walked me to the door, I thought about the pickle I had gotten myself into. "I wonder," I said, trying to make amends, "whether your son and his wife would be interested in attending a dinner party being given by the Iranian ambassador at his residence next Friday."

"They'd love it," she said, obviously pleased.

On the drive back to town, I calmed down enough to wonder: How *does* one organize a bank? Instead of heading for my office downtown, I stopped at a pay phone to ask my secretary to reschedule a couple of appointments I had that afternoon. As for the dinner party given by the Iranian ambassador, whom I knew well, I asked her to call the embassy's social secretary and request on my behalf to include the colonel and his wife on the invitation list for that Friday night's dinner.

I then veered off and headed straight to Capitol Hill, parked, and walked to the Library of Congress, the research arm of the U.S. government. With a staff of almost 3,000, it was the largest library in the world. I started researching the laws governing bank charters, getting more excited by the minute. The library closed at 10 that night, and I was back at 8 the next morning when it opened. By the end of the next day I was so pumped up I arranged to reschedule all my commitments for the following week. Then on Friday night I attended the Iranian ambassador's dinner. It was a pleasant affair and I sought out the Army colonel and his wife and we had a chance to chat. We agreed to schedule several meetings in downtown Washington over the following weeks.

I had gotten a good start at the Library of Congress, but it was now time to move my research to the next level. I began spending long days—which soon became weeks—at the Federal Reserve Board library. In the meantime, the colonel and I were meeting regularly about his mother's house on Route 1 south of Alexandria, Virginia. That, incidentally, was a town actually surveyed by George Washington in his teen years, but I digress. By this time, I had figured out how to structure a deal with the colonel and make it contingent on my securing a charter for a national bank from the U.S. Comptroller of the Currency.

The prospect of organizing a real bank had my excitement quotient soaring. I spent the next year preparing my application for a bank charter and meeting with the president and staff of the 5th Federal Reserve District in Richmond, Virginia. With help from a talented young architect I knew, I surveyed and documented the demographics of the proposed trade area, which I presented to the Comptroller of the Currency as an exhibit to my application.

In one of those remarkable coincidences that occur occasionally in life, I found out that my application to organize a new bank was just what the federal authorities had been seeking. They felt that the established banks had lost sight of their community obligations, and it was time to break up their monopoly by encouraging the entry of fresh blood into the field.

Soon, headlines in the *Washington Post* and the *Washington Star* announced that I had received preliminary approval to open a bank in a Washington suburb. The press had received the news before I had. The *Star* asked for an interview and then printed a photo of the rooming house I proposed to convert to the bank's head office. The news continued to be treated with great hoopla in the local press. It had been years since the residents of the Washington metropolitan area had seen anyone organizing a new bank there.

Still in my twenties, I felt this lucky break could propel me in a whole new direction, and I was ecstatic about it. Reality, however, soon intruded upon my euphoria: The responsibilities I was assuming were awesome and sobering.

I spent the next two years dealing with the endless details of the task I had undertaken: remodeling and renovating the building, putting together a distinguished roster of directors, recruiting officers and staff, and raising the bank's initial capital by selling stock door-to-door, literally, as was allowed for financial institutions.

Rushing headlong into this undertaking left precious little time for me to make a living in law practice—something I had blithely overlooked in my enthusiasm for this venture. That year, my total income was a paltry $1,700. As Ann had not worked since we moved back to Washington from New York, we had to dig into our savings. In the end, however, I did not forget to put my office as the bank's executive chairman in the spacious and airy porch that had led me to spend three years organizing this new venture.

Still, when I welcomed the throng of people at our grand opening, I felt elated about the whole experience, not only for creating a new bank where it was needed, but also for blazing a trail that other entrepreneurs soon began to follow in droves. New charter applications for banks started pouring into the offices of federal and state authorities. Over the next few years, more than a dozen new banks opened their doors in the metropolitan area of the nation's capital. As a card-carrying Washingtonian, I rejoiced at the proliferation of community banks. It led to the greater availability of credit for many households and small businesses, and to continuing economic prosperity for the region. In time, these developments led to a new wave of consolidations in the financial sector, including the bank I had organized.

———···———

On the home front, Ann and I had two wonderful children. Our son Doug was born in 1961, and daughter ParyAnn in 1963. We bought a home on a picturesque lane only a few feet from the Potomac River and the C&O Canal in suburban Virginia. Proud of my new status as a father, I doted on my children and sent pictures of them to Father and Mother. They came to visit and spent weeks with their first grandchildren.

What marred this idyllic life was the rift developing in my marriage. By the time the children were three and one, Ann and I were experiencing difficulty in our relationship. We had actually been drifting apart for several years, and having the children did not change that. We separated in 1964 and divorced shortly afterwards. I moved out with Doug and ParyAnn to an apartment near American University in northwest Washington, hired a live-in housekeeper, and started a new life. Ann was free to visit the children or have them overnight whenever she was available.

Ann later married a marine engineer and moved to Pennsylvania. I made certain she was set financially, and we remained on good terms during her life. She and her new husband often attended Thanksgiving dinners with us. She died in 2005.

Chapter Thirty-Three

Attributes of Fame

On a flight to Chicago, my law partner Ed Rosse perked up his ears when he overheard two passengers seated behind him talking about Cy Ansary. Ed later told me the two were discussing my business deals in some detail.

I had gone to law school to be a trial lawyer, but with the passage of time it was becoming evident that my litigation skills were not shaping my career. The publicity about organizing the bank was bringing other opportunities, and I was devoting most of my energies to negotiating deals and acquiring companies.

I had loved practicing law, but the work was primarily advisory, serving the clients' interests. These new involvements, on the other hand, gave me the opportunity of acting as a principal. I found this role most satisfying, particularly as I often heard in my mind the echo of Father's words in his familiar cadence exhorting his children to take the entrepreneurial path in life and be our own boss.

Years earlier, while I was an undergraduate at American U., *Fortune Magazine* ran a feature called "The Urge to Merge." I devoured the article. It described how American companies were growing and expanding through acquisitions. Most were major corporations doing so as part of their strategic expansion plans. Few people in the country were making financial acquisitions in the 1950s and '60s, but that is the field to which I was increasingly devoting my time and loving it.

After his experience on the plane, Ed Rosse opined that I'd no longer be able to hide my light under a bushel. He was making a joke, but it was true that my financial activities were attracting local attention. Washington was a government town, and indigenous business consisted mostly of banks, utilities, retailers, and the like. The great wave of real estate development that eventually saw the Washington metropolitan area grow from half-a-million people to over six million was not yet the centerpiece of daily fare in the newspapers. The press and the media were eager for stories about financial deals, and my professional involvements were often covered. People in town were starting to recognize my name. I was not entirely comfortable with the loss of my privacy but the upside of all the attention lifted me, at least temporarily, out of my discomfort.

A vice president at American University invited me to lunch on the campus. I was on the alumni list but not particularly active. I thought he'd be soliciting a contribution but I accepted anyway. There were also a couple of faculty members at the lunch, but what surprised me was the fourth individual on the AU side. It was Don Bittinger. Tall, trim, and articulate, he was the popular chairman and CEO of Washington Gas Light Company. I had heard of him. He had a great reputation in town. Now I was wondering what was going on. Over a sandwich and a small salad the two faculty members held forth about the state of the university and how far it had come since its financial difficulties after 1945. During World War II, I was intrigued to learn, the campus had been used for "government research," a euphemism for the training of spies.

Then Don Bittinger took over. He talked at length about his own connection with the governance of the institution and mentioned several other prominent Washingtonians who were similarly involved. I had heard of all of them. They comprised a *Who's Who* of the business leaders of the region. Maybe I was being slow, but I still had no clue to what this was about. I was convinced it was a pitch for money. Once they made it, I would thank them for the lunch but let them know they'd be disappointed with the size of my contribution. The truth—which I'd keep to myself—was that I owed a lot to Columbia University for all it had done for this penniless foreign student, but I did not entertain similar feelings for my undergraduate alma mater.

Don remarked that, as an AU alum, I had attracted attention on the campus with my activities in banking, business, and law. He added that the institution needed the involvement of alumni such as myself. He explained that the university's governance structure was the province of fifty members. Smiling broadly, he then said it was his privilege to invite me to join the university's Board of Trustees.

In retrospect, I realize this sort of thing happens all the time, but for me it was totally unexpected. Immigrants often have one foot in the old country, the other in the new. They are thus emotionally pulled and pushed. I never wanted to be in that position and was prepared to spend decades fully assimilating into the American society. Feeling overwhelmed by the offer, I reached across the table and grabbed Don's hand to shake it.

Thus began an almost three-decade-long relationship with the institution. When the Chairman of the Board, a world-renowned Methodist bishop, retired in the fall of 1979, the Board voted unanimously to elect me as his successor. I felt honored, and accepted, a post I kept throughout a demanding, productive, and tumultuous decade—the longest in the university's history but also including a shocking national scandal involving the president of the university.

Over time, similar offers arrived from other organizations, some of which I accepted. One brought me into a close relationship with a family whose patriarch was a successful entrepreneur and visionary. His name was Edward T. O'Connell, Sr., and he invited me to serve on his company's board of directors. It was a family

She-Goat, 1952,
by Pablo Picasso

enterprise, and it published newsletters in various fields, including several in the nascent computer industry. At the time, it was the second largest newsletter publisher in the U.S. I very much admired the father and accepted his invitation. During the heyday of my acquisition spree, he gave me a gift of a piece of sculpture by Pablo Picasso with the endearing inscription

"The Ansary Goat Eats Everything"

referring to my appetite for corporate acquisitions. Ed used to joke that acquiring companies was "like popcorn for Cy. He just can't get enough of it!" On another occasion, on my birthday, he presented me with a vault for my office with the inscription "The Ansary National Bank" in gold lettering on the door. That was before I had actually organized a bank.

⸻

By the mid-1960s I had accumulated several new companies, and the responsibility of overseeing them caused me to rethink my career path. When I went back to the office after the Christmas holidays in 1967, I asked all the lawyers in the firm to gather around. I told them I was leaving the practice of law. There was suddenly a hubbub of murmurs: "What is going to happen to us?" I told them I was giving them the practice—the client accounts, the cash in the bank, the receivables, the law library, everything. "What will you be doing?" was their second question. I was switching from law to finance, and going into the business of acquiring companies full time, I told them.

It seemed as though all I was doing in those days was giving things away. Okay, I confess. It isn't a good business model, but the blame for my behavior lay with my mother's parenting. She may have never heard of Benjamin Franklin, but she believed, as did he, that what we do for our fellow man commends us to God. In the midst of her frugal existence, Mother drilled that philosophy into all her children—a sort of "it is better to give than to receive" axiom. Of course, she had no experience with the take-no-prisoners model one encounters in the modern business environment. Or in politics.

Chapter Thirty-Four

A Storybook Romance

Friday, April 25, 1969, was a pleasant spring day in Washington, sunny and warm with clear skies. The Japanese cherry trees were in bloom around the Tidal Basin and the Jefferson Memorial. Richard Nixon was President. "The Age of Aquarius" was No. 1 on the Hit Parade, and NASA was frantically putting the finishing touches on the first Apollo mission for a thrilling manned landing on the moon scheduled for early summer.

My own days that spring were no less frantic. They were a blur of endless tasks and a million personal and professional demands. My life was *not* ruled by the need to excel and the drive of ambition. Rather, bedeviled by the existence of several major unfilled management slots in my company, I felt it was an accomplishment just to keep my nose above water. In the midst of it all, I was blithely unaware that something unexpected might be in the offing for me.

As usual, I was up at five that morning and met my friend Bill Cooper for a five-mile jog on the American University track. Bill's dog, a lovable dachshund, accompanied us but didn't do much running. He had only three legs, having lost one in an accident. Bill had fashioned a two-wheel attachment to the dog's back, enabling him to move without pain. By the way, Bill's T-shirt read:

So Many Women, So Little Time.

A bit of doctor humor. He was an ObGyn and president of the

Medical Society of the District of Columbia. Most often, half a dozen other friends joined us on the run.

Afterwards, I took Doug (seven) and ParyAnn (five) to school—my most cherished routine as a single parent—before heading to the office.

As I drove downtown, I was preoccupied with plans for the dinner party I was giving on Saturday night. The guests were a veritable *Who's Who* of Washington, and I wanted to be a good host. I was wondering whether I should ask Maryam, Hushang's wife and my favorite sister-in-law, to help out. Hushang was now the Iranian ambassador to the U.S. He and Maryam lived on Massachusetts Avenue, Washington's embassy row, only a short distance from me. I looked forward to spending weekends with them and their children, Nina and Nader. Earlier, Barry had been in Washington for a brief visit. When I drove him to Dulles Airport, his last words of brotherly concern before boarding his flight were "Cyrus, you are in your thirties. When are you going to settle down?" He meant well, but he was asking why I wasn't getting married, and that was the last thing on my mind.

It was a busy day at the office that Friday. As usual, keeping tabs on the companies in my conglomerate kept me hopping. I had evening plans and rushed out at six to pick up my date. We then drove about twenty miles to Olney, Maryland, where I had made reservations at the Burn Brae Dinner Theater to see *Damn Yankees*, a musical comedy based on Doug Wallop's novel, *The Day the Yankees Lost the Pennant*.

"Would you mind," the perky hostess asked upon our arrival, "being seated with other guests at a communal table?"

We had confirmed reservations, so I was surprised. But it was no problem. "That would be fine," I told her.

In the dim light, she led us to a table for eight. The others were already seated, and one of them, an attractive young woman, was in the middle of a story. I heard her mention Arthur Andersen and perked up my ears. At the time, that was one of the Big Eight accounting firms. It also happened to be the auditing firm for my company, and I knew most of the people in its Washington office. Piecing the story together, I gathered she had graduated with "a great degree," then eagerly went out to apply for a job at Arthur Andersen. After several interviews, they called to say they were impressed with her qualifications and were prepared to make her an offer if she'd come in. Elated, she rushed excitedly to their office, thinking the job was hers. It was, but not the one she had in mind.

"They wanted me as their receptionist," her voice took on a momentary forlorn tone, "to answer the phone and direct the visiting firemen."

It was a depressingly familiar story. At times, gifted women with good education entering the professional world were in for disappointing experiences. When they applied for positions for which they were amply qualified, they were often passed over or sidetracked into lesser jobs.

I remembered that there were few well-paying jobs for women when I was growing up in Tehran, but the news coming out of that country now mentioned women serving in the Cabinet and in Parliament.

I shook my head to come back to the woman telling the story. Distracted by her looks and her animated delivery, I had lost my train of thought. Oh yes, coming in the middle, I wanted to ask about her "great degree."

"What was your degree in?" I asked.

No introductions having been made, her forehead creased for a moment as she looked at me for the first time, more curiosity than interest. My eyes were adjusting to the dim lighting. I noticed she had lively blue-green eyes and short light brown hair casually framing a face with a clear complexion and little makeup.

"I have a master's in business with concentration in accounting," she told me.

Now I understood. In her shoes, I would have been outraged, but I detected no edge of resentment in her tone. She seemed good-natured about the experience. Actually, she exuded an air of both vitality and innocence.

Always on the lookout for promising candidates for my company, I couldn't help asking, "Are you still looking?"

"No." She hesitated a moment as her expressive eyes lit up. "I'm now on the faculty at Montgomery College."

Startled, I realized she had inadvertently given me her contact information, but I still did not have her name.

There was a familiar face among the other guests. Her name was Helen Talbot, and she had led a group of us on a skiing trip to Aspen and Vail back in February. Helen then made the introductions. The one telling the Arthur Andersen story was Jan Hodges. On the stage, the curtain was going up and there was no chance for more table talk.

The play, a fantasy about the Senators, at one time Washington's losing baseball team, was entertaining and enjoyable. When it was over, the lights came on and we all stood up to leave. I noticed that Jan wore a light blue Eisenhower jacket, a jaunty touch to her prim and proper attire. With a ready smile and shimmering blue-green eyes, she looked graceful, at ease with herself. *I could become fond of that smile*, I thought as I left.

In the parking lot, my brand-new Ford Mustang had a flat tire. It was not the ideal time to discover that the jack in the trunk was not the right one for that model. It took an hour working in the dark to accomplish what should have taken ten minutes. It made the evening's events even more unforgettable.

Flagship was a popular restaurant on the Potomac River. It was known for scrumptious fish dishes. I had a reservation for two but there was still a wait. Jan and I were on our first date. She appeared relaxed, laughed easily, and talked about teaching, students, and faculty meetings. We were tentative in conversation, feeling our way toward becoming comfortable.

We started seeing each other regularly afterwards. A native of Kentucky, she came from a family of lawyers. She was an avid tennis player and loved the theater. She and a friend had toured Europe and the Middle East right after college, and she recounted details of her trip with the enthusiasm of a dedicated sightseer. She belonged to a ski club, had recently spent a skiing vacation in Austria, and looked fit. She had attended St. Mary's College in South Bend, Indiana, and received her Master's from Catholic University in Washington, D.C. Bright and vivacious, she had a low-key sense of humor. She lived in Silver Spring, a suburb of Washington and was an associate professor at nearby Montgomery College.

In her off hours, Jan donated time to working with severely handicapped children. She had the Mid-American values of honor, loyalty, and devotion to family and community. With an effervescence that was almost contagious, she was exactly the kind of ideal American girl I had rhapsodized about as a teenager to my audience at A. B. Davis High School so many years earlier.

Shortly after we met, Jan was appointed chair of the Business and Economics Department at the college, while I ran my conglomerate in downtown Washington. We were both busy people, but we managed to see a lot of each other. We regularly dined at the Rotunda restaurant on Capitol Hill, a popular watering hole among members of the House and the Senate. The maître d' was Iranian and took special care of us. Another favorite restaurant was Trader Vic's on K Street, with Polynesian décor, music, and blue salt-rim *mai tais*. We got to know each other's friends and colleagues at parties and took in plays at National and Ford Theaters and other local performing arts centers.

One day Jan and I happened to be driving on Massachusetts

Avenue, Washington's embassy row, and passed by the Iranian ambassador's residence. It was where Hushang had been recently ensconced, and I looked over to see if my niece and nephew were by chance playing outside. Jan noticed me eyeing the building and asked about it.

I hesitated a moment before answering. Back in Fort Worth, the boys at school insisted on tutoring me in the arcane art of impressing the girls. They cracked me up. I remembered some of their more memorable nuggets:

"Just point to a big-company name on a building as you pass by," they advised, "and tell your date 'My uncle is president of that company.'" Or "My dad owns that regional mall."

Not wishing to be branded an empty-headed braggart like my classmates had advised, I said nothing to Jan about my brother the ambassador. I just told her that he worked there. Since it looked like an ordinary house, she told me later, she naturally assumed my brother was some kind of a domestic, and she didn't want to be nosey and maybe embarrass me by asking about it.

Later on, after she met Hushang, she and I would have a good laugh about the incident.

Jan's mother, Glad Hodges, heard about us and invited me to visit Kentucky. An elegant hostess at Louisville and Elizabethtown parties, she hosted two dinner parties that weekend and I had a chance to meet many members of the Hodges family and their friends, including Jan's sister and her husband. He would later serve as a long-term mayor of Elizabethtown. I also met her uncle, who was a circuit court judge, and a cousin who had just finished law school. (Studious and brilliant, he'd later become a justice of the Kentucky Supreme Court.) Another cousin, a Marine colonel in the Reserves, was practicing law in Lexington.

Jan's father, Bill Hodges, was the epitome of the self-made American. Born into modest means, he read law on his own, took the bar and passed it, and was later elected a circuit court judge.

What was most impressive to me was Bill's entrepreneurial bent, a rarity in the judiciary. He was the prime organizer of Elizabethtown's first radio station, the first small loan company, the first cable TV company, and a host of other firsts. Unlike today's serial entrepreneurs, however, he invited local businessmen to participate in his ventures at par and never took a premium for himself. He died prematurely at fifty-nine.

Soon I started thinking seriously about Jan. To my surprise, a couple of friends tried to steer me away from her and lobbied for someone else. Then the husband of one of Jan's childhood friends buttonholed me with a matchmaking glint in his eyes to tout Jan's many virtues. I was perplexed. Was this practice of meddling in other peoples' romantic involvements a custom I hadn't heard about?

Ironically, the arguments pro and con only served to make me realize I couldn't think of life without Jan. Shortly afterwards, she and I went jogging on a Sunday on the campus of American University. The 440 track was a busy place on weekends. People played soccer in the field and tennis in nearby courts, walked their dogs, jogged, or just socialized on the bleachers. Hot and sweaty after our morning workout, we stopped by my apartment to cool off before going out for brunch. It was a relaxed and congenial respite from our busy weekdays, and I took advantage of the serenity of the moment to propose. It wasn't exactly wine and roses, and I was not on my knees, but, gracious as always, Jan overlooked the setting, smiled warmly, and said, "Yes."

We were married fifteen months after we had first met. My Methodist minister friend—the same one who had married Johan and Judy Holst several years earlier—performed the ceremony on August 1, 1970. Jan was stunning in a cream-colored, high-neck wedding gown that followed a family tradition. We had a reception afterwards in the ballroom of a popular Washington hotel with several hundred friends and family, including a few Arthur Andersen partners. I was wondering if their inclusion would mar the joy of the occasion for Jan, but she made sure they fit in.

Dr. F. Taylor Gurney, to whom I owed so much during my *Herald-Tribune* days, and Mrs. Gurney were the most honored guests at our reception. I recalled that on the train leaving Tehran as the first leg of my trip to the U.S. all the way back in 1950, I was concerned I'd never see Dr. Gurney again. I need not have worried. He was a huge presence in my life for many years afterwards. It was later that I learned he had been one of the founders of Alborz High School, and that he had taught math and science there in his youth. After I returned from the *Herald-Tribune* trip, my first stop in Tehran was to visit Dr. Gurney in his home. Later, when I began working at the American embassy, I had the pleasure of seeing him almost daily as our offices were on the same floor. By the time of my wedding, he had already retired from the U.S. Foreign Service and was living in Washington. When he died four years later, the world lost a great and dedicated humanitarian, and I lost a revered mentor and friend.

From the wedding reception, Jan and I flew to Los Angeles for our honeymoon, and I pulled a groom's classic blunder: I had recently acquired a trumpet manufacturer in Glendale, a close-in L.A. suburb, and I did not endear myself to my bride when I slipped in a few business meetings that week. Happily, I learned something new about Jan: She did not hold a grudge.

After L.A., we drove the scenic route US 101 north to San Francisco and stopped periodically to admire the spectacular views from the cliffs overlooking the Pacific Ocean.

Back in Washington, Jan and I bought a two-story red-brick colonial house in a popular section of suburban Bethesda. From the previous owner, who obviously had an eye for a pleasing and lush garden, we inherited a huge backyard filled with azaleas, forsythia, and dogwood. The family-oriented neighborhood was an oasis of calm within walking distance of one of the most dynamic capital cities in the world. Doug and ParyAnn lived with us, and Jan gave up a promising career as an educator to take care of them. The children, already quite fond of her, thought it was "too cool" having Jan as their mother.

Chapter Thirty-Five
To Sell or Not to Sell

I had a whirlwind acquisition spree for the next several years. I found myself consumed by the planning, the negotiation, and the myriad of daily details of a deal. I felt my heart pounding in my chest at the start of the chase, then there was the whirling chaos of the transaction, followed by the elation of seeing all the pieces coming together, and finally the indescribable pleasure of owning a whole new entity. The work required three-dimensional thinking and, to my unalloyed delight, I discovered I had a facility for structuring and negotiating complex transactions. For someone who had started life with modest means, I particularly relished this unexpected talent—it must have been in the Persian genes!

On the downside, the experience also provided a concentrated tutorial in dealing with doctored résumés and other perils of running a business.

I bought a building on Fifteenth Street overlooking McPherson Square in downtown Washington as a base from which to run my operations. Dealmaking was most satisfying and rewarding, and I had no trouble filling the top slots in the entities I was continually adding to my diversified portfolio, mostly by promoting promising candidates from within. I was, however, having difficulty finding qualified executives for the parent company. The glaring vacancies at that level were a troublesome consequence of my preoccupation with the acquisition side. What was obviously lacking was an experienced chief operating officer. I put the word out, and the head of one of the subsidiaries called from Grand Rapids to say he had come across a qualified candidate. He faxed me his résumé. I had to be in Chicago on business, so I asked if he could arrange for the candidate to meet me there.

At the interview, the man came across as energetic and confident. He was a career army officer who had retired as a lieutenant general. He then joined a well-known defense contractor, a public company, for five years and reported directly to the executive chairman. He mentioned several high-level projects he had worked on at the company.

The chairman of the company for whom he had worked was actually a good friend of mine, but I saw no reason to mention it at the interview. I was back in Washington the following Sunday and called my friend at home to see how good a recommendation I'd get about the candidate. Then the unthinkable happened.

"What was that name again?" my friend asked in a puzzled voice.

When I repeated the name, he was unequivocal. "Never heard of him."

Shocked, I asked if it was possible the man had worked for someone else in the organization. He said there had been only three retired army generals in the company, and he knew them well. He then wrote down the man's name and said he'd check with the personnel office. When he called back the next day, he confirmed that no one by that name had worked in the company. Perhaps noticing my discomfiture, he mentioned that phony or doctored résumés were not an uncommon fact of corporate life.

The episode affected me more than I cared to admit. Father had lived through the incredibly tough early years of his life without losing his moral compass, and I prided myself on trying to measure up to his standards. This applicant's deception was a valuable lesson, one I had somehow failed to learn earlier. Was it not Dante who said, "It is wrong to think ill of people, but seldom a mistake?"

Lesson learned, I still needed a senior executive to run the operations. I turned to a nationally recognized executive search firm. After interviewing half a dozen candidates, I settled on an impressive and articulate vice president of a major U.S. corporation. The day he started working I felt great relief. The daily burdens would now be his to manage. I'd concentrate on more strategic issues.

If only it had worked that way. By the time my number-two executive had been on board a couple of years, it became clear that he, having been used to the vast support system available to a senior executive of a major organization, was a fish out of water in a small and highly diversified operation.

There was, of course, no question in my mind that the vacancies at the top would in time be filled. That was a difficult problem but hopefully only a temporary one.

Another area needing urgent attention was finance. Still my father's son, I had inherited his aversion to debt. I had started my company with no seed money, and I still had no loans; so I was stretched quite thin in the funding of my acquisitions. Liquidity can be an issue for companies small and large, and I wanted to be proactive about it before it became a problem. The market for initial public offerings provided an attractive option. After thinking it over, I signed up with a boutique investment banking house to take my company public. A team from their office would need six weeks to do on-site due diligence before they could commit to a firm underwriting. None of this was unexpected, so I arranged for them to have access to the management at each of the sites; they could perform whatever review of the operations they deemed necessary.

To my surprise, it took them several months to complete their investigation. Then their managing director invited me to lunch to discuss their findings. I offered to have my chief financial officer and general counsel with me, but he insisted that would be premature. He just wanted to go over some items with me, one-on-one, he said. I was puzzled, but agreed.

The lunch was in the sumptuous dining room of Washington's venerable old hotel, the Hay-Adams, across Lafayette Park from the White House and facing St. John's Church, where successive U.S. presidents have worshipped for generations. My host, an accountant by training, was a short, bespectacled, paunchy man who had trouble buttoning his jacket. We spent a few minutes on pleasantries, then ordered small salads for lunch. He wasted no time getting down to business and began by complimenting me on the kind and composition of the companies I had put together. Most, he said, fit together well. There were opportunities for operational synergies on the one hand, and some cross-selling on the other. He wasn't telling me anything I didn't know, but I kept quiet, waiting for him to get to the bottom line. To his credit, he got to it pretty quickly. He said his firm would be pleased to take us public, but he had an alternative proposal for me. Instead of doing an IPO, would I consider selling my interest in the company?

He caught me off guard. You don't build a brand-new enterprise from scratch and nurture it until it reached the point of being self-sustaining, only to turn it over to the first person who came along. Besides, I had turned my back on law practice and given up most of my other corporate and civic activities, all in the expectation that I'd be devoting the next thirty years to the conglomerate I had built brick by brick. There were also numerous contractual commitments and obligations, employee stock options and restricted stock, and many other issues I would not walk away from.

It was a no-brainer. It took me all of thirty seconds to turn him down flat. Time to get into the nitty-gritty of the IPO, but he would not be put off. He switched tactics and started talking about the sheer complexity of running a conglomerate, the void in key personnel, the difficulty of penetrating multiple markets simultaneously, etc. Again, nothing I didn't know. Then he asked if I'd be open to a proposal from him.

Pondering his question, I didn't realize I was totally self-absorbed for many minutes. *Is he asking me to do the unthinkable: Sell my company? What would it be like afterwards? Was my mind ready to contemplate the bright side of this offer? But wait a minute. What about all the employees? The other shareholders? How would they fare?* Wisely, my host did not interrupt my internal struggle.

I opened my eyes and told him I'd be open to a proposal and suggested that he forward it to the company's general counsel. As often happens, the formalities of the transaction consumed months and underwent several iterations.

Then I began contemplating my next move.

The author's father was A. Russol Ansary. An orphan and a runaway, he had lived in the street, slept in ducts, and was always on the run. By the time he was twenty-one, he had walked hundreds of miles across several countries in the region. Deprived of the chance to get an education, he taught himself to read and write five languages, and a smattering of two others. He finally settled with his new bride in Shiraz, a town of 30,000 population with lush gardens and beautiful sunsets.

Mother was Jamali Ansary. Daughter of a well-known landowner who had fallen on hard times in Shiraz, she never got beyond third grade. Her life was dominated by the devastating memories of the death of her mother, grandmother, and sister in a single weekend during the influenza pandemic when she was nine. The night of her wedding in an arranged marriage was the first time she laid eyes on her husband.

Tehran, the Iranian capital, shown in this photo, sits at an elevation of 4,000 feet and is built on the foothills of the snowbound Alborz Mountains, a chain that encircles the Caspian Sea. On weekends, the mountain is crowded with Tehranis climbing, picnicking, or just enjoying the distant panoramic view of the capital city. In the mid-20th century, it was a city of stark contrasts. Below left was a luxury villa in North Tehran, below right an impoverished woman doing manual labor in South Tehran.

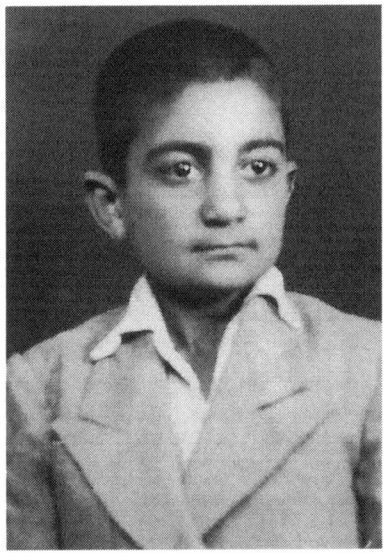

In his first year in Tehran, the author as a sixth grader ranked second in national academic competitions in the country.

The author at Alborz High School in Tehran established in the 19th century by a group of American educators.

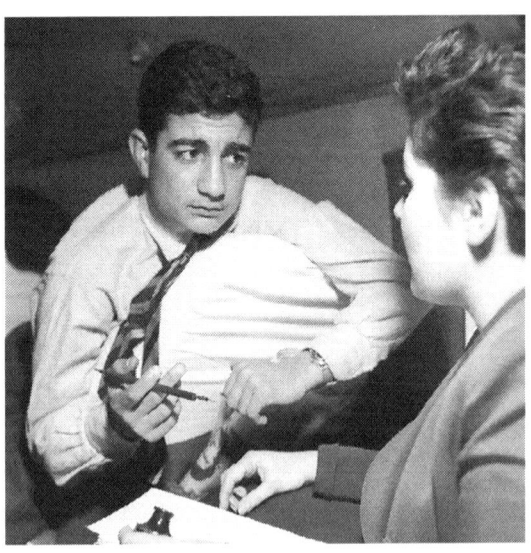

During an aerial tour of the U.S., the author, at sixteen, co-opted a Voice of America microphone to interview other New York Herald-Tribune World Forum delegates on the plane. Here he is interviewing U.S. delegate Harriet Hirsch. The interviews were later aired on Voice of America.

The New York Herald-Tribune World Forum for High School Students was an initiative of a major American newspaper after World War II. Helen Hiett Waller, a young foreign correspondent shown here at left, was the spark plug of the initiative. Above right, a group photo of the 1950 delegates, including the author, before they met with political leaders in various states.

The final session of the Forum was held in March 1950. It was at a packed house in the ballroom of the Waldorf-Astoria Hotel in New York, the first such event televised to a nationwide audience. The delegates were showcased. The author is speaking in this photo.

The Dallas Morning News

DALLAS, TEXAS, TUESDAY, JANUARY 24, 1950

GETS LOST, STUMPS EXPERTS

Frisky Cyrus Bit Cautious As Far East Students Visit

By WILLIAM H. SMITH

A mischievous 16-year-old from Tehran, Iran, sat down to a lunch of mashed potatoes, yams and chicken-fried steak Monday in The Dallas News cafeteria.

He and twelve other high school students from the Far East had just finished a tour of The News plant.

Cyrus Ansary picked up a fork, gently probed the yams on his dish and looked quizically at his neighbor. She was eating another strange dish called "hot tamales" which Cyrus had refused.

He smiled wisely at his decision. He tasted the yams. The smile dropped. He tasted them again. "Do you have this often?" he asked. "It's very nice," he added politely.

Although normally a very curious boy, Cyrus was being cautious Monday as the result of an incident aboard the plane which brought him here Sunday.

Cyrus saw a handle, wondered what it did and turned it. An escape hatch flew open and the wind almost blew the 4-foot-11-inch youth through the hatch and to his death, 10,000 feet below.

During the tour of The News, Cyrus managed to (1) Ask more questions about newspapering than several experts could answer; (2) apply for a job as research librarian and later as a reporter; (3) step in front of an NBC television cameraman taking pictures of the presses running (but he smiled for the camera); and (4) get lost three times from the tour, protesting each time that He"was not lost, only looking around for himself."

American food was only one of the many perplexing and yet interesting things that Cyrus and his friends had found in the United States.

The thirteen boys and girls are part of a group of twenty-three Far Eastern high school students selected by The New York Herald-Tribune to take part in a youth forum March 4 in New York City. The other ten students were delayed by plane engine trouble in Memphis Sunday and did not rejoin the tour until late Monday here in Dallas.

Cyrus' traveling companions came from fifteen Asiatic countries. Several were dressed in their bright native clothes as they got off the bus in front of The News.

Richard Htun Nyunt of Burma, who wants to be a doctor; Syed Adam Edward Hogan-Shaidali of Malaya and Supri Prakob-Santishuk of Thailand stood in the lobby and listened to a guide explain the historical murals.

Cyrus winked at a News employee and asked: "What do you think of that? Isn't it interesting?" The employee thought it was, too.

The tour wound on through the halls, rooms and even to the basement of the building. In the news room, the students watched reporters and editors preparing Tuesday's paper. In the press room they saw the block-long presses being readied for the next run.

The Dallas visit of the group is being sponsored by the Civil Air Patrol of Texas and the Dallas County Community Guidance Service.

Time for lunch came and the group was ushered into the cafeteria for hot tamales. The more cautious ordered substitutes that more closely resembled their home foods.

Monday afternoon they went for a downtown walk and had tea at Neiman-Marcus. A round of banquets and sightseeing trips is scheduled through Sunday.

"Cyrus willing, we will leave for Tennessee then," said Major Fred Mogey of Washington, who is in charge of the tour.

For touring the U.S., the delegates took off from Mitchell Field on Long Island. A mishap on the plane almost cost their lives. They were saved by the heroic actions of the captain and crew. The incident was the subject of an article the next day in the Dallas Morning News, as shown.

The Fort Worth YMCA, shown here with the author, was his home for a year while attending Paschal High School.

The campus of American University in Washington, D.C. was where the author did his undergraduate work in Economics. At right, the author upon entering Columbia University School of Law.

The author later served as Chairman of American University's Board of Trustees. Above, he is presenting an honorary degree from the university to Queen Farah of Iran.

Upon the author's retirement as Chairman of the Board of Trustees, American University established the Cyrus A. Ansary Medal to be awarded annually to a man or woman of distinction in business, government, and philanthropy. The recent recipients have included J. Willard Marriott, Jr. (Chairman, Marriott International, Inc.), Susan E. Rice (former National Security Advisor), Susan Zirinsky (President, CBS News), and Lonnie G. Bunch III (Secretary of the Smithsonian).

Jan Hodges, shown in this photo, was a native of Kentucky working as a college professor in Washington, D.C. when she and the author married. She also devoted time on weekends to helping handicapped children. She took a State Department course in Persian and became fluent in the language. The couple's children are shown below (front to back) Brad, Doug, ParyAnn and Jeff, with Winnie, the family pet.

Krupp was a German industrial enterprise with worldwide operations in heavy engineering. The news of Iran's investment in that venerable European company sent shock waves through the financial markets. Overnight, the concept went viral, causing a scramble by other oil producing countries to dig into their surplus funds for corporate investments in the West. It also led to the availability of an almost inexhaustible source of funds for the newly-minted private equity firms.

The author came up with the idea of what in time was dubbed Sovereign Wealth Funds, negotiated the Krupp transaction with its chairman (the photo at upper right) and its chief financial officer (on his left in the upper left photo), and then served on the company's Supervisory Board. The photo below is of Villa Hügel, the Renaissance-style castle that served as Krupp's headquarters in Essen.

This is not a photo of Bruce Lee and Jhoon Rhee, world-class karate experts. Amazingly, it is of two European kings the author knew, both great athletes in their own right. The one flying through the air with a side kick to his opponent's head is King Constantine II of Greece, a onetime Olympic gold medalist. The other is King Juan Carlos of Spain, also a superb athlete. The two were brothers-in-law and best friends. The author crossed paths with both.

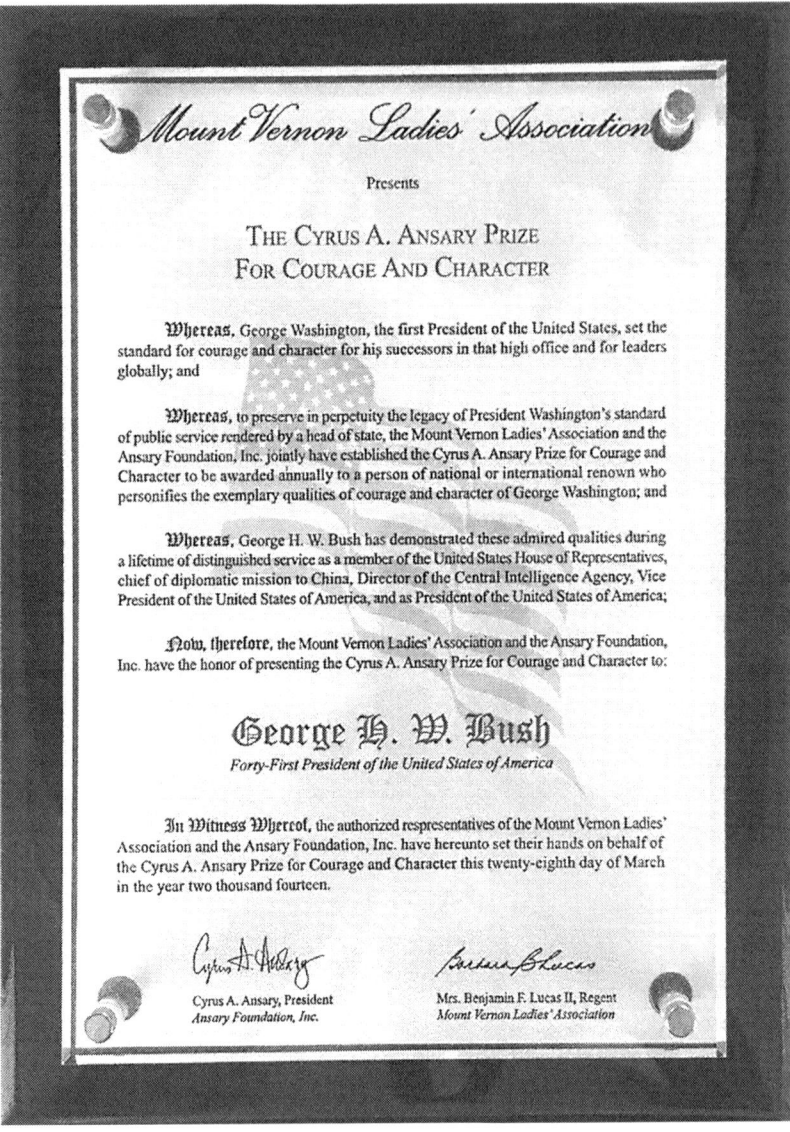

The Cyrus A. Ansary Prize for Courage and Character, awarded to former President George H. W. Bush in 2014.

Lawyer, financier, educator, and philanthropist, the author served on multiple corporate and nonprofit boards of directors. He is shown here in his downtown Washington office. The model of the Concorde was presented to him by Air France with an invitation to be the public face of the supersonic plane.

Book III

A Crowning Achievement?

The history of mankind is the history of ideas.

—Luigi Pirandello

Vision without action is merely a dream.
Vision with action can change the world.

—Joel A. Barker

Prologue

I'll tell you what became of the land I left behind...

In the 1940s, when I was entering my teens and engaging in an all-consuming decade-long struggle to find a way out of Iran, my native land was a primitive place. More than a century behind Western civilization, the nation suffered from widespread illiteracy, high infant mortality, deep unemployment, and abject poverty. Few cities had electricity, and there was extensive opium addiction.

"Iran is definitely a very, very backward nation," observed President Franklin D. Roosevelt in 1943.

The country had meager revenues from exports, much of it from the sale of Persian rugs. Children made the rugs. Their small nimble fingers were the only ones that could tie the knots of hand-made Persian carpets. Jobs for adults being scarce, the children were the family breadwinners, but they paid a high price for their sacrifice. Crouching over their looms in close quarters in cold and damp underground facilities with dim lighting, many children went blind or succumbed to disease before reaching their teens.

Despite its glaring shortcomings, Iran's warm-water ports and its strategic location on the Persian Gulf (which held 60 percent of the world's known oil reserves) made it a tempting prize. Its thousand-mile border with the Soviet Union exposed Iran to Russian agitation, assassination, and sabotage. The country was thus in a constant state of tension with Russia, and to a lesser extent with Britain.

Persia was an ancient land gone to seed, but as World War II raged on in Europe in 1941, the country installed a new king on the Peacock Throne. Perhaps this young and enlightened monarch would lead his people out of the darkness and ignorance to which they had succumbed.

"There is no glory," the young Shah proclaimed, "in ruling a destitute and unhappy people."

Chapter Thirty-Six

Awakening of a Nation

T he new king, M. Reza Pahlavi, ascended to the throne of Iran when he was twenty-two years old. He had attended Institut Le Rosey, the elite Swiss boarding school for boys on the shores of Lake Geneva known for rigorous academics and organized sports. At the time about half the student body came from the United States, but the roster of the school's alumni read like a *Who's Who* of royalty and nobility from around the globe.

The Iranian prince blossomed at Le Rosey. He became fluent in French and English, and somewhat in German. He excelled in sports, was captain of the soccer team, played tennis, and had a reputation for ultrafast ski runs down treacherous cliffs.

He collected scores of athletic trophies, but was also a serious student, particularly of French literature. He fit in well with his schoolmates and made many good friends. Once he noticed the school gardener's son being abused by a German student, he leaped to the boy's aid. The gardener's son became a lifelong friend and confidant.

Back in Tehran when he was seventeen, he underwent military training at an academy run by the French for the training of commandos and became proficient in the daredevil exploits of special ops. He also became a pilot, a skill he would later extend to the latest combat jets.

Once on the throne, Pahlavi vowed to transform Iran and bring it in line with advanced Western nations. He was aware, however, that even his own ministers saw him as a callow and romantic youth, and that they dismissed his promises as empty rhetoric.

World War II continued as a backdrop for the many urgent dramas facing the new king. In 1943, the U.S., Russia, and Britain held a conference in Tehran. It was attended by Franklin Roosevelt, Joseph Stalin, and Winston Churchill, and provided the young king with a rare opportunity to meet-and-greet with the leaders of the Allies. That they met in Tehran may have been fortuitous, but it made for a decisive turn of events for his country.

The war ended in Europe in 1945, but Iran continued to face political turmoil that threatened its survival long afterwards. With the very real danger of the country being broken up by the U.S.S.R. and Britain, no one really expected this young man to be around very long.

Few people would have believed that Pahlavi would in fact outlast all three of the leaders he had met: Stalin, Roosevelt, and Churchill.

———··———

It was February 4, 1949, and I was still a student at Alborz High School. Nearby, on the campus of Tehran University, the young Shah was attending a ceremony celebrating the fifteenth anniversary of the establishment of the university, the only institution of higher learning in the country at the time. As he started up the steps of the law school, an assassin disguised as a photographer pulled a handgun from his camera case and started blasting away at him point blank.

Hit multiple times, Pahlavi began bleeding profusely. Despite his condition, he recognized the assailant's weapon as a Belgian 6.35 automatic. He kept count of how many shots had been fired and how many rounds were left in the chamber. Weak from the loss of blood, he still managed to bob-and-weave, trying to throw off the assassin's aim. The fifth shot went through his cheek and came out of his upper lip. The gun jammed on the sixth and final round.

Belatedly, a member of his security team shot and killed the assassin, who turned out to have been a member of the communist party, reportedly acting on orders from Moscow.

From his hospital bed that evening, Pahlavi delivered a reassuring radio message to the nation. There was relief that the culprit had failed, and nationwide outrage over the communist party's activities. The incident drove the party underground, but it did not deter it from launching other attempts on Pahlavi's life. The event had dramatically revealed the miserable laxity of Iran's internal security.

Instinctively, Pahlavi knew that his country was in for a rough ride. He recovered sufficiently from his injuries to make a state visit to Washington the same year, during the administration of Harry Truman. The President, aware of Iran's problems, advised the young king to "Rule, not reign. Your country needs it."

It would be a lonely life, but Pahlavi decided to accept the President's advice. Faced with many setbacks, he continued to press his reforms. As his confidence grew, so did his ambition. He launched a variety of social services initiatives, and despite strong opposition from the Islamic clergy, granted civil and political rights to women, enabling them to begin serving at the highest levels of government and business.

By the time Pahlavi had been in office for twenty years, Iran had become a destination hot spot for businessmen and women, engineers, consultants, bankers, and others from around the world. Americans, Europeans, Japanese, and other nationals began taking up residence in Iran by the tens of thousands. In the context of global development, Iran's transformation had happened with blinding speed.

Buoyed by Iran's progress, successive U.S. administrations signed multibillion-dollar economic pacts between the two governments. "What is going on in Iran," President Lyndon Johnson said, "is about the best thing going on anywhere in the world." In 1966, the U.S. Committee on Balance of Payments elevated Iran to the level of "a developed country." *Time* magazine wrote in 1974 that the Shah had brought Iran "to a threshold of grandeur analogous to what Cyrus the Great achieved for ancient Persia." From 1963 to 1977, Iran's per capita income soared 1,100 percent. At that rate of growth, the country would catch up with Western Europe in only another decade. By 1977 the country's economy was 65 percent larger than South Korea's, 26 percent larger than Turkey's, and almost 5.5 times the size of Vietnam's.[7]

And a word about the Ansary family…

Early in his rule, the Shah made a state visit to Japan, met brother Hushang there, and urged him to return to his native land. He was most persuasive, and Hushang pulled up roots after a successful fifteen-year sojourn in the Land of the Rising Sun. In Tehran he started working in the government, and his rise in the ranks was amazingly swift.

During the administration of President Lyndon Johnson, Hushang became Iran's ambassador to the United States. With a knack for making friends in high places, he and LBJ got together periodically to play poker or gin rummy, watch movies, and socialize in the White House. He and Secretary of State Henry Kissinger also developed a lifelong friendship.

---

[7] Gérard de Villiers, *The Imperial Shah: An Informal Biography* (London: Weidenfeld & Nicolson, 1976), 287-305; James A. Bill, *The Eagle and the Lion* (New Haven: Yale University Press, 1988), 319-374.

When Hushang's tour in Washington ended, he returned to Tehran to serve in the cabinet as the minister of finance.

Brother Barry was next to give up his life in the U.S. to return to Iran. He was three credits short of completing the academic work for his master's in Industrial Management at the University of Southern California when he quit school and flew back to Tehran. There he gained control of a bankrupt textile company in a joint venture with Japan's Mitsubishi Shoji and installed his own management team. He took to the job like a fish to water, as though he had been groomed from childhood for the challenge of turning around a moribund manufacturing operation. His education at USC had not been a complete waste after all!

Barry was always traveling to Germany and Japan in search of the latest machinery for his company. He built housing, a medical clinic, a swimming pool, and a gym for the employees—a first for a business in the country. The company flourished. He then set up a subsidiary for making garments and asked sister Pary to return to Tehran to take charge of it. Mother and Father, still separated, also followed Barry and Pary there.

I too was affected by the developments in Iran but in an entirely different way from the rest of my family.

Chapter Thirty-Seven

An Earthshaking Brainstorm

It was 1972, and I was pondering the dramatically changing economic landscape in Iran. It was hard to remain aloof in the midst of all the hoopla about it in the American press. Unlike my brothers and sister, however, I had deep roots in the U.S. Jan and I were firmly ensconced in the nation's capital and considered ourselves Washingtonians. We had zero interest in changing our domicile. Nevertheless, we decided to take a little time off to visit Tehran to see what all the hype was about. We flew there with our children, Doug and ParyAnn, and our son Jeff was born there shortly afterwards.

The supercharged economic environment that greeted us as we arrived in Iran in late 1972 pushed my creative energies into overdrive. I began thinking what this new gusher of wealth could mean for that country's economic revival. I was on fire. What if Iran were to use some of its accumulating budget surplus in a daring new initiative—making judicious corporate investments in the developed world? It could buy significant minority positions in major American and European companies, propelling the nation overnight into new technologies, new markets, and new access to natural resources. The resulting long-term capital appreciation would also serve as a spectacular hedge against a future of less rosy prospects for petroleum. Wouldn't that be a giant leap forward?

It was a bold proposition, its benefits so obvious I wondered why no one had thought of it. What could I be missing?

Once I started focusing on the logistics of the idea, however, I realized the obstacles were daunting. Iran had no mergers-and-acquisitions culture. It had a barely functioning stock exchange, let alone busy and dynamic capital markets. To expect the central bankers on Ferdowsi Avenue—a most conservative lot in *any* country—to sign on to a program of buying stocks would be the height of optimism. They would be horrified, I was sure, at the notion of using government funds for making foreign equity investments. Such a cross-cultural undertaking would not even be in their lexicon. I'd better recognize right off that I could be tilting at windmills.

Even if Tehran could be persuaded to consider the idea, what would make me think the authorities in Washington, London, Paris, Frankfurt, or Ottawa would embrace such an initiative emerging from Iran? Would they take a dim view of a foreign government, particularly one from the Middle East, waltzing in to buy chunks of their flagship enterprises? A British company investing in an American corporation, or even acquiring it outright, was a routine occurrence. It did not mean a distant foreign government could pull the same maneuver with impunity.

So, there would be challenges, but that was what made the idea so exciting. And wouldn't life be dull without risk-taking? I resolved to give the project a good college try.

Returning to Washington, I hired a small staff to do preliminary research before turning to outside consultants, economists, and lawyers. First I had to find out whether *any* government in recent memory had embarked on a program of foreign corporate investments. Research revealed that a few countries did in fact possess public pension funds (notably Norway and Kuwait), but that they were run in the traditional way: They invested in safe and conservative fixed-income assets. Actually, they were using their government pension funds to buy their own government bonds. I found no record of any country doing what I was visualizing for Iran, which was confirmation that using government money to invest in foreign stock markets was outside the comfort zone of most finance ministers.

My excitement mounted as it became clear that this was an entirely novel concept. Doubt mingled with euphoria, however. I was brimming with energy at the thought of organizing such a global structure but also worried about failure. What if someone with more gravitas heard about my idea and decided to run with it? I now knew I had to tackle the obstacles to its execution simultaneously on multiple fronts. I thought I'd first try taking the gauge of local Washington sentiment before going back to the Iranians.

Strictly informally, I ran the idea up the flagpole of some well-connected friends in D.C. They were intrigued by the plan but unanimously skeptical that it could ever see the light of day. To them, the scheme was a non-starter: No public company would ever permit a sizeable chunk of its stock, let alone its control, to fall into the hands of a foreign government. Even if a company were willing to do so, it would never pass muster officially. Governments in the Western world would guard their corporate citadels and their technological secrets with the same zeal they would bring to the defense of their territories. I was dreaming if I thought they'd throw their doors wide open to corporate encroachment by a foreign government. In fact, if anyone tried, he'd be at risk of being branded a foreign agent and imprisoned.

"Don't even think about it, Cy" was the advice I received multiple times in Washington.

Things weren't exactly looking up for my brainstorm. I should have been discouraged by the sea of negative commentary, but I was not yet ready to throw in the towel. I took those remarks seriously, however. I resolved that at the proper time I'd confer not only with the appropriate officials in Washington but also with Wall Street. The stakes were high, and the challenges were indeed worth mastering.

For the present, I needed to stick to the Iranian side of the equation. That was where I needed to prove my case. Once I made some progress on that front, no matter how small, I'd then turn my attention to the U.S. side. Various countries in Western Europe would come next.

So, as General Eisenhower told Winston Churchill in World War II, one battle at a time.

I spent several months preparing a detailed report on the benefits that would accrue to the Iranian economy from a governmental program of investing in industry and technology outside its own borders. I took advantage of my membership on the Board of Trustees of American University in Washington to rope in several professors from the business school and the economics department to do research for me. The executive vice president of the university was a friend; he was also a first-rate writer. His help would be valuable in drafting the proposal. A trade association executive with extensive experience in international commerce was next in line. He too could be helpful. At a later stage, I also planned on hiring Booz Allen's consulting talents if I ran into resistance at State or Treasury or Commerce.

In preparing my proposal, I looked for specific industries where the benefits to Iran of such external involvements would be concrete and quantifiable. An obvious candidate was the oil industry. Iran had ample supplies of crude. It needed additional refining capacity, new marketing and distribution channels, and the capability to manufacture petrochemicals. These goals could be met through the careful selection of corporate acquisition and investment targets. Then there was the production of steel. To continue the dynamic growth of that industry, Iran could secure access to supplies of iron ore, manganese, nickel, and other raw materials in Africa, Australia, and elsewhere. Bank Melli, the national bank of Iran, where Father had worked for thirty years, had countrywide branching. It could extend its reach globally through acquisitions.

Investing in agribusiness abroad was equally intriguing. Iran had a soaring gross domestic product, a rapidly growing and disproportionately young population, and rising per capita income. All of these elements propelled demand for foodstuffs and agricultural commodities. Acquiring such resources abroad would assure steady supplies. And, with this program, the nation would gain the management skills and industrial know-how available in the most advanced countries.

As part of my research, I collected examples of several American companies being acquired by Japanese, German, French, and English entities. I provided details of how each country dealt with cross-border transactions. I used spreadsheets to show the financial analyses and currency aspects of such activities.

Determining how much of a budget Iran should earmark for this project was a dilemma with which I wrestled for a while. In the end, I decided to propose that the government should invest that percentage of its oil revenues that would equal the country's annual rate of inflation. Investing such funds would provide returns that should smooth the flow of oil revenues in future years.

I concluded with a strategy for putting the program into effect. I proposed that Iran's industrial investments abroad be channeled through holding companies established in countries with the most favorable business, governmental, and tax climates for such activities. To manage the oversight of these operations, I recommended obtaining corporate charters in Delaware for U.S. activities and in Luxembourg for European investments.

The end result was a book of 170 pages with many graphs and statistics as well as brief references to the laws, economies, currencies, taxation systems, etc., of the U.S., Germany, and Britain as illustrative. I titled it:

A New Initiative for the Imperial Government of Iran: A Program of External Investments

Not exactly the catchiest of titles to pull in what was bound to be a very skeptical audience, but in the haste to complete my preparations, it was all I could come up with. In any event, it was clear that the program I was proposing could only be authorized at the highest level of that government, namely Iran's prime minister himself.

Chapter Thirty-Eight

Uncle Sam and Me

While putting the finishing touches to the document, I began to think again about the possible risks in undertaking the program I'd propose to Iran. Prudence dictated that I should obtain advance clearance from official Washington. To fail to do so could easily ensnare me in a bureaucratic quagmire. The Department of Justice administered the Foreign Agents Registration Act. The Department of Commerce covered foreign investments in the U.S. The State Department and a host of intelligence agencies tracked the activities of people who purported to act on behalf of foreign governments. If I had to register as an agent of a foreign government, I'd abandon the project.

I needed to find out the attitude of the U.S. government about my proposed enterprise before proceeding any further.

Al Arent was a respected lawyer in downtown Washington. I was aware he had worked at the Justice Department. He occasionally lectured in the business school at American University, and I knew him. I described what I was working on and asked for advice. Would I have to register as a foreign agent? Would any U.S. company I approached about taking on the Iranian government as a partner find out quickly that the U.S. government would object? Specifically, how would Justice, Treasury, Commerce, and State view this program? Would every proposed transaction have to pass muster with the government? As I visualized these investments to be substantial, would they also require scrutiny by the Federal Trade Commission? Would there be any special tax considerations to take into account?

Al had questions of his own, mostly about the Iranian side of the relationship: Which ministries would be involved? What exactly would be the scope of the work? Did I visualize transactions in the aerospace and defense industries? Which banking and financial channels would be used? What would be the Iranian government's expectation of the target companies? Would the Iranians be willing to use an American institution as a trustee of the shares acquired?

Other meetings with Al followed, and he brought into the discussions another senior partner with prior government experience. Their findings were that the various U.S. government offices would not object to the program I was proposing to launch for Iran, nor my U.S.-based role in it. Iran was a trusted ally; many major American companies had lucrative contracts with Iran; and Israel had good relations with the country. The Justice Department would not require me to register as a foreign agent. Under then-President Gerald Ford, the U.S. was about to establish a Committee on Foreign Investments by executive order, and the question was whether every potential transaction would come under its purview. That would be dealt with on a case-by-case basis, Al said. As a practical matter, however, only takeovers of American companies involving national security would be blocked. Other federal statutes, such as those governing securities, did not appear to pose any particular obstacles.

Later on I would also talk informally with Ted Sorensen, a lawyer and a friend. Ted had been special counsel to President John F. Kennedy. Most of the president's memorable speeches ("Ask not what your country can do for you," etc.) and his popular book, *Profiles in Courage*, were written by Ted. Later he became a partner in a respected Manhattan law firm. He was equally encouraging about my project.

So…if the U.S. government did not pose any particular obstacles, then who would?

Chapter Thirty-Nine

Interview with a Prime Minister

It was October 1973, and I was on a night flight from Washington's Dulles Airport to Mehrabad Airport in Tehran, with a plane change in Rome's Fiumicino Airport. I was on my way to a meeting with Amir-Abbas Hoveyda, Iran's Prime Minister.

By the time the plane passed the North American landmass, the stewardess was distributing pillows and blankets to the passengers and dimming the lights. With a seat by the bulkhead, I settled down to gaze into the stygian darkness outside my tiny oval window. The dull and monotonous roar of the engines became a soporific, lulling me into an introspective state. Across my mind flashed the kaleidoscope of all the events that had brought me to this point in life. The recollections were vivid and poignant, and I was reliving them in my mind's eye. I was a seventeen-year-old again, a brand-new immigrant in America, with stars in my eyes and only a few coins in my pocket.

The stewardess was shaking me awake. We were about to land, and I needed to put up my seatback.

———•••———

I presented myself at the appointed time in Tehran for the interview with the Prime Minister. I had brought with me a copy of my proposal, and had prepared a lengthy presentation. The chief of staff brought me down to earth when he advised that I was scheduled for fifteen minutes. Then his desk buzzed and I was ushered in.

At the time of our meeting, Dr. Hoveyda had been the prime minister for almost ten years, longer than any of his predecessors. He looked to be in his mid-fifties. Of medium height, he had a plump face dominated by a Roman nose, heavy brows, and a square jaw. He also sported a small middle-age paunch. He was jovial and friendly, even folksy, the kind of image politicians strive for. With an unlighted pipe in his mouth, sitting in a leather chair behind an unpretentious mahogany desk, he exuded the kind of quiet authority that characterized some of the most confident CEO's I had known in the States.

The office was casual in decor. The books on a nearby shelf were titled in different languages. In a stand in the corner were more than a dozen canes with various metal heads and intricate carvings, but he seemed entirely too vigorous to need one. He did not have his jacket on for our meeting; it was hanging nearby with a carnation in the lapel.

I knew Hoveyda came from a modest background, and that he had a master's degree in economics from a university in Belgium and a PhD from the Sorbonne in Paris. He was fluent in English, French, Arabic, and to some extent German. It was all a far cry from the days when the country's prime minister would sit on Persian carpets on the floor and receive visitors while smoking a hubble-bubble. Nevertheless, this modern setting and the wealth of information I had collected about Hoveyda's background gave me no clue as to how he'd react to my novel investment proposal.

The Prime Minister received me with a friendly shake of the hand. His desk was remarkably uncluttered. It had only a clean brown blotter and a sculptured inkwell. Obviously a busy and well-organized person, I judged. Even though he seemed relaxed, he projected an aura of controlled energy and drive. As I'd soon learn, his clear brown eyes mirrored a sharp intellect. I presented my proposal. He asked only a couple of questions and said he'd study the book later. In the meantime, he would refer the matter to the minister of planning. He called in his chief of staff and asked him to make an appointment for me with a Dr. Majidi. That was it. I thanked him and took my leave. The Prime Minister had been courteous, but less than ten minutes had passed. I was eager to see what developed.

Barely an hour after the meeting, I received word that Dr. Majidi would be pleased to see me. As he was in Europe on government business, would I mind meeting him at the Cavalieri Hilton in Rome the following week?

Wow! These people worked fast. They also seemed to be taking my project seriously. It was the best I could have hoped for.

The following week. I flew to Rome and presented myself to Dr. Majidi at his hotel, as instructed. He was friendly and spent a few minutes socializing before getting down to business. He was a youthful and unpretentious man in his mid-forties, with wavy black hair and dark-rimmed glasses. I knew he had a PhD in law from the Sorbonne and had done post-doctoral studies in economics at Harvard. A member of the Prime Minister's cabinet, his official title was director of the Plan & Budget Organization. In my mind, I thought of him as Iran's equivalent of the director of the Office of Management and Budget in the U.S. He had the lead in drafting Iran's latest Five-Year Plan, in which the government outlined its expectations of rapid economic development for the nation. He was essentially a technocrat, exactly the kind of person I had in mind when drafting my proposal. Perhaps if I convinced him of the merits of my program, his support would get it past the natural skepticism of others.

He put me at ease and seemed eager to see my proposal. I had a copy for him. He began flipping through the pages and asked many questions about how the program would work. He ended the meeting after an hour, saying he would read my report overnight, and we'd meet again the following afternoon. It was a promising beginning. He seemed genuinely interested.

True to his word, Majidi was well prepared at our next appointment. We discussed the report, and he recommended several changes, all designed to clarify the illustrative material. We were to meet again when I had finished revising the proposal.

The hotel was glad to arrange for English-speaking secretarial help and to make an office available for my use. A well-dressed and serious middle-aged Englishwoman knocked on my door early the next morning and introduced herself as the stenographer I had requested. A no-nonsense person, she turned out to be quite efficient. Taking dictation and transcribing her notes, she worked twelve hours straight, with coffee and sandwiches brought in. I reviewed her work after she left and made corrections and revisions. The same process was repeated the next day. I reviewed everything again that evening. She then took the material home. She would bring back two copies of the finished product in spiral bindings early the following morning, in time for my noon appointment with the minister. She stayed to finish the job. It occurred to me that I wouldn't mind recruiting her for my Washington office.

Majidi took a copy of the proposal, but he had other business in Europe and was on his way to da Vinci-Fiumicino Airport. He asked that I mail additional copies to his office in Tehran. I would do so from Washington as I wanted to put the finishing touches to the book, including embossing the title in gold lettering on a royal blue cover. Putting the copies in more attractive binders than the plain gray ones I had in Rome couldn't hurt, I told myself.

A few days later in Washington I received word from Dr. Majidi's office that I was to meet with his deputy the next time I was in Tehran. I recognized that my proposal was being debated by different departments. I knew that delays were baked into the pie of government contracts everywhere. I believed my job would have been much easier if I could have pointed to a single other government with a similar program to what I was proposing. On the other hand, I was certain that the first country to come up with this plan would be the one to garner kudos in the international community.

I was encouraged by my meetings. So far, nobody had acted as though I had popped out from another dimension. Even so, I knew I was a rank amateur in the political waters of that country. I had no idea how it would all work out, nor what kind of organization I'd have to put together in the U.S. and Europe to handle the work, if my recommendations were approved.

My proposal was getting a lot of play in official Tehran but it wasn't a rocket taking off. At least, not yet. I was so convinced of the soundness of my concept that I was prepared to be patient.

I was finished in Rome but decided to do some research while still in Europe. I flew to London to meet with investment bankers I knew at Morgan Grenfell, Singer & Friedlander, and Barings. The bankers were uniformly enthusiastic and offered their services for any potential investments in Britain.

Then I was back in Tehran to make yet more presentations. My best guess was that, if everything worked out, my proposal would be presented to the full cabinet at its next meeting. Majidi's deputy volunteered that the prospect for the approval of my proposal was good. Nevertheless, I had a vague notion that the process was still fluid, and that some might be viewing my program as farfetched, perhaps even as a sort of pie-in-the-sky fantasy.

Finally the day came for my proposal to be taken up by the cabinet, called the Council of Ministers in Iran. It was a Saturday, a working day in the country, and I knew I had to stay by the telephone in case any questions came up. Conceivably, I might even be asked to attend the session personally to deal with objections and questions. In any event, I'd need to stick around to receive word about the outcome. While waiting, I remembered the stories about Howard Hughes, a corporate magnate of the mid-twentieth century U.S. He created several major companies and also dabbled in moviemaking. He was in the habit of sending word to one or more of his senior executives to wait for his call. Those were, of course, the days before cell phones. The unfortunate subordinate had to be glued to a land line, often in a hotel room in a strange city, with his meals brought in, never stepping off the premises even if it took weeks. I was glad I was not in the position of those underlings.

Waiting most of the afternoon for the cabinet's call, I soon ran out of reading material. I was wavering between optimistic thoughts of expanding my Washington staff, and pessimistically pondering the impact on my life of the project's rejection. Whether I'd be rejoicing or weeping remained to be seen.

By late afternoon my foreboding had grown and each passing hour was as long as a lifetime. The chime of the telephone came from an instrument across the room, snapping me out of my speculations. I let it ring a couple of times to compose myself, not sure who the caller might be. I picked up the receiver, and said "Yes" in a hopeful voice. It was the Prime Minister's office on the line with a message for me. It was not what I wanted to hear.

I stared grimly at the dead phone for long moments before I hung up. The skies had suddenly darkened. It was as though a heavy weight had dropped on my head. The blinding clarity of failure filled me with an overwhelming sense of futility, a suffocating tightness in my chest. I struggled to keep my pulse steady.

The Cabinet had turned down my proposal.

Chapter Forty

A Shattered Dream

I did not realize how much I had been counting on the acceptance of my proposal. Even though I knew that Iran lacked a bustling stock market or a mergers-and-acquisitions tradition, I still hoped my program would be viewed as smart and innovative rather than risky or controversial. Then I remembered that when the U.S. space program was being launched in the 1950s, some Washington politicians believed the funds would be better spent on the ground. Had similar sentiments doomed my project? Perhaps the ministers had decided to prioritize domestic investments over foreign ones, but I had no way of divining their choices.

I felt weary and sluggish. Walking in the mellow afternoon light would clear my mind. I spent the rest of that day roaming the streets. Years earlier, a few Alborz classmates and I used to study for finals by walking back and forth under a canopy of oak trees on the side of a nearby running brook. I had unconsciously walked back to the site of my youth when my proposal was rejected. A sort of emotional sanctuary perhaps, but I had always found walking to be therapeutic.

The turndown was not softened by any explanation, so I was driven to speculate about it. Was my proposal caught in the machinations of a totally unrelated political game? Was it doomed by the not-invented-here mindset prevalent in many societies? Had I been entirely too optimistic about the open-mindedness of government officials and blithely disregarded the element of risk inherent in such a new undertaking? Or had the whole thing been a mistake from the get-go?

No matter what the cause, I had to suck it up and bear the heavy expenses I had already incurred on this project. I had even picked the experienced team I'd need for it. But wasn't it sad that Iran's brightest men and women would not now be a part of the Western business culture, nor get firsthand exposure to the latest corporate governance practices?

As the sun began sinking below the horizon, I caught its last rays in a shop window. I realized I had been walking and brooding the whole afternoon. I had given the plan my all, but it had not been enough. *Ah, but it would have been most fulfilling.* It would take time, I knew, to become reconciled to my defeat. Music would help. In other circumstances I'd be making a beeline for my recording of Wagner's Ride of the Valkyries, but now I rather longed to hear the clear and lyrical tones of the great American and European vocalists whose records I had collected over the years—Plácido Domingo, Luciano Pavarotti, Beverly Sills, Maria Callas, and even the show tunes and hits of Julie Andrews, Elvis Presley, and Charles Aznavour. But they were all at my home in Washington.

I didn't particularly relish making the call to Jan with the news. She had been as convinced as I was of the validity of my proposal and as supportive as any spouse could be. She had borne my constant absences and run a large household including baby Jeff without a word of complaint. She had never questioned my turning down competing opportunities in Washington nor the large cash outlays related to this project. I was sure she'd acknowledge the disappointment but join me in the resolve to soldier on. Having her on my side meant everything. What I dreaded most was to hear her unhappy, perhaps even tearful, reaction to the news of my failure.

Feeling claustrophobic in the room, I tossed and turned most of that night. I needed to get home to my beautiful family in Washington to get my head screwed on right. That was where my island of quiet, my safe haven from a turbulent world, was located.

I was up early the next morning to make the travel arrangements: first to London and a four-hour layover at Heathrow, then non-stop to Dulles Airport. I wanted to spend time with my neglected wife and children. I did not even want to think about what I'd do next with my life. It briefly occurred to me that I could take my proposal to other governments. I knew instinctively I'd never do it. Besides, I had no reason to believe that such a program would get a better reception from the other oil-producing governments, even if I cared to deal with them. The temptation was to put my life on hold for a while, but that was a non-starter. Best to surrender to the inevitable and just go back to where I had left off before embarking on this bold but futile venture.

Back in Washington, I unloaded on Jan my tale of woe. She wisely suggested a break from professional involvements, maybe a trip to Grand Cayman Island, my favorite site for scuba diving and underwater photography. It turned out there were logistical issues to that plan. We decided instead to bundle up the children, Doug, ParyAnn, and baby Jeff and fly to Aspen for a skiing vacation. Great idea, I thought, and seized on a saying of one of my old law professors: *illegitimi non carborundum*. Good advice, not to let the so-and-sos grind you down. As Jan had diagnosed, schussing down the slopes in the cool air of the Rockies was the best cure for my malaise. When navigating the icy moguls, there was no choice but to focus on the here-and-now. I basked in the serenity of the snowy mountains, turned off my brain, and became immersed in the moment.

Holiday over, I threw myself wholeheartedly into work. I took an "of counsel" position in the downtown law firm of Jones & Baxter, which became Jones Baxter & Ansary. The campus of American University, only a mile from my home, became the focus of many of my activities. I agreed to lecture in the business school. I'd be teaching a course in corporate finance in the spring semester. The dean asked if I'd be willing to add a course in investment analysis in the fall semester. I promised to think about it. I persuaded the AU Board of Trustees to set up an Investment Committee to oversee the university's endowment, and I agreed to chair it. But the highlight of my AU activities occurred as always at five a.m. with a group run every weekday. Some days my son Doug who was quite athletic from an early age would join us.

I also went on a few boards of directors. I joined the board of First American Bank of Maryland, a state-chartered commercial bank in the Washington area, and was appointed to its finance committee. The founder of the publishing company whose board I had joined earlier now asked me to serve as its chairman, which I accepted. I became active at a performing arts center in nearby Virginia called Wolf Trap and joined its foundation's board. I also went on the board of the Washington Opera Society, served on the Woodrow Wilson Council, and became active at George Washington's estate at Mount Vernon.

I also took on several speaking engagements: I spoke at a luncheon at the downtown Washington Rotary Club, I chaired a panel at the Washington Association Executives Club, and I committed myself to give four weekly lectures on Law and Ethics at Wesley Theological Seminary.

I avoided getting involved in potential acquisitions, however. That is, until a friend confided in me in January that a local bank would consider an offer for its trust department. I was intrigued. I knew that some bankers ran their trust departments as adjuncts to their customer service, treating them as cost centers. I never subscribed to that perception. Besides, I knew the chairman of this particular bank. He and I had been involved in a transaction together. He was someone with whom I knew I could do business. The problem was that I wasn't quite ready to jump back into running companies. Still, I was inclined to consider this opportunity.

———···———

Perhaps I was overdoing it, but this potpourri of activity did keep my mind off the recent painful experience with Iran. And then, just as I was beginning to see a break in the dark cloud of my emotions, lightning struck.

Out of the blue I received word that Iran's king wanted to see me. Yes, His Imperial Majesty himself. This was stunning news.

I began making arrangements to fly to Tehran but was told to head instead to St. Moritz, Switzerland. I recalled that the Pahlavi family took a skiing vacation every winter and owned a chalet in St. Moritz. I had several days to make the meeting. I flew from Washington to Frankfurt, changed planes for Zurich, then rented a car for the drive to St. Moritz. When I checked into the Palace Hotel, a message awaited me. I was to meet the Shah the next day in the coffee shop of Suvretta House. I would have never guessed that royalty knew coffee shops even existed, let alone hold a meeting in one. Whenever and wherever, I'd go to the moon for the chance to get a new hearing on my program.

Chapter Forty-One

A Celebrity Hotel

Suvretta House was one of the most opulent hotels in the world. In its 150-year history, it had hosted celebrities and dignitaries from more than a hundred countries. I wanted to check out the place for myself before my appointment.

It was easy to see why so many high-level guests had been attracted to the Suvretta. Almost six thousand feet above sea level, it sat on an elevated plateau with a stunning view of a high Alpine valley known as the Engadine. I was sure that in addition to the magnificent panoramas, the punctilious Swiss would provide great food and meticulous service. I cast an envious eye at the skiers schussing down the perfectly groomed slopes and felt ridiculous walking around in a dark blue suit carrying a briefcase in one of the most desirable ski resorts in the world.

Ironically, it was the perfectly ordinary and barebones coffee shop of this venerable old hotel that was the scene of my first business meeting with the Shah of Iran. If one were into grand entrances, this would have been a grand letdown.

It was February 1, 1974, and I was early to the one o'clock meeting. The Shah, looking athletic and fit, showed up precisely on time, as was his reputation. I focused on what I knew about him, namely, that he was an experienced jet pilot, that he had a reputation for fast ski runs down double-black-diamond slopes, and that, in addition to English and Persian, he was fluent in French and to some extent in German.

At the entrance to the café, the king hesitated for a second, an unspoken signal to his security detail not to follow him in. I stood up as he approached. We sat at a small table facing each other, with no frills or other hangers-on. I remembered the first time I had ever seen him. I had just finished sixth grade, and he presented me with a book of Persian literature as part of the ceremony of awarding prizes to the highest-ranking performers in sixth and twelfth grades. He must have been in his twenties at the time, but his mere presence left me tongue-tied. Later, while he was on state visits to the U.S., I had overcome my awe of royalty and chatted with him at Washington functions. I was surprised how easy he was to talk to.

The trip to St. Moritz, however, was not a social occasion. No agenda had been provided, but I didn't need one. I was sure I knew the purpose of the meeting. I was being given one last opportunity to convince Iran's ultimate decision-maker of the merits of my proposal. I had carefully rehearsed my presentation, anticipated his questions, and practiced my answers and explanations. I knew I had to be persuasive and eloquent. I felt confident and ready.

I could not have been more wrong.

The Shah spent no time on pleasantries and turned immediately to the reason for the meeting. A former German ambassador to Tehran was proposing that Iran would benefit from a "close cooperation" with Krupp, an old and well-established German company. Iran was being invited to make a series of financial investments in that entity.

I had to reorient myself on the fly. Miraculously, Pahlavi appeared already sold on my concept. I could only assume he had been fully aware of my conversations with his ministers all along and had chosen this moment to intervene decisively. For me, it was a gift from the gods. I wasn't sure what feelings to experience—relief, joy, satisfaction, hope. I felt them all, trying not to close my eyes.

Better focus and think fast, I told myself. Krupp was a familiar name, but what did I know about it? It had been a major cog in the Nazi war machine in World War II. It manufactured armaments and heavy equipment. As far as I knew, it had no public shareholders. Had I not read something about the last surviving member of the Krupp family being tried and convicted at Nuremberg with the other Nazi leaders? It was a mystery to me why the Allies had not dismantled all of the Krupp operations after the war.

There were too many unknowns for me to make any intelligent comments. The Shah's schooling before World War II in Switzerland must have provided many opportunities to learn of Germany's industrial might, and particularly of Krupp, one of the country's best-known manufacturing companies. It built ships, plants, tanks, and armaments. Undoubtedly the Shah must have been immediately responsive to the approach by the former German ambassador. He asked me to work out a program for such an investment.

It was not hard to recognize the proposal's appeal from Iran's standpoint. It would gain access to heavy engineering capability and the technology for making steel—what every developing country struggling to catapult itself into the modern world would wish for. Then I had a sudden insight. Perhaps the Shah was attracted to the opportunity of developing a domestic defense industry with Krupp's help. Could that be it? To the leader of a Middle Eastern country, where regional conflicts had been a fact of life since the dawn of civilization, getting access to weapons technology would be a survival mechanism.

If there was any validity to my speculations, I could be in a real quandary. I'd better check this out with the folks at Justice and State in Washington. My earlier exemption from the requirements of the Foreign Agents Registration Act might have to be reviewed. I still had zero interest in coming under its ambit.

The king said he wanted me to look into the proposal and report back. I needed more details of Krupp's plans before I knew whether my speculations were plausible. I'd also need to assess the corporate environment in Germany, which I already knew was different in significant ways from what I was used to in the U.S. I started pondering how I'd conduct the required due diligence on this project before engaging Krupp in serious negotiation. But I didn't get far. The king was not finished with me.

He turned to another item. Ashland Oil Company had been in discussions with the National Iranian Oil Company about possible collaboration along several fronts, including a long-term supply contract.

Ashland was a familiar name to me. It was a public company headquartered in Kentucky where I had many in-laws and friends. The company was listed on the New York Stock Exchange, and I had at one time owned stock in it, as well as a couple of other oil companies. So I had some familiarity with the major players in the energy sector. But Ashland was a gatherer and a refiner; it had no exploration and production capability. I could see several advantages for Ashland in linking up with a major oil producer like Iran, but what was the attraction for Iran? I recalled that Ashland had a chemical subsidiary. That could be a plus, but did it have marketing and distribution capability in the U.S.? I'd have to check. Did its proposal include the sale to Iran of an equity stake in the company? If so, the proposal should be of great interest, but I couldn't shake a nagging question.

Why was the king asking *me* to get involved in something that was strictly the province of the geologists and petroleum experts of the National Iranian Oil Company? The oil sector was *their* patch. Could it be that he did not like what he was hearing from his own people about the proposal? If that were the case, I'd better tread lightly. Navigating my way through the Iranian government's internecine squabbles would be way beyond my pay grade. Of course, prudence dictated that I keep those thoughts to myself for the time being.

The Shah wanted me to look into it. I would be briefed about the details shortly.

There was yet a third matter, again involving a German company. There was a 14 percent interest in Daimler Benz available for purchase. I knew, of course, that Mercedes cars were popular worldwide, and that Daimler was a model of German engineering and manufacturing efficiency. Off the top of the head, I recognized this as probably a most attractive business opportunity for Iran. There were financial aspects to the other matters the Shah had mentioned, but it was clear that non-financial considerations predominated with them. In this case, I felt there could be strong financial advantages as well.

The Shah wanted me to negotiate the transaction. I would receive the contact information shortly and follow up.

The meeting over, Pahlavi stood up, offered his hand, and was gone. I sat back and took a deep breath to catch up with myself. I had kept a tight rein on my emotions before, but now I wanted to fly. I was overcome with pride at getting the chance to put my ideas into practice. I closed my eyes to savor the success after the many months of dispirited struggle and failure. It was monumentally exhilarating to find that my program would survive. Hard to get carried away with euphoria, however, if you have to focus on the details. I had plans to make, lots to do. The economist in me could see deep changes ensuing from my work, and lots of practical aspects.

Then I took a moment to review the meeting in my mind. Throughout, the king had been direct and to the point; there had been no pointless dramatics or pretentious posturing—what one might run into with some politicians. I also noticed that he had been careful not to express his own preferences, make any assessment of the proposals, or give me specific instructions on how to handle them. This could be his mode of operating with advisors and subordinates: Give them wide latitude and see how effective they would be on their own. That technique, I realized, would quickly separate the self-starters from, well, the toadies. Whatever the reason, I was grateful for his approach, as I worked better taking my own pathway in a transaction.

I found out only later that, even as the cabinet was handing me a flat-out rejection of my proposal, the Shah himself was announcing a major new initiative for Iran in an interview with a French newspaper: Making judicious corporate investments outside Iran as an aid to internal development—language that was verbatim out of my proposal. Obviously, he had been fully aware of it and had already embraced the concept I had put forth.

I also learned later that the Shah rarely had sit-down meetings with his government officials. His meetings with them were all business with a minimum of flourish and typically with everyone standing. I was told I should feel honored we had had a seated session. In a booth in a drugstore yet!

The most striking part of that meeting for me was that the Shah had treated me as though I was already on the payroll. But how? The last thing I knew was that my proposal had been turned down flat by the Council of Ministers. So I had no contract and no means of seeking reimbursement for the large outlays I had already made on this quest.

Then I remembered a previous experience of dealing with government proposals.

A longtime friend and colleague, T. Eugene Smith, and I once jointly owned two U.S. defense contractors in the Washington, D.C. area. Both companies performed "black ops" work for the government. One of them worked for eighteen months at the behest of the Pentagon and made huge outlays of its own funds on a project, but without a contract. The government wasn't sure it wanted to go forward with the project; or, even if it did, whether it would award the contract to us. It was a highly precarious position for any company but not an unusual one for a government contractor. In our case, if it did not work out, our company could have ended up in financial trouble. Fortunately, in the end it worked out fine. The experience, however, was nerve-wracking enough for Gene and me that we decided to sell both companies. The U.S. government quickly bought us out.

Recalling that experience was most helpful. When it comes to government contracting, it pays to be a patient negotiator. So it was best to keep the big picture in mind and focus on the tasks I had been assigned. Contract or no contract, I decided to jump to.

———•••———

And thus it was that on a cold day in the winter of 1974 in a plain and unpretentious coffee shop in a snowbound ski resort in Switzerland, with the humility of licked wounds but with thanks to the crucial support of Iran's ruler, I launched what became the kickoff of a whole new financial structure in the world.

Never in my wildest dreams could I have imagined that my project would trigger a stampede by many governments to invest in corporate enterprises in the advanced countries—the vehicles for which are now dubbed Sovereign Wealth Funds. I was sure this day would be commented on and written about for years to come.

Once word got out, the concept went viral, exploding onto the international financial landscape with the force of a tectonic shift. I had never anticipated the speed with which other governments, oil-producing or not, would redirect their pension funds or establish other mechanisms to jump on the bandwagon of making equity investments within and outside their borders. It was probably the most notable example of groupthink in recorded financial history. Who would have guessed that in time trillions of dollars—more than the gross domestic product of all but a handful of countries in the world—would be poured into those funds? Or that countless private equity firms, hedge funds, wealth management firms, structured-finance projects, and the like would receive much of their financing from those funds, setting off seismic changes in the capital markets and revolutionizing the corporate environment for mergers and acquisitions?

Chapter Forty-Two
Krupp, *An Exalted European Dynasty*

My first glimpse of Villa Hügel almost took my breath away. Used to the modern glass-and-steel towers that dominate the skylines of America's business centers, I was wholly unprepared for the majestic and aloof Renaissance style castle, with its splendid panoramic view of the Ruhr Valley and Lake Baldeney, that served as Krupp's headquarters in Essen, Germany. Built to showcase the wealth and power of its dynastic owners, Hügel's palatial grounds and manicured lawns rivaled the castles of European royalty. The company used the spacious dining rooms that rivaled aircraft hangars in size to entertain the kings and queens and the nobility from around the globe.

Krupp being the starting point of my investment agenda for Iran, I began the work as I had learned in the crucible of the American culture of corporate acquisitions: I put together the customary "due diligence checklist." I was requesting reams of information and documents on the company's business and its financial and operating history. Imagine my amazement when I found that Krupp doggedly refused to work that way. As far as I could make out, its senior officers believed that the celebrated Krupp brand spoke for itself. I decided not to take a hard stand at this early stage. And so my staff and I began our own research.

Shorn of its financial history, Krupp—the family and the company—had an intriguing story.

The House of Krupp was once the largest industrial enterprise in Europe. Under a distinctive logo of three interconnected rings, it produced coal and steel and heavy engineering products. In the U.S., it built factories, railroads, and a variety of machinery and equipment. During the construction of the Chrysler Building in Manhattan in the 1930s, Krupp contributed the Art Deco cap which made it the world's tallest building at the time.

The man running the company throughout World War II was Alfried Krupp, whom the European press called the richest man in the world. He was a tall man with a long oval face and a thin frame, reserved and introverted. Even among the German titans of industry, Alfried stood out as an unrivaled business innovator.

World War II ended in Europe in 1945 when the Allied powers annihilated Hitler's regime. Winston Churchill recommended that the Nazi leaders be summarily executed, but the U.S., intent on projecting an image of fairness and not that of a vengeful power, relied on American-style due process. The Nazi leaders were rounded up for thirteen trials in Nuremberg, which lasted until 1949. In the end, the U.S. convicted and executed 278 Germans for war crimes. Some have argued that Winston Churchill's way would have been less complicated and more humane.

As the last owner and manager of the House of Krupp, Alfried Krupp was arrested in 1945. He was tried, convicted, and sentenced to twelve years' imprisonment plus forfeiture of all his personal assets. He thus escaped the hangman, but the verdict was designed to leave him a pauper at the end of his sentence. The tribunal also ordered the Krupp companies to be liquidated, the machinery and equipment broken up and scrapped, and all traces of its operations eradicated. Several American companies started maneuvering to pick up the pieces.

As Alfried languished in Landsberg prison in Bavaria (where Hitler had written his infamous autobiographical book *Mein Kampf*), the tumultuous decade of the 1940s rolled into the 1950s, and the world outside his prison walls changed dramatically. The superpower rivalry had shifted to the U.S. and the Soviet Union, and a new war was starting on the Korean peninsula. Western Europe figured prominently in the struggle between totalitarian communism and democratic capitalism. With American help, the former enemies—Germany and Japan—were undergoing rapid economic revival. The German economy had already caught up with Britain.

This state of affairs happened to coincide with the unexpected entry into Alfried Krupp's hopeless existence behind bars of a man by the name of Earl J. Carroll. Mr. Carroll was an American lawyer in private practice in Frankfurt, Germany. He had a mixed record in dealing with the U.S. military on behalf of his clients. This time, coming across the Krupp case, he decided to shoot for the moon. He showed up at Landsberg prison and presented its famous inmate with an American-style contingent-fee contract. If he succeeded in getting Alfried released from prison and his property restored, Carroll would receive a fee equal to 5 percent of the value of all the recovered assets. Alfried did not hesitate, haggle, or dither. He quickly agreed.

Any port in a storm, when you are behind bars.

Carroll then prepared a petition to John J. McCloy, the American high commissioner in Germany. Described as having "the body of a wrestler and a bullet head," McCloy was a well-connected Washington/New York insider. Carroll's petition cleverly painted Alfried Krupp as callow and awkward, weak-willed and incapable of meeting the challenges of any business, let alone doing so in wartime. It was, of course, pure fiction, but it worked. Commissioner McCloy—himself an experienced lawyer—was somehow persuaded to accept Carroll's portrayal of Alfried. In a ruling that had the shattering force of a mega-ton WW2 bomb, he announced that the Nuremberg tribunal had misjudged the Krupp case, and that Alfried was a mere playboy with no head for business, a weakling who could have never stood up to Hitler.

McCloy then commuted Alfried Krupp's sentence and rescinded the order of liquidation of the company and its assets.

American reaction to McCloy's decision was explosive, but there was no appeal from it. His explanation was that his conscience had been his judge.

And so, on February 3, 1951, Alfried walked out of Landsberg prison a free man and not exactly a pauper. He was again the master of the Krupp enterprises, albeit subject to the prohibition against the manufacture of military weapons or armaments of any kind. As for Earl J. Carroll, his bet paid off handsomely. He pocketed a fee of $25 million from Krupp. Using the nominal GDP per capita method of converting currency, that would equal $665 million today.

Alfried Krupp got his company back, but the factories were in ruin after repeated Allied bombardments. He had a demoralized workforce and no resources to meet payroll. The company also had too many employees for its diminished operations, and its pension obligations exceeded its remaining assets. Only a large and immediate infusion of cash could avert the demise of Krupp. Even for a man of Alfried's caliber, Krupp's desperate posture presented formidable challenges.

Alfried's first decision was to reassure the workers. He was a man of few words, but with confidence inherited from his forebears, he would not miss this opportunity to get the troops energized. Speaking to a gathering of labor, he pledged that he would not lay off a single worker and would honor the company's pension obligations to the last pfennig. They, the workers, had always been loyal to the company, he said. He expected no less of them in this emergency. Once a Kruppianer, always a Kruppianer, he reminded them. His speech was low-key, his delivery slow and deliberate. Nevertheless, his words electrified his audience. His talk was a huge morale-builder.

Alfried then turned his attention to the company's depleted

finances. He started by lining up a syndicate of German bankers. There was not a single head of the major financial institutions in the country that would refuse his call. In quick order, he arranged for a corporate line of credit of 50 million Deutsche Marks.

Next he turned his attention to operations.

Shut out of its traditional product lines, the company now had to find new activities, and to do so on a major scale. Time, however, was not on his side. Alfried Krupp could coast on the Krupp name for only so long; he had to prove himself as quickly as possible. Here is where his business know-how soon manifested itself. He began crisscrossing the continents, traveling to Rio de Janeiro, Bangkok, Tokyo, Bombay, Ankara, Tehran, Cairo, and many cities in between. Viewing the state of the world after World War II, he shrewdly discerned a remarkable pattern emerging in the newly independent countries of the third world: They were all desperately trying to catch up with the advanced nations and harbored dreams of rapid industrialization for their economies. He, Alfried Krupp, would accommodate them. He'd lend them his engineers, he'd design their industries, he'd build their plants, and, in collaboration with German bankers, he'd finance their projects.

Using the magic of the Krupp name, Alfried began throwing lavish parties at Villa Hügel for the heads of state from around the world. Kings, presidents, and prime ministers—including, incidentally, the Shah of Iran—came through the large double doors into a giant anteroom with elaborate crystal lighting fixtures. There they were entertained at night in the grand style by immaculately attired attendants at tables with damask covers and fine linen napkins, then turned over to the Krupp sales force the next day in the more intimate meeting rooms behind the main hall. It was the most audacious marketing blitz ever devised by a company, and devilishly effective.

The press reported that Krupp had become the hardware store to the world. It was building whole factories, as well as highways, bridges, and airports for dozens of countries, and selling them earth-moving equipment, processing machinery, and every variety of engineering services. Soon the Krupp factories were humming, their revenues soaring, their profitability the envy of their competitors. Alfried had turned around the moribund company with such speed and efficiency as to leave the observers of the German scene agog at the outcome. Once again he was cited in the press as one of the richest men in the world.

By the time I became involved in Krupp in 1974, the man in control of this vast enterprise was no longer a member of the dynasty that had owned it outright for 163 years. His name was not Krupp. It was Beitz. He did not buy the company. He in fact paid nothing for it. He had originally come into the company as Alfried's chief of staff.

For Berthold Beitz, it was a carefully orchestrated case of being in the right place at the right time.

Chapter Forty-Three

An Amazing Succession Plan

Time passed while the House of Krupp enjoyed a celebrated revival. Alfried's brother, aware that Alfried was looking for a *Chef de Cabinet*, introduced him in early 1953 to a man by the name of Berthold Beitz. During World War II, Beitz had served as a sergeant in the German Army. After the war, he ran an insurance company before he had the meeting that changed his life. Basically a PR man, Beitz could be charming in a social setting, particularly when cultivating important contacts. He and Alfried shared a love of hunting. Soon Beitz quit his insurance job and started working at Krupp as Alfried's office manager.

Alfried himself was not doing so well. His years of imprisonment, with their enforced drudgery and brutality, as well as being an unwilling spectator to the hanging of so many Germans he had known or worked with, had taken their toll of his health. Shortly after Beitz started working at Krupp in November 1953, Alfried began withdrawing from public life and having less and less involvement with the arena of business. As his mental faculties diminished, he became grimly reclusive in Villa Hügel, cutting himself off from family, friends, and professional associates. Soon his sole point of contact with the outside world became his office manager, Berthold Beitz.

Beitz may have been unpopular with the Krupp rank and file, but he nevertheless became Alfried's public face and his liaison within the company and with everyone else. Alfried's diminished mental state and his reclusiveness led to Beitz assuming the role of heir apparent to the Krupp dynasty. Beitz's forte, however, was sales and public relations. The operational and financial details of running a large and complex corporation were not his focus.

Deprived of effective leadership, the company soon showed unmistakable signs of being rudderless, alarming Krupp's bankers. Beitz then put through a unique restructuring plan for the company. First, however, there was a loose end: The last surviving heir of the Krupp family was Alfried's son, Arndt von Bohlen. To ensure the success of the restructuring plan, Beitz persuaded Arndt to renounce his claim to a role in the management of the company or its ownership in return for a lifetime annual pension of two million Deutsche Marks.

The restructuring plan then proceeded to fulfilment: Fried. Krupp GmbH, the holding company for the Krupp enterprises, began operating under a supervisory board chaired by Berthold Beitz. The stock of the company owned by Alfried Krupp was contributed to an entity uncommon in Germany—a nonprofit foundation. Its board of trustees was also chaired by Berthold Beitz.[8]

Beitz thus assumed undisputed control of the House of Krupp without putting up a single Deutsche Mark of his own. It was a coup for the ages.

In the first of many visits, Herr Beitz and I met for dinner in late February 1974 in the dining room of Breidenbacher Hof on fashionable Königsallee in Düsseldorf. Beitz was a youthful sixty-year-old, tall, handsome, and fluent in English. His suit was immaculately tailored, and his dark hair was mingled with gray on the sides. This was an opportunity for the two of us to become acquainted. Getting down to business would come later. We had a table for two against the far wall, a private corner for our conversation. The

---

[8] Alfried Krupp died on July 30, 1967.

headwaiter was most deferential, obsequiously calling my host Herr von Beitz. "Von" denoting nobility prompted me to ask if he was a titled German nobleman. He chuckled and said he wasn't.

Most of the dinner was passed with pleasantries. We were trying to establish a conversational familiarity between the two of us. There would be plenty of time for serious business at a later stage when senior members of the Krupp team made their appearance. We talked about the state of affairs in Europe and the U.S. I asked if he'd tell me about his own background. He talked briefly about his days in the German army, then mentioned that he had tried to save a Jewish mother and daughter from imprisonment in World War II. The daughter had worked as his secretary before the war. The sergeant in charge would only agree to save the daughter and not the mother. The daughter refused to be separated from her mother, so both ended up in the dreaded concentration camp. It was a heart-wrenching story.

When it came to his relationship with Alfried Krupp, Beitz was expansive. He mentioned that they had met a few times while Beitz was with the insurance company. What he then added left me scratching my head. He said that Alfried was a rich playboy who devoted his life to the pursuit of pleasure. He was without commitments or responsibilities, he was shy and taciturn, and he had no head for business. He, Beitz, found Alfried's twelve-year prison sentence and the order to dismantle the Krupp factories highly unfair. He therefore took it upon himself to approach Commissioner McCloy to persuade him to free Alfried Krupp from prison and restore his ownership of the corporate assets. People applauded him for these actions, he said, but all he had done was to right a great injustice. At one of their evening get-togethers, Alfried was pensive for many minutes, silently staring at the floor and picking at his lower lip, while Beitz remained quiet and respectful. Finally Alfried looked up and offered Beitz the top job at the House of Krupp.

I was having a hard time keeping a straight face at Beitz's recital of these events; they were remarkable in several respects. His assertion that he was instrumental in getting Alfried out of prison was particularly noteworthy. I had the impression that the two of them had not met until the year after Alfried was out of prison. As for the characterization of Alfried as a playboy who had no head for business, that was right out of Earl J. Carroll's petition to Commissioner McCloy—what an advocate might conjure up in the service of his client.

The restaurant lights were muted, a pale wash of yellow that matched my perplexed mood. What I was hearing from my host differed from what I had gleaned in my own research. Nevertheless, I was determined to keep an open mind. Now what? I could relax and enjoy the evening. So I firmly put a lid on my wayward thoughts. Beitz had no clue about what was coursing through my mind, and that is how I wanted the evening to end. Besides, being underestimated by an opponent in a negotiation could be an advantage. Best to keep my doubts to myself.

I couldn't help thinking that Beitz could have achieved the same result in a different way, but then some people can be forgiven for going in for elaborate stories and plot lines. Had I failed to do all the research I had done on Krupp, I would have been mesmerized by Beitz. As it was, I found him likable and charming. Still, having had a glimpse into how Herr Beitz's mind worked, I was sure the deal would not go in a straight line and by the book. I steeled myself for some unpredictable curveballs along the way.

Before the evening was over, I recognized that Beitz would not be the one with whom I'd be negotiating this transaction. He left to his executive officers the pragmatic details of the financial and operational aspects of the deal we were contemplating. I had many meetings with him after this first event, but they were symbolic and high-level. The details were relegated to his experts to work out.

Chapter Forty-Four

Bump in the Road

Over the following weeks and months in 1974-75, I met many senior Krupp executives. The one who stood out was the chief financial officer. His name was Dr. Alfred Lukac and he had an excellent command of the financial and operational details of the company. Self-confident without being arrogant, he became the point man for Krupp in our negotiations. From him I was able to glean a realistic financial picture of the company but hardly an encouraging one. I then arranged to tour several plants, had one-on-one meetings with other personnel, and formed my own impression of the operations.

The negotiations took place in a series of sessions in various cities—Düsseldorf, Essen, Frankfurt, London, Paris, Tehran, Zurich, and New York. As usual, there were many snags, and at times the tension barometer was high. Eventually, Dr. Lukac and I worked out most of them, not to everyone's satisfaction, of course. The one that came closest to derailing the transaction related to the size of Iran's holdings.

In German companies, 25 percent ownership was a magical dividing line. If a shareholder wished to have a say in corporate affairs, he or she needed to own *more than* 25 percent. A mere 25.01 percent would do. It gave the owner the distinction of having a "blocking minority" position, a sort of veto power over the major corporate decisions.

Krupp was determined that Iran would not wield that level of influence in the company's governance. I was equally determined to secure that coveted position for Iran. I was not being an arrogant ass. I knew that without it, the Shah would be throwing away his country's money in this investment.

I was meeting at the Park Hotel in Düsseldorf with four Krupp members. I had hired a Frankfurt law firm to represent Iran, but its partners had no wish to participate in the negotiations. I understood their position—West Germany was a small country, and Krupp a powerful presence that the lawyers had no wish to antagonize. Lawyers are often blamed for deals falling apart, but in this case there were no outside lawyers present on either side. It had nevertheless turned out to be a difficult session, and an air of tension hung over the room. Soon it became clear that we were at an impasse. Finally members of the Krupp team picked up their files and departed with long faces. Some scowled my way as they left.

I was, of course, taking a risk. No one in Tehran had authorized me to handle the negotiations as I saw fit. If the deal fell apart—my first for Iran—I had no assurance that Dr. Hoveyda would shake my hand and say, "Good work, Ansary." Nevertheless, as long as I was on the job, I'd call the balls and strikes as I saw them. And, just incidentally, I was also curious about how much support I actually enjoyed from the Prime Minister.

What happened next should have been predictable, but it still caught me by surprise. Berthold Beitz tried an end run. The German ambassador in Tehran requested a one-on-one meeting for Beitz with the Prime Minister, and Dr. Hoveyda agreed. He nevertheless asked me to fly over for it.

So I was present at the meeting in Tehran when Beitz made his presentation. Dressed in his customary dark blue suit, snowy white shirt, and a pale blue tie, he was the quintessential urbane negotiator. I noticed he carefully concealed his reaction to my presence at the private meeting he had asked for. With no preliminaries, he launched into his speech. He spoke of the proud and honorable history of the House of Krupp, and how the company had prospered through nearly two centuries without permitting any outside participation in its ownership structure. How there had been many approaches, from within Germany as well as from other advanced countries. How his board wanted Iranian participation, was honored to have it, but granting veto power to a minority shareholder over major decisions would interfere with the proper functioning of the company and was not in Iran's own interest. Besides, the board would never approve it.

Beitz had started out thoughtfully and in a low voice, but as he continued he became a passionate advocate, making a heartfelt plea for sympathy and understanding. When he finished, I looked around for the flourish and the drum roll. That man, I thought, could charm the spots off a leopard. It had been a well thought out and rehearsed presentation, a virtuoso performance, and Beitz ended it by urging Hoveyda to reconsider "this crucial issue."

Beitz was like an artist who had completed painting a canvas with very attractive colors and shadings, and was now awaiting the approbation of the all-important critic, the Prime Minister of Iran. I saw myself as a mere observer at the meeting. It was not my place to render judgment on Beitz's work, and I would not offer my opinion without being asked. And yet I knew that the chairman of Krupp was a showman, adroitly sloughing off the present-day realities of his company and shifting the focus to a package in the PR wrappings he thought Hoveyda would approve. What he had described was ancient history, whereas acquisitions are all about a company's current posture and future prospects. It was a shaky chain of events on which he had built his case.

I admired Beitz's dramatic flair and his panache, but his story was hardly convincing to me. I saw it as a sophisticated form of the old razzle-dazzle. How it came across to Hoveyda I had no way of divining. He and I had had no discussion about this meeting beforehand. I noticed that his eyes, made even larger by his black-rimmed glasses, were focused unblinkingly on Beitz, and that he had listened with rapt attention to his visitor's presentation. In fact, he had greeted Beitz warmly upon his arrival, never once interrupted the long delivery, and looked properly impressed, even spellbound. The expression on his face was approving, not skeptical, and he had not looked my way even once. I was also certain that the Prime Minister was fully aware of the note of urgency in Beitz's voice when he made his passionate plea. As I absentmindedly massaged the bridge of my nose, I was burning with curiosity about how the PM would handle this. I had the unsettling thought that I could lose all credibility with the Krupp hierarchy after this session.

After Beitz completed his delivery, Hoveyda looked thoughtful for a moment as he ran his hand over the few thin strands of his hair. I had an errant thought that Hoveyda could be anybody's uncle. He took the pipe out of his mouth. A quick flash of amusement appeared in his expressive gray eyes as he seemed to come to a decision and straightened up in his chair. In that moment he amazingly lost his avuncular look. In a soft and courteous voice, he expressed satisfaction that both Iran and Krupp had been conducting the negotiations with encouraging candor. Then, in a voice of quiet authority, he began asking the Krupp chairman a series of questions about his company's financial position, its near-term business prospects, and its backlog of orders. Knowing that it was all unrehearsed, I was as surprised as Beitz. *"Wow!"* I exclaimed under my breath, *"Hoveyda has read my reports."* His grasp of the facts from my long analyses of the company was awesome. The quick mind that had made him so effective as the head of government was now on full display.

Beitz stiffened. He had not expected to get into operational and financial issues at this session. I could see him tensing up even more as he cleared his throat and folded his arms across his chest, struggling to remove any hint of disappointment from his voice. He seemed to recover with an effort and predictably tried to redirect the conversation back to his earlier comments.

In the end, Hoveyda leaned forward, pointed his index finger at Beitz, and in a voice pitched low but with no trace of malice said, "You wouldn't want His Majesty to think you are not serious, do you?"

Beitz reacted with a sharp rise of his eyebrows as his face clouded over, becoming a cold mask. His eyes tracked back to me, all pretense of camaraderie gone from his countenance. Perhaps he held me responsible for this turn of events. I took note of his bitterness but felt it was misplaced. Aware of the operational realities of his company, I felt this wasn't the battle he needed to wage. Besides, he did not have a credible argument for denying Iran the "blocking minority" prerogative. It was, after all, enshrined in German law. He then abruptly stood up, brushed away a nonexistent piece of lint from his lapel, and took his leave with all the authority he could muster in his voice to "confer with the board." By then the undisguised bitterness of his tone clearly conveyed how he felt about this encounter.

My shoulders relaxed as I exhaled with relief. A different outcome would have cut the ground out from under me in the continuing discussions with Krupp. I also recognized how Hoveyda had managed to keep his office as the head of the government for so long. He obviously knew a thing or two about handling negotiations. His performance this day definitely inspired admiration.

Elated, I too left Tehran.

I had an inkling later that Beitz gave my German lawyers hell, presumably believing they had been the source of my information about blocking minorities under German law. Beitz was mistaken. My German lawyers were hardly effective as advocates for my side. They remained totally neutral throughout the negotiations. Habit alone had made me dig deeper and research the intricate details of German corporate law.

I decided to use an American law firm in my later dealings in Germany.

Chapter Forty-Five

A Ballyhooed Transaction

I left the meeting with Hoveyda and Beitz to go straight to the airport for a flight back to the U.S. There was a two-hour layover at Paris's Charles de Gaulle Airport before I switched to a flight bound for Dulles Airport. Jan picked me up to drive me home, and I eagerly peppered her with questions about every detail of our children Doug, ParyAnn, and Jeff's activities during the hour or more we were on the way. I was looking forward to catching up, both at home and in the office, before taking off again.

It was not to be. The phone was ringing in the living room as I walked in the door, suitcase in hand. It was Diane, my assistant, informing me that the Shah wanted to see me in Paris the next day. *Wait one darn minute. I just came from there.* But no matter. Mine not to reason why.

I kissed the children hello and goodbye, gave each a big hug, then regretfully jumped in the car for Jan to drive me back to Dulles. I was barely in time to catch the last overnight flight to de Gaulle. Then, upon arrival in Paris in the morning, I checked into the Trianon Palace Hotel in Versailles. I shaved and showered and waited in the lobby for my ride to the royal audience.

It was mid-morning on June 26, 1974, when a French *gendarme* came to get me at the hotel. I was then transported in a police Peugeot escorted by two outriders, one in front, the other behind, in the wildest ride of my life. With all of their sirens screaming, they sped through the crowded Paris streets. Passersby stopped to gawk, trying to see what all the excitement was about. My police driver kept taking the turns on two wheels while I, sitting in the backseat without a seatbelt, was tossed and jostled, bumping roughly against one rear passenger door and then the other. I assumed we were late for my appointment, and one does not keep a king waiting.

I was deposited at the residence of the Iranian ambassador at 5 Rue Fortuny in Paris's 17th arrondissement. Inside, there was a mob scene in the spacious split-level foyer. There were several dozen people milling about, apparently all waiting to see the king. I heard some proclaiming a high state of urgency for their audience. I did not know them and had no way of judging the importance of their business. I had no idea why I had been summoned. The ruler of a country has more on his mind than the projects with which I was preoccupied. So I sat in a corner, feeling no urgency and content to wait my turn.

The moment the Shah walked in, the crowd quieted and parted like the Red Sea before the Israelites in the Biblical story. The group quickly made a clear passage for him. His first words were to ask where Ansary was. I stood up and followed him into a private office on the same floor. He offered his hand, then sat down and invited me to sit in the chair next to him. Dressed in a gray suit with a light blue tie on a white shirt, he looked distinguished. Also relaxed. An unbidden thought crossed my mind that he never seemed to gain any weight. Lucky fellow.

Without any preliminaries, he said, "Tell me about Krupp."

I had not expected this, but I needed no preparation to brief him on what was going on. I plunged ahead with an abbreviated version of the company's business affairs, its management, its engineering capability, and its finances. I stopped to see if he wanted me to continue. He nodded, and I gave him a rundown on the negotiations up to that point and what I saw as the thorny issues pending between the parties. I reviewed the "blocking minority" question and explained its importance. His brow arched as he listened but he let me talk without interruption. I had the impression he was already familiar with much of what I was telling him. Hoveyda must have kept him informed. Clearly, this monarch did not take refuge in his exalted position to remain above the fray. He actually seemed to relish keeping close tabs on my work.

When I finished, he did not hesitate. "I give you *carte blanche,*" he said with surprising warmth, accompanying it with a strong, calm smile and a gesture of his right hand as though awarding a prize. It was wholly irrelevant to my concerns, but I already knew that he spoke French with a perfect Parisian accent. He then stood up and repeated softly, "I give you *carte blanche.*" He was gone before I could say "Roger that."

I walked out in a daze. It was a beautiful sunny day, and cars were whizzing by in the usual daytime mayhem of Paris traffic. The king had done an extraordinary thing: He had given me a free hand in the Krupp transaction. I was grateful, but I did not feel deserving of any kudos. It was, after all, about negotiating technique and acquisition know-how. A negotiation, I reflected, is like a game of chess: Each side tries to place itself in a striking position. Still, what I heard from Iran's leader was that he gave me the choice of insisting on buying a blocking minority or not. But did he mean to do more than that? Did he give me the choice of making an equity investment in Krupp or just walking away? If this were my own personal transaction, I'd have walked away in a heartbeat. But I understood that financial gain was not the goal here. Iran had more strategic objectives. So I'd do the deal, if I could structure it as a blocking minority of more than 25 percent. I'd also insist on representation on Krupp's board for Iran.

————•••————

While negotiating the Krupp transaction, I kept rooms at hotels in two different cities. Düsseldorf was central both for the Krupp meetings and the German accounting firm I had hired. The lawyers I used for the transaction, however, were located in Frankfurt. The daily trips between Düsseldorf and Frankfurt made it convenient for me to maintain hotel rooms simultaneously in both cities. The arrangement worked out fine. Until it didn't.

At a crucial point in the final negotiations, I arrived in Düsseldorf at midnight from Frankfurt and walked into my room briefcase in hand, exhausted and ready to hit the sack, only to find it already occupied. A man and woman in various stages of undress were in the room, he standing, she lounging on the sofa. There were some items of clothing and a pair of high heels carelessly strewn around. A bottle and an ice bucket sat on the coffee table, and the man and woman held highball glasses. They were obviously shocked to see someone break into their moment of intimate relaxation. I was equally shocked by their casual presence.

To our credit, nobody threw a fit. The hotel had mistakenly removed my belongings and reassigned the room to other guests, this couple. The hotel night manager professed to know nothing about it. I insisted on staying put as the widely-distributed contact information for all the negotiating parties had the room number and it would be unwieldy to change it at this stage. The ensuing kerfuffle took hours to straighten out. I had early-morning meetings, but by late afternoon the following day I stopped by to have a serious conversation with the general manager. He was full of apologies, but had no explanation. Ironically, the incident became grist for the mill of the gossip columnists of the German press, who found it hilarious that "Ansary slept in two beds!"

———··———

In the end, Berthold Beitz and I reached agreement on all the pending issues between us. Iran achieved "blocking minority" status and appointed representative board members to several constituent entities. The first closing of this historic event took place at

Villa Hügel in Essen. To my surprise, it was followed by hours of speechmaking and dramatic flair accompanied by much celebratory clicking of champagne glasses and toasting, German style— you take a sip while locking eyes with the one you are toasting, then you bring the glass down to the level of the second button of your shirt before you break off eye contact.

For me the festivities were reminiscent of the hoopla that often accompanied a company's new listing on the New York Stock Exchange in the days before the advent of several rival exchanges.

The next Krupp closing occurred in Tehran. In a less raucous and more sedate sequel afterwards, the Shah received the Krupp team in a brief ceremony at his palace.

Soon we all settled down to the steady rhythm of collaborative governance of a complex multinational business. Iran and Krupp then joined forces in a European investment vehicle based in Zurich, in which Beitz and I shared management.

———••———

What was unthinkable had overnight become a new reality. A foreign government—one from the Middle East, no less—was now irretrievably accepted into the rarefied corporate governance structure of the West. The press and the media treated the event with worldwide coverage and nonstop commentary and analyses. And the dam having been breached, it took no time for other governments to jump on the bandwagon of taking equity positions in major corporate entities outside their own borders.

Chapter Forty-Six

German Friendships

Once the Krupp negotiations ended and the transaction closed, Dr. Lukac, Krupp's chief financial officer, called to ask for a "private and confidential" meeting with me. Perhaps a new and unexpected glitch, I surmised. What he told me, however, caused my eyes to dilate and my mouth to fly open.

He was getting married, he said, and wanted me to be his best man.

I was stunned. He and I had fought many battles over the past months, and there had been more than a few tense moments. We had been adversaries—polite and courteous, but adversaries nonetheless. Yet here he was passing up lifelong friends of his own in Germany to want me to stand by him at his wedding. I fleetingly wondered what Prime Minister Hoveyda would say about this. Would he say I must *not* have negotiated hard? Or that I was fraternizing? Unlikely, of course, so I put these thoughts out of my mind.

Lukac then embarrassed me even more by saying he wished he had a brother "like Zyrus Anzahry."

Feeling overwhelmed, I quickly said I'd be honored to be his best man.

The wedding took place a month later in a small civil ceremony. The bride was beautiful, and I unashamedly fractured the German language delivering the traditional lines before the local equivalent of the justice of the peace. After the ceremony, Ulla engulfed me in a powerful embrace and thanked me for being Alfred's best man.

This was the beginning of a lifelong friendship with Alfred and Ulla Lukac. In 1990 when East and West Germany unified, the government asked Alfred to serve as the Supervisory Board Chairman of four East German manufacturing companies. Without the marketing and competitive pressures of free economies, East German companies had been ruinously mismanaged under the Communist regime. Bonn was now determined to revitalize the business climate in the eastern part of the unified country. Alfred relinquished his role at Krupp to devote full-time to his new assignments.

Meanwhile, Berthold Beitz asked if I'd join the Supervisory Board of Krupp GmbH, the parent company. I was still pondering this offer a month later when he added yet another board invitation, this time asking me to join the Board of Trustees of the Krupp Foundation. He assured me that both boards held their sessions at Villa Hügel, that he would schedule them in the same week so there would be a minimum of travel involved for me. His assurances notwithstanding, I was not entirely comfortable with the idea. I was already on a nonstop intercontinental travel schedule negotiating other transactions. I had also taken on new U.S. board commitments unrelated to Iran and did not relish getting further tied down in Germany. Once again, Berthold Beitz used his contacts in Tehran, but this time he prevailed. So, I ended up on the Supervisory Board of Fried. Krupp GmbH, and became a trustee of the Krupp Foundation. I was told it was the first time in the 163-year history of the House of Krupp that a non-German had become a part of its governance structure.

There had been many ups and downs in this transaction, but it seemed as though there was yet one more surprise in store for me.

By this point in our relationship, I was fully aware of Beitz's unique standing in Germany—he was one of the most admired men in the country. The press and media were calling him "Mr.

Germany." He represented the country on the International Olympic Committee, and had a host of other honors too numerous to recall.

He invited me to dinner at his home soon after I accepted the directorship and the trusteeship he had offered me. He said it would be only the two of us. He lived on a tree-lined avenue surrounded by woods and parks in an exclusive residential section of Essen with easy access to the city's museums, concert halls, and the philharmonic orchestra. A mellow stringed instrument played while we ate a superb fish dinner, followed by chamomile tea, which Beitz ordered for both of us. "It will settle your stomach," he advised with a touch of fatherly concern. I was sure he had something in mind and it was not about business.

Germans did not share the casual American practice of addressing everyone by first names. You had to know someone quite well at a personal level before switching to given names. Customarily, there was a ceremony connected with this event, and it was initiated by the senior person. A much-publicized instance of this occurred when then German Chancellor Helmut Schmidt invited his longtime friend, Ernst Wolf Mommsen, then president of Krupp, to call him "Helmut." The German press had a field day with that event.

Once dinner was finished, Beitz initiated the formal ceremony that marked this rite of passage by inviting me to call him "Berthold." Irreverently, I thought there was no need to be stuffy anymore, but I kept the amusement out of my voice. Beitz was marking our transition from business associates to close personal friends. I followed custom by asking him to call me Cy. He never did. To him I was always Zyrus.

Beitz then capped the evening's event with an invitation to join his family for lunch the following Saturday on Sylt. You can't spend much time in Germany without hearing about the North Sea island of Sylt off the coast of Denmark. In earlier centuries, its beaches were the launching point for the Vikings' raids on the English coastal settlements. Sylt was now the popular playground for the country's one percent. I was already curious about the island and was glad to accept Beitz's invitation.

As it turned out, he was not quite finished. He then invited me to join my fellow trustees of the Krupp Foundation on the annual weeklong sailing trip on the North Sea. The boat, *Germania VI*, would be crewed by eighteen German college students selected each year by the captain. It sounded like great fun, but I politely declined.

As a trustee of the Foundation, I had a chance to visit the basement of Villa Hügel. Preserved in neat and dust-free chambers were many symbols of the centuries-old Krupp dynasty. There were also priceless tapestries and other souvenirs of bygone eras.

I was fighting a losing battle on board memberships. Iran next purchased a 25 percent stake in Deutsche Babcock, another German company. The Babcock & Wilcox Group was a worldwide engineering firm founded by two Scotsmen. The German arm of that group was owned jointly by British Babcock and a bank. The company was active in technologies ranging from process engineering to construction of complete industrial plants. I negotiated with Sir John King and Donald Parvin, the chairman and president respectively of British Babcock, to buy its interest in the German company for Iran. The transaction closed in 1975.

The president of the German company included in the contract a requirement that I serve on his Supervisory Board, and Iran agreed. Despite all assurances about coordinating the board meetings with Krupp, I ended up traveling to Germany several times a month, as there were always special board or committee meetings and various other functions to attend.

—•••—

Later, Alfred Lukac required bypass surgery on his coronary arteries. I tried to persuade him to have it done in the U.S. He and Ulla decided his recovery would be easier at home. He had the surgery in Hamburg. A year later, in 1992, a sobbing Ulla called to tell Jan and me that Alfred had just died in his sleep. I will always mourn my friend's loss.

As for Berthold Beitz, the last time Jan and I saw him was in 2013 in Essen. He was ninety-nine years old. Time had whitened his hair and bowed his back, but his voice still carried and he looked preternaturally perky. He said he no longer went to the office, but when they told him "Zyrus Anzahry was coming," he had to get up, shave, get dressed in a suit and tie, and make one of his rare appearances in his old office. By then Villa Hügel had been converted into the Krupp Museum, which Jan and I toured. I saw the walls adorned with photos of previous members of the Supervisory Board, including those of my own era. It was a walk down memory lane for me.

I was deeply glad to have seen Berthold. He and I had a lot of shared memories. He died two weeks after our visit, one month short of his hundredth birthday.

Chapter Forty-Seven

An Idea Goes Viral

T he investment in Krupp received big play in the media worldwide, generating heated debate over an oil-producing country using its surplus funds to acquire pieces of major Western corporations. The news also unleashed a frenzied search by other oil-producing governments for similar cross-border investments.

As for me, the business grapevine went into overdrive, and I had to prepare myself for the avalanche of invitations pouring daily into my Washington office—highly demanding but also highly exhilarating. Many were from people I did not know. Several others were from people I knew only by reputation.

André Meyer of Lazard Frères and the dean of all dealmakers wanted me to meet Umberto Agnelli, CEO of Fiat, in New York. Armand Hammer of Occidental Petroleum was inviting me to his home in West Los Angeles, and then to Oxy's shareholders meeting in the Beverly Wilshire Hotel. A New York lawyer I knew wanted to set up a meeting for me with Nick Brady of Dillon Read. I remembered he was the closest personal friend of George H. W. Bush. Jacob Rothschild, of the British branch of the Rothschild family, wanted to meet the next time I was in London. Peter Henle, Berthold Beitz's impressive son-in-law and scion of the Thyssen industrial empire, wanted to schedule a dinner meeting in Düsseldorf. The Union Bank of Switzerland wanted to set up an all-day meeting with its senior officers in Zurich. I'd want to ask them to find a Swiss bank for Iran's Bank Melli to acquire. Jack Valenti of the Motion Picture Association wanted me to meet a friend of his in New York. The economic minister of Germany was planning a trip to Washington and wanted to arrange a meeting.

Other messages included one from Sargent Shriver, President Kennedy's brother-in-law, another from Bob Sarnoff of RCA, and others from Jack Smith of General Motors, and Peter Grace of Grace and Company. The Australians were eager to sell pieces of their iron ore mountains in the country's western provinces, and the South Africans were equally interested in talking about their uranium deposits.

Perhaps the most unusual proposal was to mine manganese nodules from the Pacific Ocean floor. There were also dozens of requests for interviews from members of the press. Dealing with all of these business opportunities would require an enlarged staff, and I set off on a recruitment quest.

There were also a couple of personal matters unrelated to the Sovereign Wealth Fund I managed. Marty Hoffmann was an old friend from my law practice days. He was now Secretary of the Army under President Gerald Ford. He called to invite me to lunch. He wanted to know if I'd be willing to go to Afghanistan on behalf of the U.S. government as the head of a team to promote private-sector economic development there. I demurred but told him that if the assignment included an ambassadorship, I could recommend a friend who was highly qualified for such an initiative.

Another friend, Jack Kaufman, publisher of *The Washington Star*, let me know through one of my Columbia classmates that the two families who owned the *Star* properties, including the newspaper and magazine, radio and TV stations, Washington real estate, and more, had decided to sell the company. To me, if I was interested. I recognized, of course, that, as these were communications assets, the buyer had to be a U.S. citizen. So, the offer was being made to me personally. I was excited by this opportunity, but felt the need to make certain it would not interfere with my work running Iran's SWF. Much to my regret, I was discouraged from proceeding and had to turn down the offer.

In the ensuing weeks, there was much publicity, including articles and even books, in Europe and the U.S. about my personal role in Iran's innovative investment initiative. At the same time, my staff in Washington was deluged with calls from investment bankers from around the world offering to sell us interests in major public companies. My earlier misgivings about how my program would be viewed in the U.S. and Europe were swiftly dissipating, as my Washington staff and I continued to deal with the many opportunities that presented themselves. No introductions were necessary, and no one demanded that I sign the customary confidentiality agreements or make any other commitments before starting due diligence or embarking on a negotiation.

Shortly before the first Krupp transaction was to close in the summer of 1974, I received word that my long-overdue contract with Iran was ready for signature. A year and a half had passed since I first set out to make history with a plan to persuade a Middle Eastern government to get into the corporate investment business in Europe and America. In the interim, I had been traveling non-stop to Paris, London, Zurich, Geneva, Rome, Frankfurt, Düsseldorf, Essen, Bad Homburg, Bonn, Tehran, Nowshahr, Cannes, Los Angeles, and New York, and run up big bills for legal and consulting services and attending meetings with high-level corporate and government officials. Of course, I had personally covered those outlays.

What was striking about the delay was that the text of the contract now ready for signing was exactly what I had proposed months earlier. Unknown to me at the time, there had been much internal debate in Iran about this arrangement. Despite all my efforts, career bureaucrats were apparently never convinced.

After the contract was signed, I realized belatedly that politics may have played a decisive role in the cabinet's earlier vote turning thumbs down on my proposal. The risk-averse ministers, faced with an unfamiliar project that would be managed by an untried and unknown candidate, had resorted to a safe political solution: They kicked the decision upstairs. That way, if I failed or caused embarrassment for Iran—which could have easily happened in the kind of business we were contemplating—the cabinet would not have been blamed.

In the tortuous work of government contracting, I was not blind to another reality: I had actually negotiated several transactions over the preceding months. I had been tested in practice and not found wanting before the contract was miraculously ready for signature.

Even so, it also became clear that without the Shah's personal intervention, my proposal would have never seen the light of day. Nonetheless, once the royal approval was secured, Hoveyda rose to the task marvelously. He set up a direct reporting line to himself, arranged for me to have an office and an English-speaking secretary in the most coveted location in the Iranian government, the Prime Minister's own suite. He also gave me access to his personal staff. Then every time I arrived in Tehran afterwards, he'd immediately set time aside for a briefing from me.

The government also settled on the details of its approach to my program: A small portion of the surplus funds from the sale of crude would be earmarked for these foreign investments. There would be no outright acquisitions; only minority positions would be sought. Each potential investment would be viewed for its merits on a stand-alone basis. Board memberships would be acceptable.

One thing I was glad to see was the procedure I'd have to follow in my work. For my investment activities, I'd take instruction from the king himself. I'd also report both orally and in writing to the Prime Minister. I found out later that having an office in the Prime Minister's suite was an honor for which many Cabinet ministers would have willingly battled each other to a fare-thee-well!

I continued to staff up in Washington. Periodically, I checked to make sure I was not required to register under the Foreign Agents Registration Act. I recommended to Prime Minister Hoveyda that we formalize the external investment program by organizing the two corporations I had mentioned earlier, one in the U.S., the other in Europe. This time, Hoveyda promptly ran my proposal through channels, ensured cabinet approval, and gave me the go-ahead. I organized the European company in Luxembourg. The American side I organized in Delaware. Once both entities were up and running, I sent regular, detailed written reports to Dr. Hoveyda, and gave personal briefings to the Shah.

———•··•———

The moment the document was signed in Tehran, I called Jan in Washington to let her know the prolonged effort to secure the approval of my proposal had not been wasted. Taking care of our children, Doug, ParyAnn, and Jeff, and with baby Brad on the way, she had her hands full while suffering through the ups and downs of the preceding months with me. She was obviously relieved to hear it had not been for naught. Never mind that it was the middle of the night in Washington when I called her with the news. Celebrations are always better shared.

Investment Services International Co.

ONE THOUSAND CONNECTICUT AVENUE
WASHINGTON, D. C., U. S. A. 20036
TELEX: 248656 TELEPHONE (202) 452-1140
ISIC UR   CABLE: ISICO

June 30, 1975

STATEMENT

Imperial Government of Iran
Plan and Budget Organization
Teheran

        Travel for and on behalf of
the Imperial Government for the period
January 1, 1975, to June 30, 1975, in-
clusive, consisting of:

        Teheran-Munich (3 trips);
Teheran-Zurich (2 trips); Teheran-
London (3 trips); Teheran-Paris (1
trip); Teheran-Washington (1 trip);
Teheran-Frankfurt (1 trip); Teheran-
Rome (1 trip); Washington-New York
(23 trips); Washington-London (3 trips);
Washington-Zurich (1 trip); Washington-
Frankfurt (1 trip); Washington-Minne-
apolis (2 trips); Washington-Boston
(1 trip); Washington-St. Louis (1 trip);
Washington-Paris (2 trips); Washington-
Munich (2 trips); Dusseldorf-London
3 trips); Dusseldorf-Zurich (2 trips);
Dusseldorf-Frankfurt (2 trips); Dussel-
dorf-St. Moritz (1 trip); Dusseldorf-
Sylt (2 trips); Dusseldorf-Munich (1
trip); Dusseldorf-Rome (1 trip); Frank-
furt-Zurich (1 trip);Frankfurt-Nice
(1 trip); New York-London (2 trips);
New York-Paris (1 trip); Zurich-St.
Moritz (1 trip); Zurich-London (1
trip); Zurich-Paris (1 trip); Zurich-
Amsterdam (1 trip); Paris-Nice (3 trips);
London-Boston (1 trip); New York-
Amsterdam (1 trip).

                              L. R. Adams
                              Accountant

A typical invoice showing the author's hyperactive travel schedule
organizing the world's first Sovereign Wealth Fund.

Chapter Forty-Eight

The Dazzling Mercedes Cars

B ack when the Ansarys couldn't even afford the hubcaps on the car's luxury wheels, I had heard about the *magnificent*, the *incomparable*, the *fabulous* Mercedes-Benz.

I knew about Mercedes automobiles long before I knew that Fords or Chevys existed. As a small child, I could tell that we envied anyone who owned the car. At some level, I may have even thought that someday I too would own one.

Gottlieb Daimler and son on the 1886 motorized carriage.

Father was transferred for two years to Iran's second largest city, Isfahan, when I was three. His best friend there owned the car dealership with the Mercedes franchise, which made him the most prominent man in town. Don't ask me how Father had met him because I have no idea, but the man's youngest son was close to my age and we played together.

Over the years I had forgotten my childhood image of that opulent brand, but here I was working on buying for Iran a big block of stock in Daimler AG, the manufacturer of Mercedes vehicles. The assignment from the Shah had rekindled the old feelings of envy and excitement, but there was no room for infantile emotions in a major business transaction. I had to focus.

Daimler was a global company with a popular brand; becoming a significant shareholder in it had much allure. It could be a sound financial investment as well as one that would provide technology, management, and marketing clout for the nascent Iranian automobile industry.

According to public records, there were three major stockholders in Daimler AG. The largest block was owned by a man named Friedrich Flick, the richest man in the country at the time. Another sizable block was held by Deutsche Bank, Germany's largest and most influential financial institution.

The third block, 14 percent of the outstanding shares, was originally owned by Günther Quandt. After his death his shares were put in a trust, of which the principal trustee was his son, Herbert Quandt, the man offering the shares to Iran. Ironically, the Quandts were also the controlling shareholders in BMW, the automaker that was in head-to-head competition with Mercedes. I wondered whether this incestuous ownership arrangement had been ordained by the Nuremberg Trials after World War II, but I found no record of it.

The remaining portion of the Daimler shares, roughly 18 percent, was held by the public and traded on the Frankfurt Stock Exchange.

Herbert Quandt's office called in early March 1974 to set up a meeting in Germany, but the proposed arrangements included some cloak-and-dagger instructions more suitable for the clandestine services: I was to fly into the Frankfurt am Main Airport, arriving there at a particular date and time. There, I'd be met by a man standing by the Lufthansa counter with a red carnation on his right lapel. He would also carry a copy of the English edition of *Reader's Digest* in a conspicuous manner over his left lapel. I was told the precautions were necessary as Mr. Quandt considered secrecy essential to avoid premature publicity. I chuckled to myself that he forgot to include the sign and countersign, a required ingredient in any good spy thriller.

The need for the unusual precautions was puzzling, but I followed them to the letter. I landed in Frankfurt and found my contact. With neither greeting nor a word of introduction, the man led me to his 1974 BMW Turbo in the airport parking lot. We drove about twenty miles to Mr. Quandt's office in Bad Homburg. Characteristic of the offices of the titans of German industry, the building was located well away from the companies Quandt controlled. It was in a house with a small staff. Quandt's own office was small but remarkably well organized and uncluttered. We chatted briefly, and he invited me to dinner at his home that evening at eight.

Knowing that Germans prized punctuality, I was there at eight on the dot. Mr. Quandt met me at the door. I put out my hand to shake his, and he put out his hand with a quick, stiff motion in a different direction. It hit me that, under those startling black eyebrows, my host was blind. Amazing that I had not noticed it at our morning meeting. Now the meticulous arrangements in his office began to make sense. He knew the precise and unvarying location of every object. That way, he'd be able to grab whatever he needed. I also realized from the unusually tense handshake that Herr Quandt did not particularly care to be touched. Nevertheless, you had to admire a man who would not permit his handicap to keep him from being productive.

Over dinner, Mr. Quandt told me his family's history. His father, he said, had built a large fortune in World War I "supplying uniforms" to the German Army. After the war, "he shrewdly used his funds to invest in promising industries." He bought a potash mining company, a metalworking business, a battery manufacturer, the controlling interest in BMW, and several other entities, making him one of Europe's most prominent industrialists. After his death, his estate was placed in a trust controlled by his sons, Harald and Herbert. Harald was killed in an aviation accident eleven years before my visit. So Herbert was now the main trustee.

I had listened closely to Mr. Quandt's recital of his father's history to see how far they deviated from what I had learned in my own research about the man. I had many misgivings about what I just heard but I saw no reason to mention them.

In the following days, I represented Iran in the negotiations to purchase Quandt's Daimler holdings while several members of Quandt's management represented the Quandt Trust. His deputy was a count, a member of the German nobility. With shoes shined to a startling reflection, he wore his title with an aristocratic air that took some getting used to. On the personal level, Quandt himself also came across as brusque and imperious. Oddly, I had not noticed anything patronizing about him at the dinner in his home. Of the members of his negotiating team, the one who stood out was Max Kreifels. The principal attorney for the Quandt Trust, he was an articulate and confident negotiator. I learned later that he was Germany's most prominent corporate lawyer. He was as warmly human as his client appeared cold and humorless.[9]

The negotiations to purchase Quandt's interest in Daimler took several months. The asking price was quite reasonable in relation to the public market. I was also provided with the company's published financial statements.

For the Krupp transaction, I was using German lawyers, but this time I felt Iran would be better served by an American lawyer. One of my Columbia classmates was now a partner in a major Washington law firm. He and I discussed the transaction and I asked him to prepare the purchase agreement. He did so in an unusually fast turnaround. I reviewed the document and found it to be a thorough and professional job. Because of the peculiarities of German corporate law, I wanted to make sure that counsel included the appropriate warranties about Daimler's operations and the accuracy of its financial statements. I wanted to use the good offices of

---

[9] In time, Max Kreifels and I became friends. He visited me in Washington when he was in the U.S. On a couple of occasions, he joined Jan and me for dinner at our home. He died in an autobahn accident in 1981. He was 54.

the German ambassador in Washington to deliver a copy to Mr. Quandt by diplomatic pouch. The ambassador was glad to oblige. I took it as a given that Quandt would want to nitpick one or more of its provisions.

In the meantime, I had a surprising call from another Daimler shareholder—the holder of the company's largest block, Friedrich Karl Flick. He wished to discuss "a most confidential matter" he said. Would Iran be interested in buying his block of Daimler shares? I sensed from our conversation that he was entirely unaware of my pending discussions with Herbert Quandt. I told him I fully understood the need for secrecy and would be glad to arrange a meeting to discuss his proposal.

I was, of course, struck by the coincidence of two major Daimler shareholders choosing the Iranians as the buyers of their stock. It raised questions I'd have to ponder.

Chapter Forty-Nine

Clash of Cultures

The week after I sent the draft agreement for the purchase of Daimler stock to Mr. Quandt, his assistant called to propose a new meeting. Still puzzled over the call from Mr. Flick, I flew to Frankfurt, then drove to Quandt's office in Bad Homburg. The secretary promptly ushered me in. Apparently, the meeting was only for the two of us.

Mr. Quandt, dressed in a dark gray suit and blue tie, did not return my greeting and did not shake hands. There was nothing welcoming about him, and he remained seated in a stiff posture behind his mahogany desk after I entered. Cold and distant with obvious anger, he did not offer me a seat. The twist of his lips and eyebrows lent a fierce expression to his face. His scowl was designed to turn a Bengal tiger to jelly, I soon learned. Clearing his throat noisily, he was obviously working himself up to something dramatic.

Without preamble, he said icily, "I received your contract." He picked up the draft, waved it around, riffled through it with an air of disdain, then slammed it down on his desk. Startled, I assumed he was getting ready to vent to me about some provision in the document. Maybe his tone was harsher than he intended. Besides, ranting against lawyers was nothing new, even in the States. Whatever the cause of his fury, I wanted to get us back on track.

"This is only a draft," I assured him, keeping my voice light and conciliatory. "Let me know what bothers you, and we can talk about it." Then I unapologetically sat down without invitation.

His mouth twitched without saying anything for several minutes. In the silence, I sat still, breathing normally and puzzling over Quandt's behavior. *Could this be about money? Could he have received a more generous offer?* But he had never shown an inclination to conduct an auction, in which the seller accepts the highest of multiple bids. His earlier attempts at secrecy, requiring me to travel incognito and meet a stranger at the Frankfurt Airport, would lead one to conclude that he had not been seeking other offers. I had in fact accepted his asking price for the shares without question. In return, I had expected good-faith negotiation on the other items that might arise.

That is as far as I got in my speculations before Quandt started fidgeting in his seat, a signal there was more to come. With an abrupt movement and a bleak expression, he reached into the bottom right-hand drawer of his desk, pulled out a thin file and took out a single sheet of paper, which he brandished in my face.

Purely by reflex, I noticed that there had been no fumbling.

"Do you know what this is?" he thundered as though he was struggling but failing to control an incandescent rage.

It was a single page with only a few lines of writing and three signatures at the bottom. I leaned in to study it, but he allowed me a bare glimpse only. Nor did he give me a chance to comment.

"I'll tell you," he said as he tapped his knuckles on his desk and stood up to his full height. "This is a joint voting agreement among Deutsche Bank, the Flick family, and myself." He let that sink in for a moment, before raising his decibel level to a shout. "The three of us have majority control of Daimler AG. We have been running the company jointly under this agreement for nineteen years."

There were only the two of us in the room, but he was pitching his voice to the rafters. His conduct was setting my teeth on edge. Mt. Vesuvius was erupting; I'd wait for it to go dormant. Buoyed as he was by his multi-generational wealth, he probably felt he had no need to account for his behavior to the rock bangers—the rest of society.

"Nineteen years, do you hear?" he said, punctuating each word. "That is how we do things in Germany."

I had no chance to read the language of this so-called joint voting agreement, but I did not have to be a lawyer to know that those few lines—not much longer than the message in a Chinese fortune cookie—did not create a contractual relationship among the parties. I was doubtful that it had been designed to be an enforceable contract in the courts. Was it an arrangement, I wondered, so structured as to enable the three of them to make private decisions about a public company's affairs? I, of course, had no way of knowing.

"This is what I think of your American-style contract," he declared in acid tones with absolute finality after a pause. He then picked up the document again and, with more than a hint of malice on his face, threw it forcefully into the trash basket next to his desk.

I sat bolt upright. For a moment, all the normal office sounds faded from my conscious mind. The dominos had just whirred and tumbled into place with an audible click. Now I knew exactly what was going on, and why the theatrics. I drew a long breath, then leaned back and slowly brought my eyes up to look Quandt squarely in the face. Knowing full well that he could not see me or detect my gesture, I began reviewing for myself how we got here.

First off, it was clear that Herr Quandt's solution to any negotiating problem was to go on the attack immediately. Not often a productive approach, that. There was yet another point I thought of and again discarded as not crucial: I had noticed purely in passing that Quandt, when referring to my "American-style contract," paused on the word "American" as though he had bitten on sour fruit. It was thus easy to judge him as having anti-American prejudices. So soon after World War II, however, old animosities were easily stirred up, and anti-American feelings were not uncommon in Germany. Nevertheless, that issue was only a smokescreen at this point, as were the theatrics. What was at stake was nothing less than a titanic clash of two fundamentally different cultures.

To explain, I need to go back to the beginning:

When Quandt decided to sell his stake in Daimler, he bypassed all the obvious prospects in Europe and the U.S. Any investment banker in New York, London, Frankfurt, or Hong Kong would have done somersaults to get the chance to handle the sale for him. There probably would have been a long line of bidders for his stock. He chose instead to offer his holdings to the Iranians. Why? Was it because he figured to get a big bonanza from them? But the asking price for his shares was quite reasonable in relation to the market. In fact, in my judgment most European or American buyers could have been persuaded to pay a larger premium.

I had been puzzled about this issue from the beginning, but I had nothing to go on before. I had no need to call time-out to think it all through; it had just crystallized in my mind. I could now guess what had set off Quandt's brouhaha.

There were two crucial elements in this unfolding drama, and they need explanation:

One was that in Germany, as in a few other European countries, public corporations operated under a law that granted to labor unions the right to have equal representation with the shareholders on a company's board of directors (called the supervisory board in Germany). The inevitable conflicts between the two board factions gave rise to frequent tensions at the governance level. This state of affairs inevitably made digging into German corporate reports a dicey undertaking.

The other crucial element in this picture was that, according to Mr. Quandt, the three largest shareholders in Daimler had been operating for years under a "joint voting agreement." Whether they were functioning outside the scrutiny of the public shareholders, the union representatives, and the full supervisory board of Daimler AG, I had no way of knowing. At this point, the precautions Quandt had taken to ensure the secrecy of our meeting, the timing of the recent call from Mr. Flick, and Mr. Quandt's explosive reaction to the provisions of my draft contract all took on special significance.

When he called my proposed draft an "American-style contract," was it possible that he was really objecting to the American system of transparency in the governance structure of corporations, the full disclosure in public filings, and respect for the rights of minority shareholders?

Of course, I still did not know exactly what had caused the sudden stampede for the exits by two of the three major shareholders of this venerable old company, but it was not necessary for me to know any details. I had enough for a working hypothesis.

It was now reasonable to assume that what had attracted Quandt to offer his shares to the Iranians was *not* to get a big bonanza. Rather, it was because he was sure they would be so awed by the cachet of Mercedes-Benz that they would jump at the chance to own some stock in the company. Or perhaps he had been reluctant to open himself to purchasers who might have wanted to dig into his father's wartime activities, but I had no way of knowing about that either. In any event, what he had gotten instead was an "American-style contract" requiring him to give very specific warranties about the company's financial and operational history.

If Quandt were seeking an unsophisticated purchaser, he did not have far to look. The investment landscape was littered with them. Unfortunately for him, my Washington colleagues and I knew deep in our souls that taking published corporate reports at face value—no matter what the country—was not the route to making judicious investments.

Even aside from unsophisticated buyers from the Middle East

or elsewhere for his shares, Quandt did have another alternative, as unpalatable as that may have been to him: Deutsche Bank could have been an ideal buyer of his stock, regardless of what, if any, non-public actions the triad may have taken.

Deutsche, Germany's largest financial institution, was the eight-hundred-pound gorilla in this scenario. It extended its reach into a huge segment of the German economy. It would shock Americans to learn that the German system permitted banks to buy into their customers' businesses, a practice rife with apparent or potential conflict of interest. Every time a company would try to borrow money, it ran the risk of exposing itself to pressure to give up a chunk of its equity to the bank in addition to the payment of interest on its loan.

I was incredulous to find that German banks owned substantial stakes in the country's major corporations and had representation on their supervisory boards. In fact, the banks reportedly held 50 percent of the chairmanships of those entities. I found myself admiring the wisdom of the U.S. laws that prohibited the incestuous intermingling of the industrial and banking sectors. Even in Germany, there was much criticism of the existing system. Nevertheless, Deutsche Bank was the only one with the heft-and-clout to deal decisively with whatever possible fallout there might be from the arrangement Quandt had mentioned.

Under the circumstances, I was glad to extricate my client from this transaction. Quandt himself was giving Iran an out. Nevertheless, his behavior had been inexcusable, and I should not let it pass. I stood up. "Deal breaking," I said curtly, "no matter what the pretext, will not sit well with the government I represent." Without another word, I walked out but not before noticing that Quandt had crossed his arms on his torso in smug satisfaction.

On the drive back to Frankfurt, I speculated that Quandt might have already lined up another buyer for his shares. If he did, I'd bet my last dollar that it was a prospect who required no contractual warranties. I was also certain that any announcement coming out of his office would follow the same pattern on which he had embarked since the beginning of this project. After all, you wouldn't want the man to turn human on you. It would shake your faith in immutable things like the sun rising in the east and the stars coming out at night.

I was not disappointed. Three weeks later, German newspapers carried the story that the Kuwait Pension Fund—seemingly just restructured as the Kuwait Investment Authority—had acquired an equity stake in Daimler AG, accounting for 14 percent of the company's stock, from the Quandt Group, and that "the Kuwaitis had outbid the Iranians to acquire the shares!"

Shortly afterwards, Deutsche Bank announced that it had purchased a 29 percent block of Daimler shares from the Flick family for 2 billion Deutsche marks. Alfred Herrhausen, president of the bank, could also not resist planting some innuendoes of his own at the expense of the Iranians. "The farther east Germans go to do business," he pontificated while wrapping himself in the country's national flag, "the more suspicious they should be of the honesty of the other party."

Chapter Fifty

Scourge of Bribery

T he mysterious stranger who showed up unannounced in my Washington office in the fall of 1976 was a tall man with a thin face and pointed chin. He was dressed in a dark blue suit, white shirt, and blue tie speckled with white dots. He gave off an aura of deep anxiety, as though he was carrying out a troublesome task. He did not respond to my greeting and remained standing.

Without any preliminaries, he told me his name and offered me his passport to prove he was who he said he was. I gave it only a cursory look. It was a Swiss passport, and he was listed as a lawyer with a Zurich address. I returned it and asked what this was about. Ignoring my question, he asked to see *my* passport.

Impatient with all the mystery, I told him Americans did not routinely carry passports within the U.S. and asked again why he had come. He sounded almost pleading when he asked if I'd bear with him. I noticed his eyes were roving over the various photos, diplomas, and honors on the wall behind me, and finally lighted on my U.S. Supreme Court admission certificate, which he scrutinized for a moment. As a lawyer himself, he had perhaps found something familiar on which to focus. Apparently that certificate was not entirely satisfactory proof of my identity, but after a long pause his face showed resignation and acceptance.

His inner turmoil notwithstanding, the man only hesitated another moment before reaching into his briefcase and taking out an 8½x11 white envelope, which he handed to me. It was sealed with original wax, the old-fashioned way, such as one would see on a royal commission with a signet ring. I had not seen a wax seal in years. Without another word, he turned around and scurried out of my office. I called after him to wait while I opened the envelope, but he wouldn't slow down. Whatever his mission, he had completed it. He was quickly out the door.

Curiouser and curiouser.

"Hmm," I observed as Diane, my assistant, stood watching with a dubious look on her face. "This is extraordinary."

"It wouldn't be dangerous," she asked with obvious concern. "Would it?"

I turned the envelope over and peered at it nervously. I told myself I had been reading too many cheap mystery stories, but actually there had been several much-publicized incidents of poisonous anthrax envelopes sent to prominent Washingtonians at the time. Even though this package was delivered by a person who had identified himself, I still felt I had to be cautious. The envelope had the feel only of paper and was odorless. It was also thin enough to feel what was inside.

Without any more hesitation, I asked Diane for a large pair of scissors and slit open the envelope. It contained a single sheet of paper. Under the letterhead of a major Swiss bank was a lone paragraph. It said that the bearer was entitled, "upon the completion of an envisaged transaction" to receive the equivalent of roughly $20 million in various European currencies. It was signed by two of the bank's managing directors.

I was flabbergasted. *Hot damn!* The favorite exclamation of my old boss, Judge Charles R. Richey, had sprung unbidden into my mind after all those years. I was staggering as it sank in—I was being bribed, presumably to make certain that an "envisaged transaction" reached closure. However, the letter gave no clue to the identity of whoever thought I was for sale.

By this time, offers of new deals for Iran were building up momentum like a summer storm, and there were dozens of transactions in the works. Of the multiple deals with which I was busy at the time, several were large enough to tempt bribery of this magnitude, but which one?

As often happened, my Aha! moment came in the middle of the night. I woke up from sound sleep to realize that I should have immediately recognized the man behind this bribery scheme. Only one man I knew was capable of this kind of shenanigan, the man peddling a slice of a nuclear power company. And it wasn't the first time for him to pull something underhanded.

The latest buzzword in the energy sector in the mid-1970s, nuclear power generation was creating a hoopla and grabbing market share. A company specializing in the field had offered Iran the opportunity of becoming a major shareholder in it, and I was asked to investigate. It was a new field for me; I faced a steep learning curve. I started out by using a multi-pronged approach. While my staff analyzed the company itself, I visited several European cities to get a grounding in the technologies involved. I obviously had to defer to the experts on the merits of the competing nuclear reactors.

My contact with the company offering the investment opportunity was a man I'll call Hans. He was short, built like a bulldog, and kept up a barrage of conversation with the intensity of an onrushing freight train. I had to spend many sessions with him over several months. In our last meeting in his office, there was also a woman in attendance. Hans introduced her as a member of the staff. I had not seen her before, but as she remained quiet throughout the discussions, I paid little attention to her.

The session lasted all day and was over at 5 p.m. By then, I was already skeptical about the investment being offered to Iran. I'd want to discuss it with my staff in Washington before announcing my decision to the company. As I started to leave, Hans said the woman would accompany me to my hotel. "In case you should have any additional questions," he explained.

"That is very kind," I replied, "but not necessary."

"No trouble at all," he said expansively. "We have to move things along."

"All right," I said, not wishing to be ungracious. "Thank you."

In the car, I took a good look at the lady, whom I'll call Helga. She was young, maybe in her early thirties. She was blond, attractive, and well dressed.

Feeling uneasy, I wondered what was going on. *Never mind. Let's get on with the business at hand.* In a conversational tone I started asking Helga about the operation of the company's heavy water reactor. Her brow knotted. She said it was not her field. I switched to the financial side, and then the administrative part of the company. She professed ignorance each time, in a tone that indicated she was puzzled by my questions. It became clear she knew virtually nothing about the business. I smiled wryly in spite of myself.

So… the 'honey trap' is not just used in the clandestine services, is it? I asked myself rhetorically. Offended, I put on a pleasant face until we got to my hotel. I said goodbye and got out of the car.

Hans's capacity for skullduggery seemed to know no end. First a honey trap, and now an outright bribe. I reflected on this first experience of being on the receiving end of a tainted offer. Wouldn't it be wonderful, I mused, if we all lived in a corruption-free world? I always believed that once corruption spreads its malignant tentacles into a society, it is virtually impossible to uproot.

So now what to do?

The Shah happened to be on a state visit to the United States at the time and was staying at Blair House. Called the world's most exclusive hotel, it is located across Pennsylvania Avenue from the White House and is used to host foreign dignitaries visiting U.S. presidents. I received word that Pahlavi would like me to join him for lunch there the next day. We'd have a private one-on-one afterwards.

The lunch was small. There were only the king, his queen, and their personal physician who was also their longtime friend. We talked about personal and family matters, and everyone was relaxed and in good humor. The king was treating me like a family friend. The meal, prepared by the Blair House chef, was excellent, with lots of vegetables. Jan would have approved.

Afterwards, Pahlavi and I went up to a study on the second floor. We had a lot to cover, but I showed him the letter from the Swiss bank and told him my suspicions about its origin. His immediate reaction was to ask for my assessment of the proposal from the nuclear power generator. I took a few minutes to talk about the competing technologies involved and mentioned that the last word on which would emerge as the dominant reactor had not yet been written. Nevertheless, the experts I had consulted had serious reservations about the viability of the particular technology being offered to Iran. I felt that was the reason for the bribe, I added.

I had the impression I was carrying coal to Newcastle. I was not telling the Shah anything about the technologies involved he didn't already know. Once I stopped talking, he did not hesitate. He directed me to terminate the negotiations with the company.

A week later, I visited the bank in Zurich that had sent the bribery letter, accompanied by a government lawyer from Tehran. As the two of us rode the elevator in the bank building, another man happened to ride up with us. Another bank customer, I assumed. He was old and totally bald. I thought he looked familiar but couldn't place him. No matter.

When we got off, I asked the receptionist if we could see either of the two managing directors who had signed the bribery letter. We were ushered into a small office and introduced to one of them. I made the introductions, then showed him the letter.

The managing director's eyes lighted up. "How would you like to have the money?" he asked.

Before I could answer, he launched into a presentation on the benefits of using the bank's numbered accounts as a repository of the funds. He was just getting warmed up when I interrupted.

"I'm returning the letter to the bank," I said.

He was incredulous. "You don't want the money?" he almost yelled in disbelief.

I confirmed that I did not. I thought he was still shaking his head as I took my leave. He was obviously unused to what had just happened. In his experience, I suppose, no one had ever turned down such a bribe.[10]

I left the gentleman's office, the lawyer from Tehran trailing behind.

Going down the elevator, it dawned on me who had ridden up with us. The bald man was Maurice Chevalier, the French actor who was equally well-known to American audiences. I wondered what had happened to the full head of hair I remembered from the last movie I had seen him in several years earlier.

---

[10] Using the relative shares of GDP, that would equal roughly $318 million in 2020.

Chapter Fifty-One

A Potpourri of Deals

Adeal that by all accounts should have been sealed, but wasn't, involved Ashland Oil Company. I saw it as a great opportunity for Iran, but through the intransigence of an old man—one who had no background in the oil industry—it never reached closure.

Ashland Oil was headquartered in Ashland, Kentucky, and was listed on the New York Stock Exchange. Although smaller than the major international oil companies, it enjoyed a good reputation for its refining operations and the distribution of its oil products. It had a chemical subsidiary and a network of gas stations. It wanted to secure a long-term source of crude through a transaction with Iran in the mid-1970s.

Ashland's president, Orin E. Atkins, and two senior vice presidents met with me over several months in Washington and New York. The proposed arrangement was a strategic partnership between Iran and Ashland, and the company was fully prepared to sell Iran a 25 percent equity stake and arrange for full board representation afterwards. It would simultaneously enter into a long-term fixed-price supply contract with the National Iranian Oil Company.

When the time came to sign the documents, however, the NIOC chairman balked. There was a tradition in Iran that when a prime minister was finally put out to pasture, he was given an honorary role as chair of the national oil company. Inexplicably, the chairman objected to the deal I had carefully negotiated with Ashland. His objections made no sense, as they seemed to focus on the physical appearance of the refinery parking lot. I was mystified. We were discussing a strategic relationship, and the NIOC chairman was complaining about the landscaping outside one of Ashland's buildings. Nevertheless, he was a former prime minister, and swimming in the deep political waters of the country was far beyond my expertise.

Much to my regret, I was never able to shake the NIOC out of its position. So I struck out on Ashland. Ironically, the price of crude in the proposed contract would have been near its all-time high. Prime Minister Hoveyda and I were in accord that it had been a lost opportunity.

Unrelated to the oil industry, however, there were by then scores of new proposals in the works. Spanning the continents, they originated in Australia, Britain, Canada, France, Germany, Italy, Senegal, South Africa, and the United States. Most involved major public companies, but there were a couple of joint venture proposals involving extractive industries. All entailed extensive travel and due diligence for my staff and myself. Several reached closure, some others I referred to various government departments in Iran for handling and disposition. It is, of course, the nature of acquisitions and investments that one does not swing at every pitch.

Occasionally, there was an outlier that was easy to deal with. One was from a prolific Italian movie producer by the name of Dino De Laurentiis. He was introduced to me by Jack Valenti, whom I had known in Washington when he was the special assistant to President Lyndon Johnson. At this point, Jack was president of the Motion Picture Association of America. He invited me to meet with his Italian friend, who had "an interesting proposal," and I accepted. Mr. De Laurentiis, sitting behind a desk that rivaled in size the YMCA swimming pool in Fort Worth, wanted Iran to finance a film starring Gregory Peck. In fact, he had a draft contract all ready for my signature. Even a cursory look was enough for me to recognize that it was an insult to my intelligence and not worth wasting time on.

Despite my best efforts, other proposals became the subject of public commentary, such as the negotiations with Occidental Petroleum Company and its publicity-prone CEO, Armand Hammer. He never met a reporter he did not try to charm, or even court.

In another case, the president of a major U.S. public company, with whom I had worked out a special deal, lost his job. I assumed it happened because of our deal, but I never had confirmation of it. He and I had negotiated the terms of Iran's participation in his company before he went out of the country to accompany his wife, a world-renowned lyric soprano, on a professional tour. In his absence, the board called a special meeting and fired him. This despite the fact that he was the son of the revered founder of the company.

Chapter Fifty-Two

A Hellenic Encounter

Even in the egalitarian societies of the twenty-first century, royalty bespeaks of rank and privilege, of homage and obeisance. Perhaps humans need symbols to celebrate and revere.

In the eighteenth century, when America was being founded by ordinary citizens, the kings and queens of Europe were deemed by statute to be the "fountains of honor" and "the sources of all rights and privileges" for their countrymen and women. Unbelievably, the law even ascribed "absolute perfection" to them. Today, there are fewer kings and queens in the world, and if anyone attributed perfection to them it would be with a wink and a smile. Nevertheless, reverence for royalty is still a strong emotion in many lands.

In the course of administering Iran's Sovereign Wealth Fund, I occasionally crossed paths with royalty. I emerged from some of these encounters believing that each was an extraordinary human being, unreservedly dedicated to the welfare of his people.

Here and in a subsequent chapter are the stories of a couple of such encounters—intriguing glimpses into the private lives of European royalty.

———•••———

Constantine II and I crossed paths by pure chance early in the spring of 1976. We met at the airport in Cannes, France, where I was in the preliminary stages of a business negotiation. I was introduced to him, and we shook hands. It was a brief encounter. I was aware that his reign as the king of Greece had ended nine years earlier when a group of army officers staged a coup in the country and drove him into exile. A military dictatorship took over, and there was an attempt on Constantine's life. Coincidentally, the assassin was apprehended by the security forces of the Shah of Iran. Being barred from his native country, Constantine chose England in 1973 as his home in exile.

A few weeks after that first meeting, I ran into Constantine again at another airport, the Lufthansa international lounge at the Frankfurt terminal. The wait for one's flight seems interminable at times, and any break would tend to ease the monotony. Sophia Loren was also waiting there, smiling at all who were ogling her. I was one of the people staring at the movie star, and almost missed King Constantine. On the way to catch my flight, I walked over and reintroduced myself to him. We shook hands and chatted for a few minutes. I had no reason to expect he'd remember me.

A month later I was surprised to receive an invitation from him to dinner at his home in London. In our brief encounters, he had come across as approachable, easy to talk to, a man with a sense of humor. I thanked him for his invitation and accepted.

I found his house on Linnell Drive in Hampstead Garden Suburb, London, predictably comfortable. Constantine himself looked fit. Queen Anne-Marie was a gracious hostess and eager to talk about her children. They had three, two sons who were princes of both Greece and Denmark, and a daughter of similar rank. Of the two other guests at the dinner, one was a Greek shipping tycoon, the other a young Greek who introduced himself as an inventor and regaled us with stories about his creations.

It was an entertaining evening. As I prepared to leave, Constantine walked me to the door and asked if I could meet him in his office in Mayfair the next morning. "Of course," I said.

When we met the following day, he asked for a favor. He said he had been given an opportunity to make a major investment in a new project. Would I be willing to look into it for him? He provided the background material and said he would be grateful for any advice.

I agreed to do as he asked.

Constantine spoke softly, but I could discern that he was hopeful about the results of my research. For a member of the European royalty to want my expertise on a potential investment was an honor, but also a puzzle. *The press must be exaggerating my abilities.*

Back in Washington, I mustered the requisite resources to examine the project. Ten days later, we all came back together to discuss our findings. There was unanimity that the proposal was entirely without merit. I gathered up the necessary evidence to document our conclusion and prepared to report back to the king.

The next time I was in London, we met again, and I gave Constantine the rundown on our investigation and our unequivocal conclusion. He was shocked. I had given him unpleasant news. He thanked me for saving him from making a big mistake and was gracious in his disappointment.

King Constantine II and the Queen were permitted to return to Greece in 2007 with their children. Their adult children, working as commoners, have been highly successful in various fields in Europe and America.

Chapter Fifty-Three

Talented Royalty

This was one time when I didn't think fast enough and dropped the ball.

Juan Carlos, the king of Spain, was born in 1938 in Rome, where he spent his early years during his family's exile. At nine he was sent to Spain to continue his schooling. Later, he underwent military training there. In the years that followed, he became fluent in English, French, Portuguese, and Italian in addition to his native Spanish. He learned competitive sailing and became a pilot and an amateur radio operator. He hunted big game, practiced the martial arts, skied in the Alps, and delighted in riding his motorcycle incognito in Madrid.

In 1962, Juan Carlos married Princess Sophia, the daughter of King Paul of Greece and Queen Frederica. The young couple then moved into Zarzuela Palace in the mountains of El Pardo, near Madrid. Built in the seventeenth century, the palace had undergone several renovations. At the time of the wedding, Zarzuela was a two-story structure with an office, dining room, library, large living areas, and gardens, fountains, and terraces.

Earlier, Spain had been ravaged by a civil war that started in 1936 and ended when World War II erupted in 1939. It pitted the communists supported by the Soviet Union against the fascists supported by Hitler and Mussolini. The fascists won, and their leader, Francisco Franco, became the country's dictator. He did not, however, choose to abolish the monarchy. He affirmed it and in 1969 formally named Juan Carlos his successor. Franco died on November 20, 1975, and Juan Carlos acceded to the throne two days later. Expected to follow dictator Franco's mold, he began instead to transform Spain into a modern democracy.

It was the summer of 1976, and my staff and I were knee-deep in projects for Iran and running hectic travel schedules. Into this mayhem came an invitation to have lunch with King Juan Carlos at his home. Not my usual fare, it caught me by surprise. (My Texas friends would accuse me of walking in tall cotton!) I had no real idea to what I owed this honor, but I did not hesitate to accept.

As it happened, I was already committed to several business meetings in London, so I scheduled a brief detour to attend the royal luncheon. I had always wanted to visit Spain, but I'd not be there this time to watch the bullfighters twirling their capes.

I took the night flight from Dulles to Madrid-Barajas Airport, then checked into a nearby hotel upon arrival. I barely had time for a quick shower and change before the concierge rang to say the car was there to take me to Zarzuela Palace. On the way, I kept craning my neck to see the sights. A shame I wouldn't have time to see the many cultural attractions of the Spanish capital.

And then I thought of my old friend, John Safer.

—··—

I was barely out of my twenties when John Safer and I met in the early 1960s. He was already a successful banker, lawyer, and developer. There had been a small luncheon at a downtown Washington club, about a dozen of us around the table, guests of a local luminary. John sought me out afterwards, and we chatted on the way to my office, a block away.

We met again for lunch the following week. We had a lot to talk about. He was a banker, and I had just organized my own commercial bank in a Virginia suburb. He was a lawyer, Harvard Law, and I too was a member of the bar. He was deep into real estate while I only had small interests in a shopping center and a commercial building. He was chair of the executive committee of a major bank holding company and thought I should be interested in what was going on.

I noticed something unusual about John at lunch. The entire time we were talking, he was playing with his cloth napkin. He would fold it, twirl it, bend it, and mold it into one shape and then another. It was only later that I found out John was also a serious sculptor.

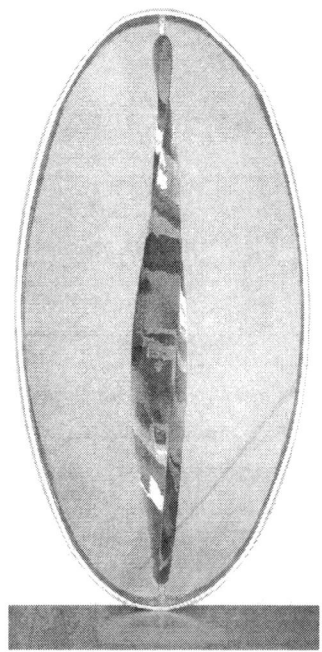

Limits of Infinity
by John Safer

Over the many years that John and I knew each other, his fame grew internationally. His sculptures appeared in museums, galleries, and embassies throughout the world. He had a large piece in the lobby of the U.S. Department of State, another in the quad at Harvard University, a huge one at the entrance to the Smithsonian National Air and Space Museum, and many more. His wife Joy and my Jan also became good friends, and John made a piece especially for Jan's fortieth birthday.

During his tenure in office, President Gerald Ford, knowing that King Juan Carlos was an art connoisseur, presented Safer's *Limits of Infinity* to him as a gift of state. It was a magnificent work that I knew well and which the king placed at Zarzuela Palace. Knowing my friend's piece was there would make my visit to Madrid even more meaningful.

I snapped out of my reverie as we pulled into the palace driveway. I saw a tall well-dressed man standing in front of the steps of the palace. He had his right hand in the pocket of his suit jacket and was looking in my direction. He was alone. It took me a moment to realize, to my disbelief, that it was the king himself. He looked athletic and fit. I jumped out of the car and walked over. He took his hand out of his pocket, smiled, and offered it to me to shake. He led me up the few steps to a small study off to the left. I expected to be sitting at a lunch table, but it turned out that the meal was a couple of hours away. The king wanted us to get to know each other first. He introduced me to the queen. We exchanged a few pleasantries, and she left us alone. The royal couple were openly affectionate toward each other—always a good sign.

"Did you notice," the king asked lightheartedly, "that I had my right hand in my jacket pocket when you drove up?"

I said I had noted it in passing.

"Let me show you what I was holding in my hand."

He took a tiny pistol out of his pocket. "Your FBI made this for me," he said. "It fires a single shot and can pass any security check."

I did not hold it, but I assumed it was made of plastic. Since he and I had never met, Juan Carlos explained, he had to be cautious while waiting for me on his driveway. He did not mention it, but I already knew that he was also a martial arts expert, a skill I always admired.

The king asked about me, my family, my background, and my current professional activities. I gave him a brief rundown. He was attentive as I spoke and did not interrupt. He then switched to politics and the trend toward socialism in Europe. He became particularly animated when he talked about Spain's political situation. He talked about the problems facing his country and the thorny situations he faced as the head of state. It was easy to see why Juan Carlos was a popular monarch—he had the polished demeanor of one—and his love of Spain came through in blazing colors. He brought up some of the sensitive pending issues with which a modern Spanish king had to contend, and I felt privileged that he would discuss them with me.

Lunch started at about 2:15 p.m. In addition to the queen, the king had also invited the head of Iberia Airlines, a confidant. The lunch lasted until 5:30 p.m. In the course of the conversation, the king returned time and again to the pending political posture of the Spanish government and his plans as events unfolded. The lunch had a very personal flavor, and Juan Carlos spoke openly about the events in his country. I felt I was a witness to history.

I had enjoyed the august company of my host, but lunch was over and I was ready to take my leave.

Back at the hotel, I took care of some cables and telexes and had a small garden salad for dinner. I was in bed and asleep by 10 o'clock local time. I had several high-level meetings lined up starting early the next morning in London and a reservation for a 6 a.m. flight out of Madrid. I ordered a wake-up call for 4:15 a.m.

The ringing of the phone jolted me awake. The bedside radio said it was a little after 11 p.m. Gathering my wits about me, I said "hello" and immediately recognized the caller's voice. It was the *basso profondo* of none other than King Juan Carlos himself. He wanted me back at the palace.

"Cyrus, come on over," he said. "We are going to watch a cowboy movie and then have dinner."

I had been awakened from deep sleep, but if you work in the international arena as I did, you become inured to sleep interruptions. I did not fail to recognize that the caller was not just a member of the palace staff passing on a message to me. By being on the line himself, the king was treating me as a personal friend again, asking me to join him and his family for some nighttime fun.

For an anguished moment I did not know what to do. I took a deep breath and tried to marshal my thoughts. I had to think fast. Say the movie started at midnight and lasted until 2 or 2:30

in the morning. The dinner would start sometime after the movie ended. Spanish dinners, I was sure, were not to be rushed. What about my London meetings that had been scheduled weeks in advance? This was before cellphones, email accounts, and messaging. There would be no way to get to the people in time to cancel my appointments. Those traveling from other countries would already be there. I was caught in a real bind.

It was clear the king was inviting me to a party that would last until morning. We would be having dinner in the dark hours between midnight and dawn. That was not what was troubling me. I was no stranger to all-nighters. Hell, I had pulled quite a few in my day—in school prepping for finals, in combat exercises in the Marines, and in law practice. Even though staying up all night had lost its excitement for me long ago, sleep deprivation was nothing new in my life. The trouble was that I could see no way to fit this highly enticing social occasion into the rush-rush business schedule to which I had committed myself. My heart said dinner with the king and queen of Spain. My mind said I had other urgent obligations. This was one of those rare moments when you must choose between two magnetic poles. To my everlasting regret, I chose the line of least resistance.

King Juan Carlos was patiently waiting for my answer. There was no easy way to do this.

"Would Your Majesty give me a rain check? Much to my regret, I have unavoidable commitments tomorrow. I could be back next week, or whenever your schedule permits."

I deserved a swift kick in the pants for not allowing more time for the Madrid trip.

There was silence on the phone, then a new voice came on. He did not introduce himself. Probably one of the king's intrepid aides. He only said, "We regret you cannot join us. Good night."

Poetry, Ansary, I muttered sheepishly to myself. *Stick to Persian poetry.*

Perhaps I had made a colossal blunder. Undoubtedly, there'd be many who would condemn my behavior as evidence of a lack of proper upbringing. One simply does not turn down an invitation to dinner and a movie personally delivered by a king in his own country. You need not grovel to royalty, but what possible excuse was there for being disrespectful? To say I had a heavy schedule of high-level meetings in London, and that they took priority over socializing, would be viewed as the ultimate ill grace. *Mea culpa.*

After those difficult few minutes, sleep was no longer an option. I knew all the arguments against my conduct that night, but I also knew in my soul that, under the same circumstances, I'd do it again. My behavior may not have been smart, but a part of me admitted that it was the only alternative.

Belatedly, it occurred to me why I had received such friendly treatment from King Juan Carlos. I had assumed it had to do with my work on behalf of Iran's Sovereign Wealth Fund, but in reviewing the day's events in retrospect, it was clear that the king had zero interest in what I was doing for Iran. So what was going on?

"Aha," I thought. It was not the first time my mind had worked too slowly. Juan Carlos was married to Princess Sophia, the daughter of King Paul of Greece and Queen Frederica. The king of Spain was the brother-in-law of another king. In this case, an ex-king, the one with whom I had had dinner only recently in London, Constantine II of Greece. The two were not just in-laws, they were close friends. They shared many common interests, including family connections to other members of the European royalty and deep interests in European political and military affairs. It was no coincidence that the luncheon invitation to Zarzuela Palace had come only a short time after my last visit with Constantine in London. Undoubtedly, that was why King Juan Carlos had treated me as though I were a trusted friend.

In a life filled with bloopers and misjudgments, I had to account for this as one of my dumbest moves. Still I found something to smile about in this episode. I resolved to note in bold capital letters the genealogy of any royalty I happen to run across in the future.

Several years later, my business partner, J. William Middendorf II, a former U.S. Secretary of the Navy and former ambassador to the European Community, wrote a march honoring King Juan Carlos. Bill's marches were well known. He said he wanted to play it at the palace in Madrid, and asked if I would arrange it, "since you know the king, Cy." I thought the king would never want to hear from me, but I didn't reveal my misgivings to Bill. I sent a telex to the palace, asking if His Majesty would receive my partner to play a march dedicated to him. The reply came quickly, informing me that the king would be pleased to receive Secretary Middendorf and that all the arrangements would be made for the army band there to play the march.

Another instance of the magnanimity of royalty.

Chapter Fifty-Four

Royalty, American Style

Royalty of a different sort happened to cross my path at another time. It put the spotlight on a most interesting, but less public, face of the American society.

To begin at the beginning, the government of Senegal had proposed a joint venture with Iran to develop West Africa's fertilizer market, and I had been asked to investigate. I had spent a busy week in Dakar, Senegal, meeting with President Leopold Senghor (who also happened to be a well-known poet in French), Prime Minister Abdou Diouf, and their economic team. Two of my Washington colleagues stayed on in Dakar while I flew on to Paris for another week of negotiations, this time with a South African group.

I was now looking forward to my flight home. My reservation was for a seat by the window in the first row of a regular commercial flight bound for Dulles Airport, and I settled in once on board. It would be a seven-hour flight, and I planned on spending the time working on the accumulated pile in my briefcase. I took out the first file before putting my briefcase in the overhead rack. The stewardess then announced there'd be a delay in takeoff, waiting for a last-minute passenger to arrive.

The passenger who finally made her appearance nearly a half-hour late happened to have the seat next to me. She was small and sprightly, grey-haired, and simply dressed. I promised myself I wouldn't encourage her if she tried to initiate a conversation.

From the first moment she sat down, however, the lady started talking. Not *to* me, but *at* me. She never bothered to introduce herself, nor to ask who I was, where I was coming from or going to. You know, the customary conversational gambits of fellow travelers. She was talking about a lot of people using their first names, and I could not figure out why she thought I'd want to hear all that.

Soon the stewardess began serving lunch, a roast beef sandwich and a large raisin bran cookie for dessert. Still keeping up a cacophony of one-way conversation, my seatmate gulped down her sandwich in short order. As soon as she sampled the cookie, she called the stewardess over.

"I love your raisin bran cookie," she said. "I'd like a bag of them to take home."

"Oh sorry," the stewardess said, "we don't have any more." She sounded genuinely regretful. I thought that was that as the stewardess turned away.

"But wait," the stewardess said turning back. She hesitated a moment, her brow knitting in thought. "I'll see what I can do," she said and went to her station.

She came back a few minutes later holding a small brown bag that was obviously empty. I was watching this tableau, puzzled by what she had in mind. I did not have long to find out. She reached across my seatmate, over to me, and with a quick "excuse me," unceremoniously picked up my as-yet-untouched cookie and put it in her bag. She then moved on without a backward glance. Nonplussed, I stared at my empty plate, confused by what had just happened.

The stewardess's next stop was to the passengers across the aisle and then to every passenger in our section. I did not hear her give an explanation to anyone, but by then she had a bag full of raisin bran cookies.

She came back to my seatmate, gave her all the cookies, and said, "Here you are, Mrs. Kennedy."

Suddenly, all the names my seatmate had been throwing at me

in her talk—Teddy, Ethel, Sargent, Peter, Eunice, etc.—made sense. This lady was Mrs. Rose Kennedy, the mother of the slain President John F. Kennedy. Her son-in-law, Sargent Shriver, was the U.S. ambassador in Paris at the time, and she was returning to Washington after a visit to him.

As I said, royalty of a different sort—American style.

Chapter Fifty-Five

Debut of a Supersonic Plane

A mazingly, this time it was the computer that picked me. It was inevitable that the avalanche of press and media coverage would bring attention from unaccustomed sources. I spent a portion of my time fending off new involvements. Occasionally, one was colorful enough to make an impression.

The Paris Air Show at Le Bourget Airport is a must-see annual extravaganza of the latest developments in air travel. It lasts a week and attracts mobs from around the world. In 1973, four years after Neil Armstrong walked on the moon, a new supersonic aircraft made its maiden voyage at Le Bourget with more than two hundred thousand spectators. The plane was the star of the show that year.

Earlier in 1947, a celebrated test pilot, Chuck Yeager, was the first to break the sound barrier in an experimental plane. Achieving the same speed in a commercial aircraft was the next dream. In 1956, France and Britain joined forces to translate it into reality. Their teams of aeronautical engineers worked seventeen years to pull it off. The result was a plane called the Concorde, meaning "harmony" in French and aptly named because it had required the collaboration of traditional rivals Britain and France. When finally launched, it cut transatlantic flight time in half. Taking account of changes in time zones, a passenger leaving London arrived in New York before he or she departed.

The Concorde then began ferrying passengers between Washington, D.C., and London or Paris. It traveled at an altitude of forty to fifty thousand feet and at more than 1,350 miles per hour. From Washington's Dulles Airport to London's Heathrow took three hours and fifteen minutes. A passenger could look out the window and see the curvature of the earth. Crashing the sound barrier caused a loud *ka-boom* which could shatter windows on the ground, but not inside the plane. Passengers never had to worry. Their ride was perfectly smooth, and for the first time the flight path showed on a screen in the cabin. It was luxury travel and a huge thrill.

———···———

With a heavy travel schedule, I was rarely in my Washington office. On one such occasion, Diane, my assistant, said a woman from Air France wanted to talk to me. Diane had tried to brush her off, but the caller was insistent and said it was personal. I took the call reluctantly. The woman introduced herself and immediately proceeded to tell me about a major advertising campaign the airline was planning to launch shortly. It would feature the photo of a businessman above the caption, "The Concorde was a lifesaver for me, because...." The ads would appear in *The Wall Street Journal, The New York Times, Business Week,* and either *Forbes* or *Fortune.*

Before I could say "I'm glad for you, but what does this have to do with me?" she jumped in to say the airline wanted to build its campaign for the promotion of the supersonic Concorde around me. It'd be my photo in the ads, and the quote would be from me.

Well, I never!

Once over the surprise, I was intrigued by the prospect. I loved the plane. It had indeed been a great timesaver for a constant traveler like myself. I had flown in it with both airlines, Air France and British Airways, and I could only say good things about the experience. The ride was as smooth as glass, the service inside the plane was always superb, and the food rivaled what the best chefs in London or Paris could provide. I had never had any kind of incident in the plane, and I certainly would want other travelers to hear about the Concorde.

On the other hand, I already needed twenty hands to fulfill my load under the contract with Iran. All of us in the office were literally working at capacity. Besides, I knew that once the campaign was launched in these popular publications, I'd become the public face of the Concorde. At some other point in my life, I'd welcome the chance, but now…

I had hesitated long enough. To the Air France lady, I said I was flattered by her company's offer and thanked her profusely, but I sincerely regretted that I was not available to participate in the project. I was constantly traveling, had a full schedule, etc.

"But that's exactly why we picked you," she interjected.

"Why *did* you pick me?" I was naturally curious.

"We didn't. It was the computer that selected you."

"Could you tell me on what basis?"

"Because in the first eighteen months that Air France flew the Concorde out of Dulles Airport for Paris's Charles de Gaulle, you were on our plane sixty-eight times."

She caught me by surprise. Considering that I also flew the British Concorde in and out of London during the same period, that made the total an ungodly number.

"Wow!" I blurted out. "Really?"

"Yes," she said, and then added, "and we didn't find anyone else who came close to your record."

That blew my mind. I thanked her and hung up with some regret.

Chapter Fifty-Six

End of an Engagement

L ooking back on the program I set up to introduce a Middle Eastern government into the Western corporate scene, I revel at how quickly that initiative transformed the investment world in fundamental and far-reaching ways. The idea of governments investing their pension funds or excess revenues in industrial or real estate projects outside their own borders, once considered shocking heresy, had now become commonplace.

It was fully thirty years after the debut of Iran's External Investment Program that a clever finance professional coined the term "Sovereign Wealth Fund" for the innovative program I had initiated in 1974. The term caught on overnight. By then most countries had already organized their own SWFs; even some states in the U.S. (notably Alabama, Alaska, Colorado, Idaho, New Hampshire, New Mexico, North Dakota, Oregon, Texas, Wyoming, West Virginia, Wisconsin, and others) had joined the parade, scouring the world in competition with foreign governments for investment opportunities.

The flood of new money that thus became available was staggering; it enabled many pension funds and private equity firms to acquire substantial corporate portfolios. It is not surprising, therefore, that SWF managers have been universally welcomed in every gathering of financial and economic heavy-hitters from around the world ever since.

The Norway and China SWFs are now the largest in the world, each with $1.35 trillion at this writing. Altogether the top 100

SWFs (including 11 based in Africa) account for more than $11 trillion. China, for one, uses its funds as adjuncts to its strategic international initiatives. Others focus on financial goals, even buying stakes in sports teams, entertainment, and the arts. The top five SWFs own over 31 million square feet of real estate in New York City alone.[11]

I can hardly take all the credit for the creation of the Sovereign Wealth Fund phenomenon. It was Pahlavi, the last king of Iran, who saw the benefits of the program I had proposed not only for his own country but for the world at large, and set it in motion. I only knew him in the narrow context of my work, but up close and personal, he was indeed an exceptionally visionary leader. He had a knack for inspiring people to reach far beyond what they would otherwise expect of themselves. His passion for the welfare of the nation he ruled was genuine and infectious. He came close to pulling Iran into the ranks of the world's developed nations.

———•••———

The most satisfying part of my work for Iran was a purely personal one. It was the opportunity of seeing my brother Hushang and his family regularly. It was psychic income. I stayed with them in their beautiful home in suburban Tehran whenever I was in town. Because of the Iranian government's anti-nepotism policy, Hushang was not officially involved in my work, but he and I spent many evenings talking about personal and professional matters, sometimes far into the night. He was, of course, not only skilled in operating in Iran's political environment, but he was also a consummate dealmaker in his own right. And, despite the obvious merits of my original proposal, I knew in my

---

[11] Sovereign Wealth Fund Institute, March 2023.

ODYSSEY OF HIGH HOPES

bones that I was also the beneficiary of the personal credibility my brother enjoyed in the government after the years he had worked there.

Richard Helms was a family friend long before he became Director of Central Intelligence. He was a true intelligence professional. After he left the CIA, President Nixon appointed him ambassador to Iran. He returned to Washington in 1976 and for the next two years spent a portion of his time as an unofficial senior advisor in my office.

Iran underwent a revolution in 1979, which ended the Pahlavi dynasty and replaced it with a religious dictatorship. I felt terribly sad for the country. The Shah, ensnared in regional rivalries for domination of the Middle East, had found himself suddenly without any U.S. support under President Jimmy Carter, and lost his throne. In the throes of malignant melanoma that had metastasized to his liver, he died in Egypt shortly afterwards. He was sixty years old.

"Is that you, Maggie?"

This was the heading of an article in *USA Today* about the first-ever compilation of a directory providing contact information for government officials worldwide that I had just published. "Maggie" was Margaret Thatcher, the British prime minister at the time. With a gee-whiz-you-won't-believe-this slant, the reporter was showcasing the availability of the bedside phone number of a major head of government.

My work running the Sovereign Wealth Fund had convinced me there was great demand for a more workable method of identifying and gaining access to government officials worldwide than what existed at the time. Collecting the data on fifty thousand cabinet and sub-cabinet officials in one hundred and sixty-eight countries, however, turned out to be a laborious undertaking. Diane, my long-term assistant, volunteered to lead the effort. I organized a company to handle the project and installed her as its president.

The first step was to identify and recruit several dozen "stringers" who'd perform the necessary research for their own country. What none of us had anticipated was that some of the stringers would be placed under arrest on charges of espionage as happened in several countries. Or, that a few other governments would impose conditions on the release of the requisite information. The most difficult of this group was China; it unabashedly refused to cooperate unless we agreed to drop Taiwan from the compilation.

The end result after three years was a series of directories of government officials worldwide. Surprisingly, it turned out that the governments themselves constituted fully two-thirds of the customer base.

Epilogue
A Golden Ring, A Lasting Memento

In the latter part of the twentieth century I continued serving on corporate boards, including the chairmanship of several mutual funds in New York and Los Angeles. I also regrettably, but respectfully, declined an invitation from President Reagan's White House to come in for an interview about serving on the Federal Reserve Board. I then joined two other financiers to establish Middendorf Ansary & Harrison. Bill Middendorf was a former secretary of the navy, Stan Harrison a former president of Ford Aerospace. Both had numerous other honors to their credit. As for their politics, Bill was a dedicated Republican, Stan an active Democrat. We decided to give back to the country some of what we had received. We then switched from finance to philanthropy.

To encourage interest in investments, I gave out many prizes to high school students in the Washington area. Later Jan and I set up college scholarships for deserving students, and several nonprofit organizations in which we were active gave out various awards and medals in our names. The roster of recipients comprised a number of distinguished Washingtonians of various ethnic and racial backgrounds and political persuasions.

———•••———

Father died in 1986 while he was visiting Barry in France. He was buried in Chateauneuf-Grasse. I had always known that I loved and admired him deeply, but I had never fully appreciated his heroic strength in the face of overwhelming early hardships. He continued to maintain his integrity and honor throughout a difficult and demanding life. With his children, he did his best to set us on a path to decent and promising adulthoods.

In 1975, while working on Iran's Sovereign Wealth Fund, I eagerly traveled to Shiraz to visit my great aunt Baji. I had missed her deeply. The small town of my childhood had grown to an unrecognizable metropolis of 1.5 million people. My great-aunt was hospitalized with Alzheimer's and did not recognize me. She died shortly afterwards.

Mother died in 2002 in Los Angeles. After her death, sister Pary moved to Washington, D.C. Brother Barry had sold his company in the mid-1970s, after which he retired to London where he and his three daughters still live. He is now an English citizen and a world-class tournament bridge player.

Hushang left Iran just before the revolution of 1979 with only the shirt on his back. His home, his funds, and all other assets were left behind. He started from scratch in New York, but with worldwide connections and his experience in finance, his rise to the top was preordained. He is only old in years but otherwise remains the same intense, driven, and charismatic brother I knew as a child. Still punching above his weight, he is one of the rare breed of U.S. political insiders who maintain close relationships with Democrats and Republicans at the highest levels. A busy globe-trotting philanthropist now, he lives in Houston and New York.

———·:·———

This has been a glorious journey for me. I have lived to the full the bright and shiny dream I harbored when I set out for America. I have basked in the joys and navigated the sorrows this land has brought me. After fifty years of marriage, Jan and I are sometimes as giddy as teenagers when we are together. We have grown ever closer, still deeply in love. We can often read each other's mind, and communicate volumes with just a look. I'll never forget the first time we met. With light brown hair cut short and swept back from her forehead, twinkling blue-green eyes, and a radiant smile, she almost took my breath away. Over the years I have never stopped marveling at my good fortune in winning the hand of this extraordinary woman. Now, of course, she and I take pride and pleasure in our offspring. Our children and their spouses, Doug and Nancy, ParyAnn and Kevin, Jeff and Karen, and Brad are educated, decent, and responsible adults. They are an integral part of the Ansary Family Office and continue to bring us endless joy. We are also surrounded by their fun and lively children, Ashley, Chris, Eric, Evan, Justin, Kelsey, Linnea, Maxi, and Will. Our love for our family consumes us, filling us with endless pleasure in our daily lives.

Father's precious ring, which he passed on to me in a deeply emotional moment when I was a seventeen-year-old on my way to the U.S. for the second time, has served as a comforting bond with him through the years. I still touch it often and rejoice in the solace it brings, just as Father's touch did for me as a small child.

It has been a blissful life for this once-penniless immigrant, and I owe it all to America, the fabled land to which the whole world owes much for its moral achievements, respect for human dignity, and unique contributions to the betterment of life on our planet.

For me, America will always be the hope of the world.

Acknowledgements

Prodded for years by my wife Jan to write my memoir, I finally gave in. It is now the repository of the three distinct slices of my life, Books I, II, and III.

Earlier, while busily engaged in my professional affairs, I grabbed every spare moment over a fifteen-year period to write a book about George Washington. I saw him as a man "not of an age but for all time." Having spent most of my adult life steeped in financial and entrepreneurial endeavors, I brought a new perspective to the study of our first Presidency. To my amazement, I found that no historian had ever recognized Washington's unique contribution to the American economic system. Several historians with whom I spoke were shocked by my description of Washington as a consummate serial entrepreneur long before that term ever came into use.

Thus was born *George Washington: Dealmaker-in-Chief: The Story of How the Founder of Our Country Unleashed the Entrepreneurial Spirit in America.* Deeply researched, it describes how Washington set the United States on an economic trajectory that has won for the nation the highest standard of living in the world. Once alerted to this facet of Washington's prolific life, other historians quickly jumped on board and the concept went viral.

After that book was published in 2019, I had run out of excuses to Jan. I then set out on a two-year project to write *Odyssey of High Hopes.* With snippets dredged up from dormant memories and old records came new insights about long forgotten events: teachers who set me on the right paths in learning, total strangers who went out of their way to help, and second chances I did not deserve. There was also the haunting recognition of my countless mistakes in the course of many new experiences. To write about these events was also to relive their painful moments, of which the list was long.

I could not pass up this opportunity without noting the love and devotion of Jan in this as in all things. I also acknowledge my debt to my editors, Peter Kilborn, Jeff Alexander, and Melissa Holbrook Pierson; my long-term executive assistant, Jenny Krieg; and my son Brad Ansary, who took a special interest in the work from its inception and then assumed charge of the publishing process.

Cyrus A. Ansary
June 2023

for reading this book. Hope you enjoyed it.

You would make the author very happy if
you'd write a review on Amazon's
Odyssey of High Hopes page.

Image Credits

Cartoon, Stas Drawkman via iStock, detail.

She-goat © 2022 Estate of Pablo Picasso / Artists Rights Society (ARS), New York.

North Skyline [Tehran], Kaveh Kazemi / The Hulton Archive Collection via Getty Images.

Helen Hiett, Bettmann / Bettmann Collection via Getty Images.

The World We Want, Don Rice / Associated Press, New York Herald Tribune.

Summer Morning of American University, Friedheim Quad and Hurst Hall, Jeff Watts, ©American University.

Villa Hügel, Image c13-12, Aerial view of the Villa Hügel in Essen 1994, D-luftbild.de.

Royal Spanish Doings, David Lees / The LIFE Picture Collection via Getty Images.

The Shah skiing in Alborz Mountains, Dmitri Kessel / The LIFE Picture Collection via Getty Images, detail.

Krupp logo from the front grill of a pre-1965 Krupp two-stroke truck, Stahlkocher via Wikimedia Commons.

Limits of Infinity by John Safer, David Finn / The John Safer Collection, Washington, D.C.

All other images appear courtesy of the Ansary Family Collection.

Index

Kissinger, Henry, 264
Kleinman, Ada, 116-117, 142
Kreifels, Max, 332
Krupp, Fried., GmbH, *250*, 288-290, 295-300, 301-304, 305-309, 312-313, 317-318, 319-321, 323, 325, 332
Krupp, Alfried, 296-300, 301-302, 303-304
Krupp Foundation, 302, 318, 320
Kuwait Pension Fund, 268-269, 341

L

L'Association des Amis de la Culture Française, 50
Lazard Frères, 323
Limits of Infinity, sculpture, 359
Lincoln, Abraham, President, 87, 185-186
Liss, Eric, v, 379
Liss, Evan, v, 379
Liss, Linnea H., v, 379
Loren, Sophia, 354
Lukac, Alfred, 305, 317-318, 321
Lukac, Ulla, 317-318, 321

M

Majidi, Dr., 277-278
Mansour Attia, Hamed, 116-117, 141, 142
Marcus, Stanley, 173-174, 184
Marriott, J. Willard, Jr., 248
Martin, D. B., 169
McCloy, John J., 297-298, 303, 304
McGhee, George, 115
McMahon, Brien, 123
Meyer, André, 323

Middendorf Ansary and Harrison, 377
Middendorf, J. William, II, 364, 377
Miller, Hank, 120-121
Mixon, Miss, 193-194
Mojtahedi, Dr. Mohammad Ali, 71-72, 73, 74, 87, 98-99, 102
Mommsen, Ernst Wolf, 319
Montgomery College, 230-231
Montgomery Ward, department store, 163-164, 166, 172, 173
Mostmand, Mehdi, 59
Morsi Ali, Berlanta "Bella," 116, 141-144
Motion Picture Association of America, 323, 350
Mussolini, Benito, 357

N

Naples, Italy, 140, 147-151
National Iranian Oil Company, 290, 349-350
Nat Mai, Yadana, 115
Neiman-Marcus, department store, 173-174
Nemazee, Mohamed, 206
Nemazee School, 29, 89, 206
New York City, 69, 71, 75, 84, 96, 97, 105-106, 108, 111, 113, 115-116, 119, 120-121, 123, 140, 148, 151-152, 186-187, 196-197, 207, 208, 209, 219, *245*, 274, 296, 297, 305, 323-324, 325, 338, 349, 369, 374, 377, 378
New York Herald-Tribune, 69-70, 71, 73, 75, 76, 79, 81, 84, 87, 95-97, 105, 108, 111, 119, 120-123, 125-126, 130, 209

Drawing on substantial new material, *George Washington: Dealmaker-In-Chief, The Story of How the Father of Our Country Unleashed the Entrepreneurial Spirit in America* gives a riveting account of how our First President put in place in America an economic system that enlarged the dreams and opportunities of Americans, led to a flourishing entrepreneurial climate, and is an inspiring tale for our time.

What readers are saying:

★ ★ ★ ★ ★ This is a superbly-written and very thoroughly researched historic book. The author reveals in well versed detail the hitherto little-known entrepreneurial nature and deal making achievements of our first president..... Reads like a suspense novel.

★ ★ ★ ★ ★ This is a truly wondrous book, written by someone who ably serves as an expert guide to George Washington's contribution to America. It evidences deep research.... Indeed, it's one of the best books I've ever read of very many books on George Washington.

★ ★ ★ ★ ★ Engaging and thoroughly researched book.... Ansary's background in finance provides a unique perspective on Washington's entrepreneurial life and his economic legacy. There could be no better example of President Washington's dealmaking genius than his building of an entire city—the nation's capital—without a penny of federal money.

★ ★ ★ ★ ★ I'm thinking about starting a personal campaign to get everyone I know who cares about this country to read this book.... the book is a pleasure to read.

★ ★ ★ ★ ★ "What Americans had done...was to transform a European device for exclusive aristocratic profit into an unparalleled opportunity for wealth creation of the masses." In this thoughtful book, the author takes us on a journey, in part, to discover how and why this happened. It's a wonderful and fascinating read and one I highly recommend.

★ ★ ★ ★ ★ "I look forward to reading future works by this skillful author."

Made in the USA
Monee, IL
09 November 2024

b98dd43a-048f-411d-9b32-327fdc0746d7R01